STRATEGIES FOR CHANGE
Logical incrementalism

The Irwin Series in Management and
The Behavioral Sciences
L. L. Cummings and E. Kirby Warren   Consulting Editors
John F. Mee   Advisory Editor

STRATEGIES FOR CHANGE

Logical incrementalism

JAMES BRIAN QUINN

William and Josephine Buchanan Professor of Management
The Amos Tuck School of Business Administration
Dartmouth College

1980

Homewood, Illinois 60430

ISBN 0-256-02543-6 (paperbound)

ISBN 0-87094-220-4 (hardbound)

Library of Congress Catalog Card No. 80-82098

Printed in the United States of America

0 K 5 4 3 2 1 0 9

To my wife,
The kindest and most beautiful
person I have ever known.

Preface

In recent years three disturbing tendencies have developed in formal planning within major enterprises:

First, planning activities in such enterprises often become bureaucratized, rigid, and costly paper-shuffling exercises divorced from actual decision processes. In many organizations their primary impacts have been: (*a*) to expand the scope of capital and operational budgeting procedures, (*b*) to extend formal performance measurements to new activity areas, and thus (*c*) to achieve greater central control over operations. Instead of stimulating creative options, innovation, or entrepreneurship, formal planning often has become just another aspect of controllership—and another weapon in organizational politics.

Second, most important strategic decisions seem to be made outside the formal planning structure, even in organizations with well-accepted planning cultures. This tendency is especially marked in highly entrepreneurial or smaller enterprises. However, as one closely observes well-managed large companies over extensive time periods, it becomes increasingly apparent that this might well be a characteristic of good management practice and not an abrogation of some immutable principle.

Third, much of the management literature and technique associated with planning has concentrated on developing more sophisticated models of a system that is not working the way the model builders think it is—or should be—operating.

Properly integrated into other decision and political processes, formal planning can make many important contributions to effective management of large enterprises and avoid many of the rigidities suggested above. But often this requires a very different approach from that recommended in much of the management literature.

Instead of following rigidly prescribed formal planning practices, this book suggests that managers in major enterprises tend to develop their most important strategies through processes which neither formal planning paradigms nor power-behavioral theories adequately explain. Such managers *consciously* and *proactively* move forward *incrementally:*

1. To improve the quality of information utilized in corporate strategic decisions.
2. To cope with the varying lead times, pacing parameters, and sequencing needs of the subsystems through which such decisions tend to be made.
3. To deal with the personal resistance and political pressures any important strategic change encounters.
4. To build the organizational awareness, understanding, and psychological commitment needed for effective implementation.
5. To decrease the uncertainty surrounding such decisions by allowing for interactive learning between the enterprise and its various impinging environments.
6. To improve the quality of the strategic decisions themselves by systematically involving those with most specific knowledge, by obtaining the participation of those who must carry out the decisions, and by avoiding premature momenta or closure which could lead the decisions in improper directions.

This book attempts to document why these managers act as they do and to explore the implications of those actions for managers and students of strategic planning.

Acknowledgments

In any work of this scope there are far too many people involved to thank each one individually. Nevertheless, I would like to acknowledge the special assistance given me by those who went far out of their way to be helpful. Among these are: Jeremiah O'Connell, Bohdan Hawrylyshyn, and Max Daetwyler of Centre d'Études Industrielles; Eugene Cafiero and E. W. Gaynor of Chrysler Corporation; Richard Hofmann, Warren Hayford, and Robert Hatfield of Continental Group; Sigurd Andersen of E. I. DuPont de Nemours; Norton Belknap, Thomas Barrow, and George Piercy of Exxon Corporation; Charles H. Bell, James McFarland, Verne Johnson, and John Gerlach of General Mills, Inc.; Henry Duncombe and F. Alan Smith, and E. M. Estes of General Motors Corporation; Irwin Goldman and John Horan of Merck and Co.; William Borns of Mobil Oil Corporation; George Weissman of Philip Morris Corporation; Alastair Pilkington, Lord Pilkington, and B. N. Tyler of Pilkington Brothers, Ltd.; William Spoor, E. H. Wingate, and G. Dunhowe of Pillsbury Co.; Robert Marschalk of Richardson-Merrell, Inc.; P. G. Gyllenhammar, H. Frisinger, L. Malmros, B. Ekman, and B. Joenssen of Volvo AB; and T. Trolle, J. Goldman, D. Pendery, C. Mayo and G. White of Xerox Corporation.

Among the academic community, several people were especially helpful. Dean John W. Hennessey kindly arranged my sabbatical leave for the project and helped review the work in its developing stages. Robert James, Charles Summer, L. L. Cummings, E. Kirby Warren, Liam Fahey, Mariann Jelinek, Robert Guest, and Raymond Miles also reviewed the work in some of its various stages and offered most helpful insights. Mariann Jelinek also did the interviews in Texas Instruments and made her publications available to me for review. She also kindly helped in the writing of two cases and counseled me in the early stages of the project, for which I am most grateful. Otherwise, I made all interviews myself and wrote up all the supporting cases with the able research assistance of Marcia Baldwin, James Williams, and Peter Melendy. Finally, I would like to thank my wife, Allie, for many nights of patience; and Jean Lightfoot for handling so swiftly and well the endless typescripts, redrafts, and footnote controls during the entire project.

James Brian Quinn

Contents

1
The study, issues, and definitions

THE STUDY, ISSUES, AND DEFINITIONS

In the late 1950s and early 1960s I shared with many others the view that more rational planning structures could improve decision making in large organizations. To this end, I investigated the various developing theories of planning and sought the pragmatic causes of successful and unsuccessful long-range planning in large enterprises. Based on these studies, I published some early papers suggesting how better formal planning could benefit corporations, particularly in the development of their research and technical capabilities. These led to extensive consulting assignments helping large companies and government groups implement such methodologies. In most cases, better planning did seem to help top managers in important ways. Planning extended time horizons, forced an integrated look at total commitments, generated new data about the future, involved more people in longer term thinking, developed a systematic methodology for communicating about the future, and provided a better framework and rationale within which to evaluate individual proposals and budget options.

ORIGINS OF CONCERN

As time went on, however, I noticed three disturbing tendencies. *First,* the planning activity often tended to become a bureaucratized, rigid, and costly paper-shuffling exercise. In many companies, its primary impact was to expand the scope of capital and operational budgeting procedures, to introduce formal measures to new areas of performance, and thus to achieve greater central control over operations. Instead of stimulating creative options, innovation, or entrepreneurship, formal planning often became just another aspect of controllership—and another weapon in organizational politics. *Second,* most major strategic decisions seemed to be made outside the formal planning structure, even in organizations with well-accepted planning cultures. This tendency was especially marked in entrepreneurial and smaller enterprises. As I observed my client companies over long time periods, however, it became increasingly apparent that this was also a characteristic of good management in large organizations and not an abrogation of some immutable management principle. *Third,* much of the management literature on planning seemed bent on developing ever more sophisticated models of a system that simply was not working the way the model builders thought it was—or should be—operating. In fact, their purported "normative" solutions began to appear highly questionable, if not actively destructive, in many instances.

STRUCTURE OF THE STUDY

Consequently, I took a sabbatical leave in 1977, with the kind support of the Associates Program of The Amos Tuck School (Dartmouth College) and the Centre d'Etudes Industrielles (Geneva, Switzerland), to investigate how real companies actually arrive at their strategic changes and how this fits into accepted formal planning and management concepts. I selected companies for study based on five criteria.

1. They had to be large (multiple billion dollar) companies.
2. They had to either be undergoing important strategic changes or have recently completed such shifts.

3. They had to allow me sufficient access to top levels to obtain desired data.
4. They had to be balanced among several different industry characteristics: consumable goods, basic processes, high technology, and consumer-durable industries. Both industries and companies were purposely chosen to represent a variety of technologies, time horizons, and national versus international dimensions.
5. The sample had to include at least two companies meeting these criteria in each industry.

The following companies generously cooperated: General Mills, Inc., and Pillsbury Company (consumable products); Exxon Corporation and Continental Group (basic processes); Xerox Corporation and Pilkington Brothers Limited (advanced technology); and General Motors Corporation, Chrysler Corporation, and Volvo AB (consumer durables). Quotations or statements attributed to cooperating companies are derived from the case studies that are the data base for this book. For simplicity, only one footnote reference in each chapter will be made to each of these cases.

Interview design

Within each company, I tried to interview at least ten people who were most involved in the strategic changes studied. Prior to interviews, I conducted an extensive survey of secondary source data about each company. I used a standardized typed sheet of questions to guide each respondent and to ensure adequate and comparable coverage. Because each situation was unique, however, interviews tended to flow around issues rather than the structure of the questionnaire. Each interview lasted about two hours. In interviews, respondents were first asked what they thought were the most important shifts the company's strategic posture had undergone during the period under study. They were then asked to trace how—to their knowledge—each change had actually come about. Respondents, of course, tended to focus on the changes with which they were most familiar. Within each change, I used a standardized framework of questions to ensure coverage and comparability. In most cases I was allowed to tape interviews. In some I had to use shorthand notes, which were immediately redictated. Typescripts from these tapes became the base documents for all quotations.

Verifying and publishing data

I then tried to prepare a 25–35-page case summarizing each company's experience, with appropriate quotations of individual executives' viewpoints. For these cases (as well as for interview purposes) my research assistants prepared a large secondary source data file on each company. In addition, I asked for primary source documentation whenever this seemed appropriate. These sources became part of a several-level check on interview data.[1] *First,* cross-checks were both built into individual interviews and made among the comments of two or more respondents. *Second,* both primary and secondary source data bases were used to confirm or challenge people's memories about facts, sequences, or the timing of events. *Third,* quotations were cleared with each individual quoted or paraphrased. Whenever possible, the source is identified in the case and in this text; but even when its origin had to be disguised, each quotation was cleared with its initiator. Nearby paragraphs were also shown to the interviewee to confirm the context of his or her remarks. *Fourth,* each individual case was reviewed for factual errors by the company involved. *Fifth,* as the cases were appropriately cleared, they were published as a data base. Some are available now; others are in various stages of preparation and clearance. No quotations are used in this book that have not appeared in secondary sources, public utterances of officials, specially approved statements, or cleared cases.

Objectives and risks

I am well aware of the risks and problems of this kind of research;[2] however, strategies emerge over periods of three to ten years, and it is physically impossible to observe all the events involved. Events in such decision processes cannot be fully replicated to set up experimental controls. Some careful descriptive research is needed on complex areas like strategy formulation just to pose questions that more refined research can later test in more detailed and controlled environments. Finally, some new insights on the broad issues of strategy formulation may be extremely valuable even if they cannot be asserted with quantitative rigor. Most respondents were intrigued by going back over their own strategy's development and tried—for their own benefit—to avoid superimposing a post hoc logic on events. Anonymity in interviews and the right to clear quotes allowed people to respond candidly. Although I did lose some richness when a few individuals later cleared their quotes, the reasons for such changes were generally quite obvious, and we could usually work out a compromise wording that conveyed the intended meaning but protected the individual.

The objective of field work was to describe and document the dynamics of the actual processes of strategic change, as realistically perceived by those most knowledgeably and intimately involved. Using this data base, I then attempted to: (1) identify some common patterns of strategic action, (2) better understand how managers in complex situations really did act, (3) obtain their insights as to why they acted as they did, and (4) compare their actions and perceptions with the viewpoints expressed in prevailing theories. These are summarized in the next several chapters. I hope that this book and its related documents will provide a basis for building stronger and more complete theories about strategy formulation and strategic processes. Out of this effort and other research, I trust, will flow more useful normative guidelines for those who must participate in such processes.

Style, detail, and access

Hoping to appeal to businesspeople, public policy makers, and educators, I have tried to write each case and the book in a readable style, rather than with the deadly passive tenses and couched phrases that are supposed to convey objectivity—yet are merely the trappings of objectivity and not the essence of it. I have tried to document and present all conclusions with thoroughness and care. But they are *my* conclusions; I can only encourage people to look at my data base and see whether they could conclude otherwise. To the extent the companies allow, the data base will be open; but in some cases clearances are pending, and in others legal and internal political considerations have limited the data I can disclose. As they are cleared, of course, all the cases will be published for review.

Each chapter in the book has been set up as an integral unit in itself—to be published separately as an article or to be assigned as a classroom exercise for business students or executive programs. The subject of strategy is so embracing that no attempt has been made to cover all its aspects in this short book. Instead, the reader is assumed to be knowledgeable about where to locate detailed methodologies for product positioning strategies, forecasting, environmental scanning, program evaluation, formal planning structures, game theory, negotiation and bargaining procedures, coalition management, and so on. References are provided to major sources only. Even the extensive bibliography at the end of the book only scratches the surface of possible references on all potentially related topics. Nevertheless, one hopes it will help lead those readers, who so wish to find more detailed references.

Military concepts and formal planning

Chapter 5 on formal strategic planning methodologies requires some special comment. Having implicitly criticized many formalistic aspects of planning, I felt an obligation to suggest explicitly how such planning could be made stronger both conceptually and as an integral component in the logical incremental mode of strategy formulation. I hope the reader will forgive a somewhat long allusion to an ancient classical strategy and to the evolution of military-diplomatic strategic concepts. But no set of readers could be expected to be familiar enough with any particular historical incident—or to this stream of literature as a whole—to draw pertinent inferences without my providing at least some detail. The question was merely how much.

Executives are generally intrigued by the insights the classical strategic theorists offer relative to their own strategies. Yet I find little specific reference to classical principles in the modern management literature, and I repeatedly see formally developed business strategies that ignore basic strategic axioms to the point of embarrassment. Formal strategies should at least be tested against the criteria these axioms suggest as relevant. When they are, the quality of most formal business strategies can be vastly improved. The thought processes necessary to generate thorough strategies and fulfill these axioms are quite properly an integral portion of the logical incremental process of strategy formulation.

SOME DEFINITIONS

Because the words *strategy, objectives, goals, policy,* and *programs* may have different meanings to individual readers or to various organizational cultures, I have tried to use certain definitions consistently throughout the book. For clarity—not pedantry—these are set forth as follows:

A **strategy** is the *pattern* or *plan* that *integrates* an organization's *major* goals, policies, and action sequences into a *cohesive* whole.[3] A well-formulated strategy helps to *marshal* and *allocate* an organization's resources into a *unique and viable posture* based on its relative *internal competencies* and *shortcomings,* anticipated *changes in the environment,* and contingent moves by *intelligent opponents.*

Goals (or objectives) state *what* is to be achieved and *when* results are to be accomplished, but they do not state *how* the results are to be achieved. All organizations have multiple goals existing in a complex hierarchy:[4] from value objectives, which express the broad value premises toward which the company is to strive; through overall organizational objectives, which establish the intended *nature* of the enterprise and the *directions* in which it should move; to a series of less permanent goals that define targets for each organizational unit, its subunits, and finally all major program activities within each subunit. Major goals—those that affect the entity's overall direction and viability—are called *strategic goals.*

Policies are rules or guidelines that express the *limits* within which action should occur. These rules often take the form of contingent decisions for resolving conflicts among specific objectives. For example: "Don't use nuclear weapons in war unless American cities suffer nuclear attack first" or "Don't exceed three months' inventory in any item without corporate approval." Like the objectives they support, policies exist in a hierarchy throughout the organization.[5] Major policies—those that guide the entity's overall direction and posture or determine its viability—are called *strategic policies.*

Programs specify the *step-by-step sequence of actions* necessary to achieve major objectives. They express *how* objectives will be achieved within the limits set by policy. They ensure that resources are committed to achieve goals, and they provide the dynamic track against which progress can be measured. Those major programs that determine the entity's overall thrust and viability are called *strategic programs.*

Strategic decisions are those that determine the overall direction of an enterprise and its ultimate viability in light of the predictable, the unpredictable, and the unknowable changes that may occur in its most important surrounding environments. They intimately shape the true goals of the enterprise. They help delineate the broad limits within which the enterprise operates. They dictate both the resources the enterprise will have accessible for its tasks and the principal patterns in which these resources will be allocated. And they determine the effectiveness of the enterprise—whether its major thrusts are in the right directions given its resource potentials—rather than whether individual tasks are performed efficiently. Management for efficiency, along with the myriad decisions necessary to maintain the daily life and services of the enterprise, is the domain of operations.

Strategies versus tactics

Strategies normally exist at many different levels in any large organization. For example, in government there are world trade, national economic, treasury department, military spending, investment, fiscal, monetary supply, banking, regional development, and local reemployment strategies—all related to each other somewhat hierarchically yet each having imperatives of its own. Similarly, businesses have numerous strategies from corporate levels to department levels within divisions. Yet if strategies exist at all these levels, how do strategies and tactics differ? Often the primary difference lies in the scale of action or the perspective of the leader. What appears to be a "tactic" to the chief executive officer (or general) may be a "strategy" to the marketing head (or lieutenant) if it determines the ultimate success and viability of his or her organization. In a more precise sense, tactics can occur at either level. They are the short-duration, adaptive, action-interaction realignments that opposing forces use to accomplish limited goals after their initial contact. Strategy defines a continuing basis for ordering these adaptations toward more broadly conceived purposes.

A genuine strategy is always needed when the potential actions or responses of intelligent opponents can seriously affect the endeavor's desired outcome—regardless of that endeavor's organizational level in the total enterprise. This condition almost always pertains to the important actions taken at the top level of competitive organizations. However, game theorists quickly point out that some important top-level actions—for example, sending a peacetime fleet across the Atlantic—merely require elaborate coordinative plans and programs.[6] A whole new set of concepts, a true strategy, is needed if some people or nations decide to oppose the fleet's purposes. And it is these concepts that in large part distinguish strategic formulation from simpler programmatic planning.

Strategies may be looked at as either a priori statements to guide action or a posteriori results of actual decision behavior. In most complex organizations (for reasons to be cited), one would be hard pressed to find a complete a priori statement of a total strategy that actually is followed. Yet often the existence of a strategy (or strategy change) may be clear to an objective observer, although it is not yet apparent to the executives making critical decisions. One, therefore, must look at the actual emerging *pattern* of the enterprise's operant goals, policies, and major programs to see what its true strategy is.[7] Whether it is consciously set forth in advance or is simply a widely held understanding resulting from a stream of decisions, this pattern becomes the real strategy of the enterprise. And it is changes in this pattern—regardless of what any formal strategic documents may say—that either analysts or strategic decision makers must address if they wish to comprehend or alter the concern's strategic posture. This is a major theme of this book.

Politics, power, influence, and authority

One could become endlessly tangled in the nuances of the terms *power, influence,* and *authority.* I have tried to use the terms consistently, yet without excess pedantry, in keeping with the social psychological literature. *Influence* enables a manager to shape the actions of one or more other persons. The manager's capacity to influence may come from any of a variety of *power* sources: (1) a degree of personal expertise that causes others to defer to his or her judgment, (2) a "personal charisma" that causes people to follow the manager's lead, (3) the "referent power" one bestows upon an individual or group by conforming to their norms, or (4) the "legitimate power" normally attributed to a person in the executive's role.[8] The delegated right to use legitimate power I refer to as *formal authority.*[9] Individuals may also accrue *informal authority* through their own personal persuasiveness, personalities, or interpersonal skills.

Political behavior, as used here, consists of activities undertaken primarily to increase an individual's or group's referent or legitimate power. Individuals and groups tend to seek power because it is pleasurable in itself and because it gives them more control over their organization or its external environments.[10] Achieving increased political power may or may not make more people dependent on the manager, but it does give the executive a greater capacity to influence events. Political behavior is thus normal for any ambitious person.[11] The term is not generally used in a pejorative sense here, although some of its manifestations—like hiding agendas, screening information, or creating dependencies—may not be among an executive's most attractive activities. The development and use of power, authority, influence, and politics are natural adjuncts to the processes needed to formulate, shape, and implement major organizations' strategies, and they are so treated here.

NOTES

1. For a good discussion of the many problems of case research, see R. C. Snyder and G. D. Paige, "The United States Decision to Resist Aggression in Korea: The Application of an Analytical Scheme," *Administrative Science Quarterly* (December 1958-59), pp. 340-78.

2. For discussions, see H. Mintzberg, D. Raisinghani, and A. Théorêt, "The Structure of 'Unstructured' Decision Processes," *Administrative Science Quarterly* (June 1976), pp. 246-75; and E. H. Bowman, "Epistemology, Corporate Strategy, and Academe," *Sloan Management Review* (Winter 1974), pp. 35-50.

3. This portion of the definition agrees well with R. F. Vancil, in "Strategy Formulation in Complex Organizations," *Sloan Management Review* (Winter 1976), pp. 1-18.

4. H. A. Simon, "On the Concept of Organizational Goals," *Administrative Science Quarterly* (June 1964), pp. 1-22.

5. N. G. Nicolaidis, in "Policy-Decision and Organization Theory," D.P.A. thesis, University of Southern California, Los Angeles, 1960; and W. H. Newman, in *Administrative Action: The Techniques of Organization and Management*, 2d ed. (Englewood Cliffs, N.J.: Prentice-Hall, Inc., 1963) develop the useful differences between policy and goals in some detail.

6. J. Von Neumann and O. Morgenstern, *Theory of Games and Economic Behavior* (Princeton, N.J.: Princeton University Press, 1944); M. Shubik, *Games for Society, Business, and War: Towards a Theory of Gaming* (New York: Elsevier, 1975); and J. McDonald, *Strategy in Poker, Business and War* (New York: W. W. Norton & Company, Inc., 1950).

7. H. Mintzberg, "Research on Strategy-Making," *Academy of Management Proceedings, Thirty-second Annual Meeting,* August 13-16, 1972, pp. 90-94.

8. J. R. French and B. Raven develop this typology of power in "Bases of Social Power" in D. Cartwright, ed., *Studies in Social Power* (Ann Arbor: University of Michigan Press, 1959), pp. 150-67.

9. This is the concept originally developed as "vested power" by Mary Parker Follett in H. C. Metcalf and L. Urwick, eds., *Dynamic Administration: The Collected Papers of Mary Parker Follett* (New York: Harper & Brothers, Publishers, 1941).

10. W. R. Nord, "Developments in the Study of Power" in W. R. Nord, ed., *Concepts and Controversy in Organizational Behavior* (Pacific Palisades, Calif.: Goodyear Publishing Co., 1976).

11. J. S. Livingston, "Myth of the Well-Educated Manager," *Harvard Business Review* (January-February 1971), pp. 79-89; and P. C. Cummin, "TAT Correlates of Executive Performance," *Journal of Applied Psychology* (February 1967), pp. 78-81.

2
The logic of
logical incrementalism

When I was younger I always conceived of a room where all these [strategic] concepts were worked out for the whole company. Later I didn't find any such room. . . . The strategy [of the company] may not even exist in the mind of one man. I certainly don't know where it is written down. It is simply transmitted in the series of decisions made.

Executive Statement
In General Motors Corporation:
The Downsizing Decision Case

THE LOGIC OF LOGICAL INCREMENTALISM

My data suggest that when well-managed major organizations make significant changes in strategy, the approaches they use frequently bear little resemblance to the rational, analytical systems so often described in the planning literature. This literature clearly states what factors should be included in a formally defined strategy[1] and precisely how to analyze and relate these factors step by step.[2] In addition, many articles have described in some detail how to apply this "formal planning approach" to strategy formulation for specific businesses.[3] Its main elements include the following:[4]

1. *Analyzing one's own internal situation:* strengths, weaknesses, competencies, problems.
2. *Projecting current product lines'* profits, sales, investment needs, etc. into the future.
3. *Analyzing selected external environments* and opponents' actions for opportunities and threats.
4. *Establishing broad goals* as targets for subordinate groups' plans.
5. *Identifying gaps* between expected and desired results.
6. *Communicating* planning assumptions, goals, and policies to the divisions.
7. *Generating proposed plans* from subordinate groups with more specific target goals, resource needs, and supporting action plans.
8. Occasionally *asking for special studies* of alternatives, contingencies, or longer term opportunities.
9. *Reviewing and approving* divisional plans and summing these for corporate needs.
10. *Developing long-term budgets* presumably related to plans.
11. *Assigning implementation* of plans to specific groups.
12. *Monitoring and evaluating* performance for emphasis presumably against plans, but usually against budgets.

Formal planning—just a building block

Although the formal planning approach is excellent for some purposes, it tends to focus unduly on measurable quantitative forces and to underemphasize the vital qualitative, organizational, and power-behavioral factors that so often determine strategic success in one situation versus another. It can easily become a rigid, cumbersome routine, used primarily as a basis for financial control, rather than a creative direction-setting challenge. Designing strategies in terms of the military-diplomatic principles and "thrust matrices" outlined in Chapter 5 can make the formal analytical approach much more effective than it usually is as a corporate strategic framework. Even then, however, such planning can be only one of many building blocks in a continuously evolving structure of analytical and political events that combine to determine strategies in large institutions.[5]

For good reasons, strategies in such institutions tend to emerge in ways that differ quite markedly from the usually prescribed textbook methodologies. The full strategy is rarely written down in any one place. The processes used to arrive at the total strategy are typically fragmented, evolutionary, and largely intuitive. Although one can frequently find embedded in these fragments some very refined pieces of formal strategic analysis, the real strategy tends to *evolve* as internal decisions and external events flow together to create a new, widely shared consensus for action among key members of the top management team.[6] In well-run organizations, managers proactively guide these streams of actions and events incrementally toward conscious strategies embodying many of the structural principles described in Chapter 5. Far from being an abrogation of good management practice, the rationale behind this kind of incremental strategy formulation is so powerful that it—rather than the step-by-step formal systems planning approach so often espoused—probably provides the best normative model for strategic decision making.

The power-behavioral approach

Recognizing the limits of the formal systems approach, another group has provided important insights on the crucial psychological, power, and behavioral relationships in strategy formulation. Among other things, this group's efforts have enhanced understanding about: the multiple goal structures of organizations,[7] the politics of strategic decisions,[8] executive bargaining and negotiation processes,[9] satisficing in decision making,[10] the role of coalitions in strategic management,[11] and the practice of "muddling" in large-scale decision making, especially in government.[12] Unfortunately, many power-behavioral studies have been conducted in settings far removed from the realities of strategy formulation. Others have concentrated solely on human dynamics, power relationships, or organizational processes and ignored the ways in which systematic data analysis shapes and often dominates crucial aspects of strategic decisions. Finally, few have offered much normative guidance for the strategist.

A new synthesis

The observations that underlie this book suggest that a synthesis of various behavioral, power-dynamic, and formal analytical approaches more closely approximates the processes major organizations use in changing their strategies.* Managers purposely blended these processes together to improve both the quality of the decisions and the effectiveness of their implementation. Although the processes they used at first appeared to be disjointed or "muddling," they actually embodied a strong internal logic that is consistent among companies and among action sequences within individual companies. Upon analysis, this logic appeared to embrace many central elements of both the formal systems planning approach and the power-behavioral approach. But neither of these paradigms adequately characterized the way successful strategic processes operated. Instead, my studies showed that:

1. Effective strategies tended to emerge from a series of strategic formulation subsystems.[13]† Each subsystem involved a somewhat different set of players, information needs, and time imperatives. Each attacked a specific issue of corporate-wide importance (like product

---

*As used in this book, the term *processes* simply refers to the sequence of steps, relationship transformations, and interpersonal and intellectual transactions needed to reach an end state or outcome.

†As used here, the term *subsystem* refers to a grouping of activities and decisions interacting principally toward the accomplishment of one major strategic goal. Each subsystem has its own discrete timing and information imperatives yet

line positioning, technological innovation, product diversification, acquisitions, divestitures, government-external relations, major reorganizations, or international posture) in a disciplined way.[14] Yet for good reasons, optimal strategies within each subsystem tended to demand incrementalism and opportunism in their formulation.

2. The logic patterns underlying the formulation of effective strategies for each subsystem were so powerful that they could serve as normative approaches for creating these key components of strategy in large organizations.[15] Yet the timing imperatives and internal pacing parameters of each subsystem rarely matched the precise needs of other simultaneously active strategic subsystems.

3. Because each subsystem had its own cognitive limits[16] and process limits,[17] its strategies tended to be arrived at logically and incrementally. Consequently, the total enterprise's strategy—which had to deal with the interactions of all the subsystem strategies—was also arrived at by an approach most appropriately described as "logical incrementalism."

4. In the hands of a skillful manager, such incrementalism was not muddling. It was a purposeful, effective, proactive management technique for improving and integrating both the analytical and the behavioral aspects of strategy formulation.[18]

This chapter will suggest the logic behind several important subsystems for strategy formulation in industry and outline some of the management and thought processes executives in large companies use to synthesize them into effective corporate strategies. I—like others—have frequently observed similar incremental practices in large government or semipublic organizations. Since these have been documented elsewhere, this chapter will principally use examples from private industry.

Critical strategic issues

Certain "hard data" decisions (e.g., on product market segmentation, plant location, build or purchase alternatives, financial access and capital cost, or internal financial alloca-

---

is dependent on other subsystems in some important ways. Each subsystem tends to involve a different set of people, but these sets are generally not established as discrete organizational units solely pursuing that one major strategic goal. Instead various top-level executives are often part-time members of several such sets, each developing a different subsystem's strategy and involving different support groups in the process.

tions) have been covered extensively in the analytical literature about business strategies.[20]* Consequently, I will not try to treat the details of these strategic subsystems here. Executives in my sample identified other "soft" changes as having at least as much importance in shaping the overall strategic postures of their concerns. Most often cited during this study were changes in the company's:

1. Degree of diversification (whether induced internally or through acquisitions).
2. Approach to divisional controls and divestiture.
3. Overall organizational structure or basic management style.
4. Relationships with government or other external interest groups.
5. International posture and relationships with foreign governments.
6. Innovative capabilities or personnel motivations as affected by growth.
7. Worker and professional relationships reflecting changed social expectations and values.
8. Past or anticipated capacity to deal with its technological environments.

When executives were asked to "describe the processes through which your company arrived at its new posture" vis-à-vis each of these critical domains, several important points emerged. First, few of these issues lent themselves to quantitative modeling techniques or perhaps even formal financial analyses. Second, successful companies used a different subsystem to formulate strategy for each major class of strategic issue, including market segmentation, capital access, and capital cost strategies; yet these subsystems were quite similar among companies even in very different industries (see Diagram 1). Third, no single formal analytical process could handle all these strategic variables simultaneously on a planned basis. Why?

---

*Although such decisions are not value-free, sufficient quantitative data exist to seriously confine and constrain alternatives, once goals are specified. Nevertheless, even for these decisions, the wise manager pays serious attention to motivational factors, power positions, credibility of data sources, consensus building, and the other essential preconditions to effective implementation.

Diagram 1
Strategies form in subsystems (involving different people, skills, goals, information, and timing imperatives)

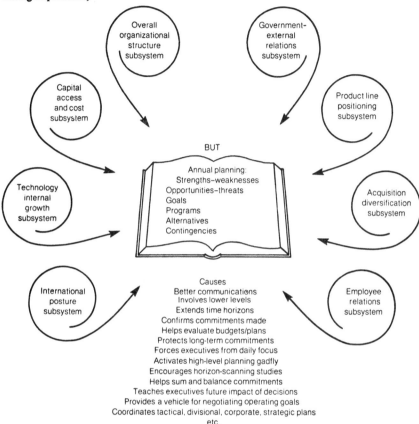

PRECIPITATING EVENTS

Often external or internal events over which managements had essentially no control would precipitate urgent, piecemeal, interim decisions that inexorably shaped the company's future strategic posture.[21] This phenomenon was clearly observed in the decisions forced on General Motors by the 1973-74 oil crisis,[22] the shift in posture pressed upon Exxon by sudden nationalizations, and the dramatic opportunities presented to Haloid (Xerox) Corporation and Pilkington Brothers Limited by the unexpected inventions of xerography and float glass.[23, 24]

In these cases, analyses from earlier formal planning cycles contributed greatly as long as the general nature of the contingency had been anticipated. They broadened the information base available (as in Exxon's case), extended the options considered (Haloid-Xerox), created shared values to guide decisions about precipitating events in consistent directions (Pilkington), or built up resource bases, management flexibilities, or active search routines for opportunities whose specific nature could not be defined in advance (General Mills, Pillsbury).[25] But no organizatıun—no matter how brilliant, rational, or imaginative—could possibly foresee the timing, severity, or even the nature of all such precipitating events. In this sense, they were truly unknowable. Further, when these events did occur there might not be time, resources, or information enough to undertake a full formal strategic analysis of all possible options and their consequences. Yet early decisions made under stress often meant new thrusts, precedents, or lost opportunities that were difficult to reverse later.

Broadly formative, yet tentative

Recognizing this, top executives often consciously tried to deal with precipitating events in an incremental fashion. Early commitments were kept broadly formative, tentative, and subject to later review. In some cases, neither the company nor the external players could understand the full implications of alternative actions. All parties wanted to test assumptions and have an opportunity to learn from and adapt to the others' responses.

- Such behavior clearly occurred during the 1973-74 oil crisis. The oil companies made no precipitous strategic moves. As they shifed supplies to other areas, they considered the interests and potential actions of customer governments, producer governments, and those with potential military power. No governments made sudden moves that would have been impractical to retract. Many of the oil-producing countries, despite the embargo, enforced their restrictions and increased posted prices tentatively until they could tell whether the cartel would hold, how the customer nations might respond, and what the true options of the oil companies might be. Despite considerable rhetoric, all parties maintained their flexibility of movement. These interactions improved the quality of decisions for all.

Flexibility and participation

Even under extreme pressure, effective top exectuves often consciously delayed initial decisions, or kept such decisions vague, to encourage subordinates' participation, to gain more information from specialists, or to build commitment to solutions. They were extremely sensitive to organizational and power relationships and consciously managed decision processes to improve these dynamics. Even when a crisis tended to shorten time horizons and make decisions more goal-oriented than political, these executives consciously tried to keep their options open until they understood how the crisis would affect the power bases and needs of their key constituents.

• General Motors' top management only incrementally realigned its various car lines as it understood, step by step, the way in which the oil crisis and environmental demands would affect the viability of each existing divisional or dealership structure. In the aggregate, these changes amounted to the greatest shift in balance and positioning among GM's automobile lines since Alfred P. Sloan, and management was deeply concerned about the way its decisions would influence the power and prosperity of various groups. Yet it is virtually impossible to determine a point in time when a decision on specific elements of the strategy—much less the total strategy shift—occurred.

In other cases, added information had to be combined with phased political moves to secure a desired outcome. Without time for a formal strategic analysis, well-made crisis decisions could establish or maintain lasting favorable relationships or allow the enterprise to move into advantageous new permanent positions. Or, if improperly made, they could severely inhibit future options. Further information has a value, and incrementalism often helped buy this at a low price.

● I was in the office of the president of Esso-France in 1968 when strikes suddenly paralyzed the country, Paris was shut down by political rioting and turmoil, and it appeared that a major revolution might be possible. Our discussions were interrupted several times by announcements that one or another of Esso's facilities in France had been taken over by various activist groups. When I suggested that the president might like to end our conversation to take some specific action, he quietly replied, "No, that won't be necessary. Right now we must merely find out what is going on. Then we must wait until the situation clarifies enough to know what to do." He was correct. Although all public services, including transportation, were shut down in Paris and the countryside, it took several days to clarify the demands of the activists, to understand the forces at play, to participate effectively in coalitions, and to see if management teams could take over activities formerly performed by workers. In the meantime, it was essential not to precipitate actions that would have had negative long-term strategic consequences.

To improve both the information content and the process aspects of decisions surrounding precipitating events, logic dictates and practice affirms that they are normally best handled carefully and consciously incrementally, to make decisions as late as possible consistent with the information available and needed.[26]

INCREMENTALISM IN STRATEGIC SUBSYSTEMS

Incrementalism is used frequently in other widely different contexts; for example, neither the potential producer nor the user of a completely new product or process (like xerography or float glass) can fully conceptualize its ramifications without interactive testing. All parties benefit from procedures that purposely delay decisions and allow mutual feedback. Because of this, companies like IBM and Xerox have formalized the concept into "phased program planning" systems.

They make concrete decisions only on individual phases (or stages) of new product developments, establish interactive testing procedures with customers, and postpone final configuration commitments until the latest possible moment. As a result, many new products occupy a quite different strategic position than initial analyses would have suggested. Such interactive adjustments in early product positioning strategies are common in smaller companies where added information is vital to survival. For example, Howard Head's first metal skis became "cheaters" for beginning skiers, rather than racing skis.[27] And Haloid's first xerographic devices were used primarily to make offset masters.

Interactive learning and innovation

One of the greatest possible errors in managing technical programs is to freeze plans too soon. The whole process of design and development needs to be oriented to invention, innovation, and change. One wants to adopt the best currently available technical solutions and to adapt to the customers' most current perceived needs. Consequently, the process needs to be designed to make decisions with the quickest possible feedback from the marketplace and technical communities.[28] Logic dictates that this information be introduced into the development process for as long as possible—until truly fixed commitments must be made for plants, buildings, or major equipment. Early commitment to PERT charts or detailed schematic designs essentially assumes no new knowledge will be discovered during the development process, no inventions will be made, and no new design concepts will be worthwhile.

● In this regard, it is interesting to contrast the essential chaos and incrementalism of Pilkington's development of float glass—or the way many successful small entrepreneurial ventures operate—with the rigid planned assumptions of the U.S. fusion power program. The latter comes complete with progress check points and schematic drawings for buildings out to the year 2000. While such planning is comforting for bureaucrats and formalists, its results can be positively counterproductive. The assumption that no relevant basic science discoveries or technological inventions will be made in the next two decades can become a self-fulfilling prophecy. The stimulus to invention is lost. Psychological commitments to results and fiscal commitments to alternatives are almost certainly suboptimum. And people begin to "prove the plan," rather than to discover and solve the problems associated with controlled fusion systems.

Highly adaptive learning interactions with outside information sources and strong incentives to use the information obtained are among the primary reasons why high-morale, small companies (like Intel or KMS Fusion, Inc.)[29] can so often outdesign larger electronics companies (like Fairchild or RCA) or huge planned bureaucracies (like the American and Russian atomic energy establishments).

One also finds that an incremental logic applies—for somewhat different reasons—in attacking many other critical subsystems of corporate strategy. Conscious incrementalism often helps in three important process dimensions: (1) coping with the varying lead times and sequencing arrangements demanded by interacting major decisions, (2) overcoming important political and informational barriers to needed changes, and (3) creating the personal and organizational awareness, understanding, acceptance, and commitment needed to implement strategies effectively. Managers cannot isolate each of these processes and deal with their imperatives separately and in a completely orderly fashion. Instead executives must move forward incrementally, integrating all three parameters each time a crucial step in any of the three processes allows.

Diversification subsystems

Strategies for diversification, through either R&D or acquisitions, provide excellent examples. The formal analytical steps needed for successful (internal or acquisition) diversification are well documented.[30] They include:

1. Clarifying the overall objectives of the corporation.

2. Setting forth broad goals for the diversification program within these overall objectives.
3. Defining specific criteria that acquisitions or developments should meet.
4. Systematically searching out new product or acquisition candidates.
5. Setting priorities for pursuing these.
6. Evaluating specific candidates in technical, operational, and financial terms.
7. Pricing acquisition deals or controlling R&D projects for adequate returns.
8. Planning the integration of the new division or line into the enterprise.
9. Implementing its integration and following up to see that intended yields are realized.

However, the precise directions in which R&D may project the company can be understood only step by step as scientists uncover new phenomena, make and amplify discoveries, build prototypes, reduce concepts to practice, and interact with users during product introductions. Similarly, only as each acquisition is sequentially identified, investigated, negotiated for, and integrated into the organization can one predict its ultimate impact on the total enterprise.

● When Pilkington Brothers, Ltd., introduced float glass, it would have been difficult to anticipate that float would cause the organization to decentralize, go into a diversification-acquisition program, change its paternalistic management style, professionalize its management ranks, become a more truly multinational company, and ultimately move from a private to a publicly held company. One could have foreseen a few of these dimensions in 1958, when float was introduced, and have built flexibilities and resource buffers to take advantage of opportunities as they developed. However, logic dictated that Pilkington test the success of its new process at increasing scales and for different products, see how the market place accepted its product, improve the flexibility of the process before installing numerous plants worldwide, and allow plate competition to settle into new patterns before converting to the other specific dimensions of its ultimate strategy.

Acquisitions and joint ventures like those with British Indestructo Glass, Perkin-Elmer, and other specialty glass manufacturers could only occur opportunistically as those companies became available for sale or developed new products of interest to Pilkington. As the product line diversified, more decentralization, formal planning, and professional management became natural demands. And incremental changes in the tax environment, age structure, and financial fortunes of stockholders led to Pilkington's 1970 public offering. The general nature of many of these strategic thrusts could be foreseen a few years before the actual event. However, the specific nature, timing, and integration of each opportunity had to occur incrementally.

Similarly, the specific shape and form of General Mills' or Pillsbury's acquisition strategies could be determined only as individual candidates became available.

• General Mills very carefully laid out criteria for its (1969 era) acquisition program in the classic manner. Out of this came two thrusts. One was to expand in food-related areas, and the other was to develop new growth centers based on General Mills' skills at marketing to the homemaker. The informal feeling was that the great majority of resources should go to food-related areas. In fact, almost the reverse occurred. Over the next five years General Mills invested something like $450 million in new businesses, and most were not closely related to foods.

Food related fields had become highly competitive. Available companies were not market leaders, were prohibitively priced, or were foreclosed by the FTC for antitrust reasons. As a result, the corporation had a good selection of candidates in the nonfoods area and few in related fields. By 1973, General Mills had diversified into a dazzling array of new areas from creative crafts to fine clothing, with high impact on its strategic posture.

A step-by-step approach is clearly necessary to guide and assess the proper timing and strategic fit of each internal or external diversification candidate.[31] The actual net vector of such strategies will ultimately be determined by how all the diversifying pieces blend together—a fact that can rarely be determined until the pieces themselves are known and in place. Incremental processes are also required to manage the crucial psychological and power shifts that ultimately determine the program's overall direction and consequences. These processes help unify both the analytical and behavioral aspects of diversification decisions. They create the broad conceptual consensus, the risk-taking attitudes, the organizational and resource flexibilities, and the adaptive dynamism that determine both the timing and the direction of diversification strategies. Most important among these processes are those outlined below:

Generating a genuine top-level psychological commitment to diversification. General Mills, Pillsbury, and Xerox all started their major diversification programs with broad analytical studies and goal-setting exercises designed both to build top-level consensus around the need to diversify and to establish the general directions for diversification. Without such action, top-level bargaining for resources could have continued to support only more familiar (and hence apparently less risky) old lines, and this could have delayed or undermined the entire diversification endeavor.

Consciously preparing to move opportunistically. Organizational and fiscal resources must be built up in advance to exploit candidates as they randomly appear. A "credible activist" for ventures must be developed and backed by someone with commitment power. All successful acquirers among the companies studied created the potential for profit-centered divisions within their organizational structures, strengthened their financial controllership capabilities, took action to create low-cost capital access, and maintained the shortest possible communication lines from the acquisitions activist to the resource-committing authority. All these actions integrally determined which diversifications actually could be made, the timing of their accession, and the pace with which they could be absorbed.

Building a "comfort factor" for risk taking. Perceived risk is largely a function of one's knowledge about a field. Hence, well-conceived diversification programs anticipated a trial-and-error period during which top managers were likely to reject early proposed fields or opportunities until they had analyzed enough trial candidates to become comfortable with an initial selection. Early successes tended to be "sure things" close to the companies' past (real or supposed) expertise. After a few successful diversifications, managements tended to become more confident and accepted other candidates—farther from traditional lines—at a faster rate. The way this process was handled affected both the direction and the pace of the actual program.

Developing a new ethos. If new divisions were more successful than the old—as they should be—they attracted relatively more resources and their political power grew. Their most effective line managers moved into corporate positions, and slowly the company's special competency and ethos changed. Finally, the concepts and products that once dominated the company's culture might decline in importance or even disappear. Acknowledging these ultimate consequences to the organization at the beginning of a diversification program would clearly have been impolitic, even if the manager both so desired and could have predicted the probable new ethos. These factors had to be handled adaptively as opportunities presented themselves and as individual leaders and power centers developed.[32]

Each of the preceding processes interacted with all others (and with the random appearance of diversification candidates) to affect action sequences, elapsed time, and ultimate results in unexpected ways.[33] Complexities were generally so great that few diversification programs ended up as initially envisioned. Consequently, wise managers recognized the limits to systematic analysis in diversification and used formal planning (1) to build the comfort levels executives needed for risk taking and (2) to guide the program's early directions and priorities. They then modified these flexibly, step by step, as new opportunities, power centers, and developed competencies merged to create new potentials.

• Several executives at Xerox described that company's acquisition of Diablo, Daconics, and Versatec in the same

way. "The Flavin Committee's work and other earlier discussions about the information field had defined certain
concepts and 'stand-alone' hardware as interesting and
relevant. Each of the three acquisitions then 'came in over
the transom.' . . . For example, we became aware that
Daconics would be willing to sell out to a big company.
Various people knew we had an interest in acquiring such a
company, and they brought it to us. . . . The acquisition
did not change our strategy; it just helped us implement it
more rapidly. The marketplace for information systems
was undefined. There were certain questions to be resolved.
Would there be centralized logic? Shared logic? Decentralized logic? The best way to find out about such a marketplace is to engage in it. Daconics and Versatec were already
in these markets earning revenues, and Versatec was already
profitable. This made them inexpensive bets. You could
acquire experience, knowledge, and products quickly. You
could both make a profit while you learned and avoid the
initial development costs of entry."

Divestiture subsystems

Similar practices governed the handling of divestitures.
Divisions often dragged along in a less-than-desired condition
for years before they could be strategically divested. In some
cases ailing divisions had just enough yield or potential to be
viable. In others, they represented the company's vital core
from earlier years, the creations of a powerful person nearing
retirement, or the psychological touchstones of the company's past traditions.[34]

Again, in designing divestiture strategies, top executives
often found that they had to reinforce vaguely felt concerns
with detailed data, build up managers' comfort levels about
issues, achieve participation in and commitment to decisions,
and move opportunistically to make actual changes. In many
cases the precise nature of the decision itself was not clear at
the outset. Executives often consciously made seemingly
unrelated personnel shifts or appointments to affect the
values of critical groups. Or they might initiate a series of
staff studies to generate awareness about a problem or accep-

tance of the need for new solutions. Only after a series of such partial moves might the outlines of the ultimate divestiture strategy become clear.

Executives might then instigate goal assessment, business review, or planning programs to provide broader forums for discussion and a wider consensus for action. Even then they might wait for a crisis, a crucial retirement, or an attractive sale opportunity to determine the timing and conditions of divestiture. In some cases, decisions could be direct and analytical; but when divestitures involved the psychological centers of the organization, the process had to be much more oblique and carefully orchestrated.

• When General Rawlings became president at General Mills, he had his newly developed Staff (Corporate Analysis) Department make informal presentations to top management on key issues. Later these were expanded to formal Management Operating Reviews (MORs) with all corporate and divisional top managers and controllers present. As problem operations were identified (many "generally known for a long time"), teams of corporate and divisional people were assigned to investigate them in depth. Once needed new data systems were built and studies came into place, they focused increasing attention on some hasty post-World War II acquisitions.

First to go was a highly cyclical—and unprofitable—formula feeds business for which "there was no real heavy philosophical commitment." Then followed some other small divisions and the low-profit electronics business "which the directors didn't feel very comfortable with because it was so different. . . ." At the time, this business was headed by a recently appointed former Finance Department man "who had no strong attachments to electronics." Only then did the annual reports begin to refer to these conscious moves as ones designed "to concentrate on the company's major strengths." And only then, despite earlier concern, frustration, and discontent about its commodity aspects, could the traumatic divestiture of flour milling—the core of the company's traditions—be approached.

Before finally selling off a division, companies would frequently "dress up their finances," spinning out inventories, absorbing overheads at corporate levels, and cutting back on technology, plant maintenance, and other "invisibles." To maintain the morale of those in the division, such changes were often made to appear like the beginning of a turnaround as the division improved its financial profitability and returns. Certainly, managers could not announce in advance their intention to sell off the division. Otherwise, specialists would leave the division and make it unsalable.[35] Sometimes, in fact, the company gave the division a trial period in its new trappings to see whether it could be continuously profitable before making the final decision to sell it off. In strategic terms, such a decision represented an important choice: "To be willing to make a planned withdrawal if necessary." However if resources were available and the division put up a good fight, it might be asked to hold its position or even advance. Such decisions—often markedly affecting the parent entity's total strategic posture—were logically made incrementally.

The major reorganization subsystem

It is well recognized that major organizational changes are an integral part of strategic changes. In general, the observation is that "organization follows strategy."[36] My data showed, however, that major reorganizations themselves sometimes constituted the central element of a strategy change. Sometimes they preceded and/or precipitated a new strategy, and sometimes they helped to implement a strategy. But like many other important strategic decisions, macroorganizational moves were typically handled incrementally *and* outside the formal planning processes. Why?

Their effects on personal or power relationships precluded discussion in the open forums and reports of formal planning. In addition, major organizational changes had timing imperatives (or process limits) all their own. In making any significant shifts, top executives had to think through the new roles, capabilities, and probable individual reactions of the many principals affected. They might have to wait for the promotion or retirement of valued colleagues before consummating any change. They then frequently had to bring in, train, or test new people for substantial periods before they could staff key posts with confidence.

Such incrementalism was especially noticeable during major strategy shifts such as that brought on by William Spoor at Pillsbury.

• Bringing in a whole new quantitative, goal-oriented, management style, Mr. Spoor had to see how new individuals—regardless of how enthusiastic they might be about the new regime and/or successful under the old—tested out under new circumstances. Without the devastating morale consequences of a "clean sweep" of experienced personnel, Spoor had to develop his new organization incrementally as people understood and performed in their new assignments, as his own confidence in individuals grew or abated, and as his new control systems pointed out performance factors that were not previously apparent. In addition, the organization had to be shaped around the management capabilities of people acquired in new acquisitions or lost in divestitures. Clearly, these matters could be neither foreseen in detail nor expressed in broad planning meetings.

During such testing periods, top executives might substantially modify their original concepts of the entire reorganization as individuals' potentials, performance, personal drives, and relationships with other team members developed. Because this chain of evaluations could affect the career development, power, affluence, and self-image of so many, top executives tended to keep close counsel in their discussions. They negotiated individually with key people and made final commitments as late as possible to obtain the best match-ups between people's capabilities, personalities, and aspirations in their new roles. Rarely, if ever, did all these events come together at one convenient time, particularly at the moment annual plans were due. Instead top executives moved opportunistically, step by step, selectively moving people toward a broadly conceived organizational goal, which was constantly modified and rarely articulated in detail until the last important psychological and structural pieces fit together.

Major organizational moves might also define entirely new strategies that the guiding executive could not fully foresee at the outset.

• When Exxon began its regional decentralization on a world-wide basis, the Executive Committee placed a senior officer (and board member) with a very responsive management style in a vaguely defined "coordinative role" vis-à-vis its powerful and successful European units. Over a period of two years this man sensed problems and experimented with voluntary coordinative possibilities on a pan-European basis. Only later, with greater understanding by both corporate and divisional officers, did Exxon move to a more formal "line" relationship for what became Exxon Europe. Even then the move had to be coordinated step by step with similar experimental shifts to regionalized consolidations in other areas of the world. All these changes together led to an entirely new internal power balance toward regional and non-U.S. concerns and to a more responsive worldwide posture for Exxon.[37]

• At General Mills, General Rawlings and his team of outside professional managers actively redefined the company's problems and opportunities in ways the prior management could not have. Once the divestitures noted earlier were made, the funds released were used for acquisitions, thus automatically increasing the visibility and power of the controllership-financial group. Similarly, with fewer large divisions competing for funds, the consumer food groups rapidly increased in their importance. This ultimately led to a choice between these two groups' leaders for the next chairmanship of the company—and hence for control over the corporation's future strategy.

In such situations, executives might be able to predict the broad direction, but not the precise nature, of the ultimate strategy that would result. In some cases, such as Exxon, the rebalance of power and information relationships *became* the strategy, or at least its central element. In others, such as General Mills, organizational shifts were primarily means of triggering or implementing new strategic concepts and philosophies. But in all cases, major organizational changes created unexpected new stresses, opportunities, power bases, information centers, and credibility relationships that affected both previous plans and future strategies in unanticipated ways.[38] Effective reorganization decisions, therefore, should allow for testing, flexibility, and feedback. Hence, they should —and from my observations usually do—evolve incrementally.

Incrementalism is especially necessary for organizational changes that reflect dramatic shifts in the company's ethos or involve substantial infusions of outside management.

- Mr. Geneen's takeover of IT&T is a classic example. Geneen obviously had a clear idea of the broad structural changes he wanted to make to obtain more effective control at IT&T. However, he first had to install a new control system which could measure performance in the terms he sought. To obtain effective information, he had to install a cadre of competent and loyal people in staff positions at the corporate level. He had to maintain confidence in and improve the profitability of the company's existing divisions at the same time that he was preparing to sell off some, was convinced that the management of others must be replaced, and was testing to see whether some of the company's existing executive force might not thrive under a new system. New acquisitions had to be grouped and regrouped, their managements weeded out, and their control practices changed. Divisions would have to be bought, sold, or developed opportunistically as they became available (or hopeless), or as political environments shifted.[39]

With so many "unknowables" involved in major organizational changes, incrementalism—working toward a broadly and flexibly conceived framework--was the dictated logic.

The government-external relations subsystem

Almost all companies cited government and other external activist groups as among the most important forces causing significant changes in their strategic postures during the periods of the study. However, when asked "How did your company arrive at its own strategy vis-à-vis these forces?" few companies at that time had cohesive strategies (integrated sets of goals, policies, and programs) for government and external relations other than lobbying for or against specific legislative actions. To the extent that formal strategies did exist, they were piecemeal and ad hoc and had been derived in a very evolutionary manner. Yet again, there seemed to be very good reasons for such incrementalism. The following quotations offer the two best short explanations of the way these practices develop.

- "We are a very large company, and we understand that any massive overt action on our part could easily create more public antagonism than support for our viewpoint. It is also hard to say in advance exactly what public response any particular action might create. So we tend to test a number of different approaches on a small scale with only limited or local company identification. If one approach works, we'll test it further and amplify its use. If another bombs, we try to keep it from being used again. Slowly we find a series of advertising, public relations, or community relations actions that seem to help. Then along comes another issue and we start all over again. Gradually the successful approaches merge into a pattern of actions that becomes our strategy. We certainly don't have an overall strategy on this, and frankly I don't think we devote enough [organizational and fiscal] resources to it. This may be our most important strategic issue."

- "I [the president] start conversations with a number of knowledgeable people. . . . I collect articles and talk to people about how things get done in Washington in this particular field. I collect data from any reasonable source. I begin wide-ranging discussions with people inside and outside the corporation. From these a pattern eventually emerges. It's like fitting together a jigsaw puzzle. At first the vague outline of an approach appears like the sail of a ship in a puzzle. Then suddenly the rest of the puzzle becomes quite clear. You wonder why you didn't see it all along. And once it's crystallized, it's not difficult to explain to others."[40]

In this realm, uncontrollable forces dominated. Data tended to be very soft, often could be only subjectively

sensed, and might be costly to quantify. The possible responses of individuals and groups to different stimuli were
very often difficult to determine in advance. The number of
potential opponents with power was likely to be high, and
the diversity in their viewpoints and possible modes of attack
was so substantial that it was physically impossible to lay out
probabilistic decision diagrams that would have much meaning. Results were unpredictable and the costs of error
extreme. Even the best intended and most rational-seeming
strategies could be converted into disasters unless they were
thoroughly and interactively tested.

- In the 1960s General Motors found that technical discussions of cost-versus-benefit trade-offs were useless against
  demagogic slogans like "smog kills" or "GM is the worst
  polluter in the world." It publicly resisted some early attempts to impose pollution standards, stating that they
  were "beyond the state of the art." Then after successfully
  completing the costly and risky development of the cata-
  lytic converter, GM had its earlier concerns thrown in its
  face as "foot dragging" or "lying" about technical potentials. As one executive said, "You were damned if you did
  and damned if you didn't."

  Only after prolonged interaction with regualtors, legislators, and public-interest groups did GM truly understand
  the needs and pressure potentials of its opponents. Area by
  area it learned to communicate better with various major
  interests. Only then could it identify effective patterns for
  dealing with all parties.

For such reasons, companies will probably always have to
derive major portions of their government-external relations
strategies in an experimental, iterative fashion. But much
more formal strategic thinking is needed by most companies.
Clear goals defining the dimensions of principal thrusts,
developing a unity of command on this issue, creating a sufficient time horizon to be effective, dealing with the basic
social and psychological forces behind potential opponents'
actions, and developing needed coalitions with like-minded
(nonbusiness) groups are the minimum prerequisites of such

a strategy. Most companies' incrementalism in this sphere could be much more proactive—and less reactive—than it often has been in the past. Favorable public opinion and political action take a long time to mold. And active, continuous commitment of intellect and resources is required to shape this opinion without creating more counterpressures than progress.

There is a developing body of knowledge about how to influence political action. Unfortunately, however, most companies did not use this knowledge to manage their strategic processes in the political realm with the same astuteness they demonstrated in more familiar environments. Once potential approaches were experimentally derived—without destroying needed flexibilities—more cohesive planning could have ensured that the resources committed were sufficient to achieve desired goals, that all important polities were included in plans, and that rigorous and adaptive internal controls maintained those high performance, attitude, service, and image qualities that lent credibility to the strategy. Still, no matter how well such formal techniques may be utilized, some testing, feedback, and dynamic development will probably always be necessary because of the complexities involved. Logical incrementalism is likely to remain the essential thread linking together the formal information gathering, analysis, testing, awareness building, consensus broadening, coalition creating, and other behavioral and power dynamic actions needed to achieve an effective strategy in this realm (see Chapter 4).

FORMAL PLANNING: A COMPONENT IN CORPORATE STRATEGY

For good reasons, managements derived strategies for each of the previous major issues through separate strategic subsystems; that is, different people, considerations, and methodologies dominated each. Each subsystem had its own pacing parameters that were different from the others. As they approved final decisions for each subsystem, top managers tried intuitively to integrate actions into a cohesive whole. However, the imperatives of a given moment might easily drive any one of the subsystems out of synchronization with the others. Examining and maintaining the potential meshing of the various subsystems with ongoing operating commitments was one of the main functions of formal corporate planning. All companies in the study did have some form of formal planning procedure embedded in their management direction and control systems. These seemed to serve certain essential functions; in a decision-making sense, they:

1. Formalized and calibrated strategic decisions already made.
2. Provided a systematic means for evaluating and fine-tuning annual budgets.
3. Formed a basis for protecting longer term investments and commitments that might otherwise have been driven out by budgetary pressures
4. Helped implement strategic changes once decided on (for example, coordinating all elements of Exxon's decision to change its corporate name).

All these were important functions; however, formal planning systems rarely formulated a corporation's central strategy. Perhaps the most important contributions of formal corporate planning systems were in the "process" realm:

1. They created a network of information that would not otherwise have been available.
2. They periodically forced operating managers to extend their time horizons and see their work in a larger framework.
3. They required rigorous communications about goals, strategic issues, and resource allocations.
4. They systematically taught managers about the future so they could better intuitively calibrate their short-term or interim decisions.
5. They often created an attitude about and a comfort factor concerning the future; that is, managers felt less uncertain about the future and consequently were more willing to make commitments that extended beyond short-time horizons.

6. They often stimulated longer term "special studies" that could have high impact at key junctures for specific strategic decisions.[41]

Special studies

In fact, in the companies observed, formal planning contributed most directly to significant change when it was set up as a "special study" on some important aspect of corporate strategy.

- In 1958, when it became apparent that Pilkington's new float glass process would work, the company formed a Directors Flat Glass Committee consisting of all internal directors associated with float glass "to consider the broad issues of flat glass [strategy] in both the present and the future." The committee did not attempt detailed plans. Instead, it tried to deal in broad concepts, identify alternate routes, and think through the potential consequences of each route some ten years ahead. Of some of the key strategic decisions, Sir Alastair later said, "It would be difficult to identify an exact moment when the decision was made.... Nevertheless, over a period of time a consensus crystallized with great clarity."

- In the late 1960s, after the extraordinary success of the 914 copier, Xerox's Chairman Wilson and President McColough began to worry about the positioning of their total product line. At their request the company's engineers worked with the product planning department to evaluate a series of experimental products (which were then in development) from which top management could choose. These groups developed a series of strategies (from A through Q) concerning these alternative products—where to concentrate and where to deploy lesser resources. Top management chose Strategy Q, which led to the development of the product lines on which the company concentrated in the 1970s. Yet many of the initial targets for product positioning, timing, and pricing were adjusted as cost and market realities became clearer.[42]

In each case there were also important precursor events, analyses, and political interactions, and each was followed by organizational, power, and behavioral changes. Such special strategic studies also represented a subsystem of strategy formulation distinct from both annual planning activities and the other subsystems mentioned earlier. Like each of these, this subsystem developed some important aspect of strategy, incrementally blending its conclusions with those of other subsystems toward an intuitively sensed whole. In fact, in all observed cases, it would have been virtually impossible to force all the subsystems together analytically to crystallize a completely articulated corporate strategy at any one instant.

Formal plans also increment

In most cases, even formal planning was actually part of an incremental process. Although individual staff planners might identify potential problems and bring them to top management's attention, the annual planning process itself was rarely (if ever in the study) the source of new key issues or radical departures into entirely different product/market realms. These almost always came from precipitating events, special studies, or conceptions implanted through the kinds of logical incremental processes described previously.

Formal planning practices themselves usually institutionalized a form of incrementalism. There were two reasons for this. *First,* in order to utilize specialized expertise and to obtain executive involvement and commitment, most planning occurred "from the bottom up" in response to broadly defined assumptions or goals, many of which were longstanding or negotiated well in advance. Of necessity, lower level groups had only a partial view of the corporation's total strategy and commanded only a fragment of its resources. Their power bases, identity, expertise, and rewards also usually depended on their existing product lines, services, or processes. Hence, these—rather than entirely new departures—should have and did receive their primary attention. *Second,* most managements purposely designed their plans to be "living" or "evergreen." They were intended only as frameworks to guide and provide consistency for future decisions made incrementally during shorter term operating cycles. To act otherwise would deny that further information could have a value. Thus, properly formulated formal plans also became part of an incremental logic.

Formal annual planning procedures provided a mechanism through which earlier strategic decisions were confirmed. Formal planning, to a large extent, provided the interface between strategic and tactical decisions. As such, planning was the sine qua non of all decentralization. Without codifying agreed-upon goals, commitment patterns, and action sequences, operating managers could not coordinate their tactics toward longer term objectives. Nevertheless, most of the important strategies that were supported by formal plans were determined in processes separate from the formal planning cycle, and most of these occurred in the types of incremental processes described previously.

Total posture planning

Occasionally, however, managements did attempt very broad assessments of their companies' total posture.

● Shortly after becoming CEO of General Mills, James McFarland decided that his job was "to take a very good company and move it to greatness," but that it was up to his management group, not himself alone, to decide what a great company was and how to get there. Consequently, he took some 35 of the company's topmost managers away for a three-day management retreat. On the first day, after agreeing to broad financial goals, the groups broke up into units of six to eight people. Each unit was to answer the question, "What is a great company?" from the viewpoints of stockholders, employees, suppliers, the public, and society. Each unit reported back at the end of the day, and the whole group tried to reach a consensus through discussion.

On the second day the groups, in the same format, assessed the company's strengths and weaknesses relative to the defined posture of "greatness." The third day focused on how to overcome the company's weaknesses and move it toward a great company. This broad consensus led, over the next several years, to the surveys of fields for acquisition, the building of management's initial comfort levels with certain fields, and the acquisition-divestiture strategy that characterized the McFarland era at General Mills.

- Xerox Corporation used several such posture analyses between 1965 and 1974. The first of these was the Strategy Q analysis described earlier. In 1971, McColough formed another committee of top-line officers to define for the company how it should develop itself around a coalescing theme, "the architecture of information," which had seemed to catch the imagination of the company. This produced a plan defining some eight business areas for the company. This was flexibly implemented through acquisition and internal development.

  In 1974, McColough asked another group, with the full support of internal staffs and external consultants, to help define for the company what its posture should be vis-à-vis many of the great issues of the times (food shortages, energy, ecology, materials supplies, the world's poor, etc.). They were to "discard every taboo, every written, stated, or believed objective of the company." They were to "write strategies and comment on strategies in a broad frame" and report to the chairman and president on these matters. The committee was to use a full array of all the available formal strategic analysis techniques in arriving at its conclusions. These primarily broadened the horizons and perceptions of the CEO and president. Specific decisions are not yet clear.

Yet even such major endeavors were only portions of a total strategic process. Values that had been built up over decades stimulated or constrained alternatives. Precipitating events, acquisitions, divestitures, external relations, and organizational changes developed important segments of each strategy incrementally. Even the strategies articulated left key elements to be defined as new information became available, politics permitted, or particular opportunities appeared (like Pilkington's "Electro-Float" invention or Xerox's Daconics acquisition). Major product thrusts conceived strategically (like Pilikngton's TV tubes or Xerox's computers) proved unsuccessful. Actual strategies therefore evolved as each company overextended, consolidated, made errors, and rebalanced various thrusts over time, and it was both logical and expected that this would be the case.

DETERMINANTS OF THE STRATEGIC PROCESS

All effective strategy formulation must deal with both the analytically quantifiable factors present and the informational shortcomings, uncertainties, unknowables, and human psychological issues that dictate incrementalism. Within observed companies each strategic subsystem had its own internal logic and its own set of pacing parameters. At certain points these called for formal analytical approaches as noted. At others social-power-behavioral considerations dominated. In all companies I found a mixture of all three of Mintzberg's "modes" of strategy formation—entrepreneurial, adaptive, and planning.[43] The particular mix of formal and informal processes a company needed depended largely on its culture or ethos, management style, organizational form, external opposition, time horizons and degree of control over events.

Some of these determinants were internal characteristics of particular enterprises and accounted for differences in practice among companies in the same industry. Others, dictated by the industry and its environment, caused relative similarities within one industry. All interacted in determining what strategic processes—and what degrees of incrementalism— were most appropriate for a particular company. Using three examples—Exxon, Xerox, and Chrysler Corporation—from different industries, the following sections will show how such factors influenced the processes each company used in its strategy formulation.*

Culture or ethos

Exxon operated in a world of huge volumes and physical movements; the world moved as much oil and coal each year

---

*Conclusions in these sections are my own observations alone. They do not necessarily represent the official policy of the companies. However, they do reflect how these companies' strategic structures seemed to perform in practice.

as the sum of all the other materials it used in commerce. And Exxon was the largest mover of energy resources in the world. The company invested incredible resources ($4 to $10 billion per year) relative to most companies, and its products influenced entire nations' internal economies, trade patterns, balance of payments, and foreign relations in ways few other industries could. The company was used to playing on the stage with world powers, and governments were inevitably and deeply involved in all its strategic considerations. The company took huge risks, losing hundreds of millions of dollars in single dry formations in the Gulf of Mexico or the Atlantic shelf. It worked among large unknowns both in the physical environment and in the way governments, markets, industries, unions, and others could react to its every action. Yet not even multibillion-dollar investments could change its course significantly in five to ten years. This environment led to: (1) a very elaborate, constantly updated formal planning activity to evaluate and control major investments; (2) a worldwide intelligence network of extraordinary proportions to help anticipate political and social trends; (3) a tentative, probing, politically responsive style of arriving at ultimate decisions concerning its external polities; and (4) a matrix-committee management structure to ensure a thorough quantitative and qualitative review of all critical issues.

Xerox Corporation, by contrast, had lived in an ethos initially created by a great invention and a product line well defended by patents. Its technology was exploding; its culture exuded confidence, daring, and a sense that one could do almost anything. It was also driven by a "what can we do next" syndrome. In its relatively protected competitive position, its management could lean back, take a long look into the future, and try to determine what future it wanted to create. This led to a series of carefully structured strategic analyses that sequentially: (1) analyzed and positioned the company's reprographic lines, (2) positioned the company within a broad concept of "the architecture of information," and (3) analyzed the impact of the world's great forces (food shortages, energy needs, health, and the environment) on the company and its potential responses to these forces. Yet because the company had attracted so many bright, ambitious young people, each of these strategic analyses had to be carefully coupled with participatory actions deep in the organization, careful consensus building, and flexible follow-up to allow invention and innovation. And as the company undertook acquisitions for diversification, this part of its strategy of necessity became more opportunistic and incremental in approach.

Chrysler Corporation had developed an ethos that could be described as: "We're number 3; we must scramble on the edge of a volatile market. But we're an engineering company. We can be tough; we can use outmoded plant and resources to do things our competitors cannot." The company had become used to centralized (sometimes charismatic) leadership at the top and to tight financial controls that drove the whole organization. "Our car line is our strategy" was a common view within the company. As a result, strategic planning had been reduced to budgetary planning. Detailed changes in auto designs were made by the chief executive officer. The company had been late to move overseas and had picked up weak acquisitions. Its non-auto units had received little strategic attention. Workers had become alienated, and the development of intermediate-level management had suffered.

To turn this situation around permanently required a mix of strategic approaches: an appealing new broad concept of the company at the top; some hard centralized decisions on unsatisfactory divisions and the concept of the automobile line itself; and a carefully coordinated, long-term, grass-roots effort to rebuild morale, management, and a new, more proactive ethos. The president led a series of discussions to bring some broader goals into focus for top management. Then a series of "Special Analytical Studies" helped determine the fate of nonauto and overseas divisions. Hard single-policy choices had to be made on subcompacts and trucks. Formal product planning helped reposition some individual car lines. Formal business plans were installed to broaden horizons at the division level. And a very long-term participative process was started to stimulate needed attitude changes deep in the organization. All these issues deserved strategic emphasis. Different approaches, time horizons, and priorities were needed for each. Their integration had to be incremental, but their cohesiveness and impact were undermined by deep differences in top-level viewpoints. Unfortunately, little was done to develop a meaningful special competency for the firm or a unified concept of the total line that was related to the new external environment—particularly the need for smaller cars, which would have directed investments away from the "more profitable" larger cars favored by the company's top financial managers and directors.

Nature of opposition

Exxon faced very different opponents from Xerox or Chrysler. Whole nations, international cartels and power blocs, complete government agencies, individual politicians, organized special-interest groups, very large utilities, huge competitors, and massive financial interests made up its opposition. Each force was powerful. Any untoward move by Exxon could create a new coalition among these forces, and individual players could be both brilliant and extremely hostile. The company had to be very responsive at local levels, yet able to use its full force to maintain some control over its destiny in international relationships. Single errors could be very costly for Exxon or its opponents. As a result its strategy concerning external forces tended to form as a slowly changing series of power relationships within the company and externally. The company constantly probed the environment, adjusting its overall posture incrementally, testing commitments each step of the way, and maintaining maximum flexibility and bargaining potentialities through diversified resource reserves, finance sources, and a localized identity (such as Exxon France) throughout the world.

Xerox's opposition, by contrast, had been mostly in the marketplace and from possible technological advances. Since the market was at first wide open with no established power centers, Xerox could pick its own positions for concentration, provided it could dominate that sector's technology. Consequently, its early (post-914) strategy rationally segmented the market, analytically selecting where Xerox should concentrate its limited resources and what points it should concede until later. Because the technology's potentials were unknown, the company maximized flexibility by hiring as many highly talented people as it could afford and allowed them a much less structured environment at operating levels than either Chrysler or Exxon could. It defended itself against threats with patents, through a very large R&D endeavor, and through incrementally developed diversification moves. As long as these defenses existed, Xerox had the lead times needed for more structured formal strategic planning. But it still moved incrementally in diversification, new product introduction, reorganization, and government-external relations spheres.

Chrysler's major opponents were well-entrenched, large, specifically identifiable entities: unions, government regulators, Ford, General Motors, and selected foreign auto makers. Each of these—and its own customers—could hurt the company catastrophically if Chrysler made significant errors. The bulk of its commitments were to plant, tooling, product introduction, and marketing costs supporting the Chrysler auto lines, which immediately had to meet the one-year "battle strategies" of each competitor. Consequently, Chrysler focused much formal planning effort on the short-term characteristics of the auto line itself. It attacked other elements of its strategy—government relations, employee relations, standardization and quality improvement programs, and others—with much less formality and with more behaviorally oriented persuasion processes. Unfortunately, the company felt so constrained by resources that it did not develop the financial, technical, and organization buffers that could have allowed it greater flexibility, more strategic control, and a longer time horizon for its overall strategic commitments.

Organization form and management style

Because of its huge scale, Exxon would have had very large divisions no matter what its organizational form. And these divisions had to be headed by very powerful people capable of running business units larger than most major companies in the world. The sheer scope of these divisions' activities defied measurement and control in detail. Each product line (oil, coal, petrochemicals, and so on) needed its own technical and functional expertise. Operating units had to respond flexibly to local needs and cultures. Yet the company needed centralized control over its capital, technology, currency positions, inter-unit shipments, and corporate image building. All this required a huge multilevel, worldwide, matrix organization with high decentralization and relatively few common strategic bonds at the center. The few strategic decisions made at the center involved huge commitments, powerful amorphous opposing forces, and incredibly long lead times. Exxon therefore had evolved a complex committee-matrix headquarters organization that brought to bear the best wisdom of many different viewpoints on any important issue.

Such systems by their nature tend to be slower, more conservative, satisficing, incremental, and political than straightline organizations. And consensus solutions with broad top-level acceptance tended to characterize corporate strategic decisions. Phrases like "The decision just seemed to emerge, it was reasonable to all of us; we had tested the water and that seemed the proper way to go" described many important decisions. Such processes predictably led to negotiated strategies with a less distinctive product or investment profile (vis-à-vis industry competitors) than one might expect at Xerox or Chrysler.[44] In fact, perhaps the key element in Exxon's strategy was establishing the bargaining power and intended bargaining limits among the corporate center, various special interests, and the decentralized regional and operating units.

At Xerox the management style was open, charismatic, and entrepreneurial. Both Joe Wilson and Peter McColough were structured, conceptual thinkers, but both had highly participative management styles. From the early days of Haloid Corp., Wilson established the practice of taking his management team on retreats to share information about the company's situation and to keep managers thinking about the future. Xerox's dominantly functional organization demanded coordination at the top and a clear strategy to guide lower level units—which were both functional and highly decentralized. Along with the other determinants described, this naturally led to a series of more formalized strategies arrived at participatively. However, as the organization became larger and more complex, more varied matrices of interest stimulated more negotiated strategies and a distinctive incrementalism in acquisition, deversification, organizational, and government-external relations strategies.

At Chrysler, Cafiero and Riccardo needed to signal a break from the old centralized management style and its overuse of financial controls. Cafiero had a very warm, human, operating style and saw "using Chrysler's well-trained people to optimum advantage" as a key strategic element in improving quality and productivity. So he began a long-term program to decentralize the company and to get active involvement in change at all levels. He started participation programs in all plants and incrementally encouraged people to experiment with change. "If anyone gets fired for [these activities], I'll rehire him with a raise," was his announced policy. He held repeated meetings, created standardization and quality improvement committees, and gave interactive seminar speeches throughout the company to create awareness, support, and consensus around needed changes. At the same time, he and Riccardo—who had a financial-accounting background—introduced more formal goal setting, business planning, and performance measurement programs throughout the organization to tighten up controls and operating routines because of resource stringencies. And based on special studies, they sold off nonautomotive, foreign, and weak divisions, built up the truck unit, refocused the compact auto line, and stayed out of subcompacts. Thus, they too mixed formalism and behavioral consensus building incrementally—but perhaps too slowly—to initiate a new strategy.

Time horizon and degree of control

Other crucial factors affecting how an enterprise approaches its strategic formulations are its time horizon and its degree of control over events. Exxon dealt with resource bases that could last scores of years, marketing outlets that would be in place for decades, refineries that took ten years to place and another three to five years to achieve returns, pipelines that functioned for decades, and so on. Data were reasonably solid for these kinds of investments, their dollar values were impressive, and the company had reasonable control over most operations once begun. Consequently, very sophisticated calculations using all the model builder's art went into positioning these investments. These were an important part of the total Exxon strategy.

Building Exxon's essential political relationships was also a long-term matter, but here there were potentials for very short-term reversals over which the company could have little control. Although Exxon had both internal groups performing political analyses and external sources to help evaluate political trends and changes worldwide, its corporate geopolitical strategy had to be "soft," behavioral, and evolutionary in nature. To achieve security for its long-term investments in each area, the company needed to identify itself with each host country's interests and become as genuinely indispensable to that country as possible. Yet simultaneously it had to stay as flexible as possible vis-à-vis each country in case a hostile political force took power. Somehow, while achieving a balance between these conflicting goals, it had to try to rationalize its investments and materials movements worldwide to optimize its own gains. Within the limits of such broad policies, the company's actual geopolitical strategy evolved continuously and incrementally, with only a few obvious thrusts—like "diversifying supply sources worldwide" or "increasing the company's presence in stable and friendly political environments"—being at all visible or stable.

By contrast, Xerox's time horizons could properly be placed at about ten years—the time to develop, introduce, and exploit a major new product line before its market was substantially eroded by next-generation technology. Any control the company had over its markets came from the concept and design of its products, their technical capabilities, and their positioning in the marketplace. Consequently, Xerox used sophisticated formal planning to specify the technical-economic-performance configuration of any new line as carefully as possible with a time horizon of a decade or more. But its technology and marketplace were changing so rapidly that the company had purposely introduced incrementalism— that is, iterative customer testing, feedback, and redesign— into the later parts of its design cycles to make sure that formal planning did not become a straitjacket on design, that innovation was encouraged, and that final product decisions reflected the latest possible information.

Chrysler Corporation's operant time horizons were dominated by its three-year design and retooling cycle for a new line and the one-year sales cycle for any given model. Consequently, there was great formality in planning these aspects of the business. But three other strategic horizons were also relevant: (1) the seven to ten years it took to build a continuing image for a complete line of cars; (2) the five to seven years necessary to develop technology, change customer attitudes, build credibility, educate legislators and regulators, and respond effectively to government regulatory moves; and (3) the three- to five-year lead time it took to lay down plants and to standardize parts for lower costs and greater quality control. Decisions in all four time frames interacted. But they all should have centered around the choice of the unifying concept and distinctive edge the car line could achieve, the very area where decisions to date have proved least adequate. This and some other crucial strategic moves required primarily qualitative judgments and highly adaptive response strategies, others demanded fixed commitments based on firm estimates, and still others—like technology— involved great uncertainties and merely built options for later choice. Thus a mixture of qualitative and formal planning, integrated incrementally and iteratively, was once again called for.

LOGICAL INCREMENTALISM

All my data suggest that strategic decisions do not come solely from power-political interplays. Nor do they lend themselves to aggregation in a single massive decision matrix where all factors can be treated quantitatively—or even relatively simultaneously—to arrive at a holistic optimum. Many have spoken of the "cognitive limits" that prevent the latter.[45] Of equal importance are the process limits—that is, the timing and sequencing imperatives necessary to create awareness, build comfort levels, develop consensus, and select and train people—that constrain the system yet ultimately determine the decision itself. Unlike the preparation of a fine banquet, it is virtually impossible for the manager to coordinate all impinging elements—internal decisions, external environmental events, behavioral and power relationships, technical and informational needs, and actions of intelligent opponents—so that they come together at any precise moment.

Can the process be managed?

Instead, top executives typically deal with the logic of each subsystem of strategy formulation largely on its own merits and usually with a different subset of people.[46] They try to develop or maintain in their own minds a consistent pattern among the decisions made in each subsystem. Knowing their own human limitations and the unknowability of the events they face, they consciously try to tap the minds and psychic drives of others in the organization who are more expert on details. They often purposely keep questions broad and decisions vague in early stages to avoid creating undue rigidities and to stimulate others' creativity. Logic dictates that the prudent and rational executive make final commitments *as late as possible* consistent with the information available.[47]

Consequently, many successful executives initially set only broad goals and policies that can accommodate a variety of specific proposals from below yet give a sense of guidance to the proposers. As they come forward, the proposals automatically and beneficially attract the support and identity of their sponsors.[48] Because they are only proposals, the executives can treat them at less politically charged levels, as specific projects rather than as larger goal or policy precedents. Therefore, they can encourage, discourage, or kill alternatives with considerably less political exposure. As events and opportunities emerge, they can incrementally guide the pattern of escalated or accepted proposals to suit their own purposes without getting prematurely committed to any rigid solution set, which unpredictable events might prove wrong or which opponents find sufficiently threatening to coalesce against.

A strategy emerges

Successful executives link together and bring order to a series of strategic processes and decisions spanning years. At the beginning of the process, it is literally impossible to predict all the events and forces that will shape the future of the company. The best executives can do is to forecast the most likely forces that will impinge on the company's affairs and the ranges of their possible impact. They then attempt to build a resource base and a corporate *posture* that are so strong in selected areas that the enterprise can survive and prosper despite all but the most devastating events. They consciously select market/technological/product segments that the concern can "dominate" given its resource limits, and place some "side bets" to decrease the risk of catastrophic failure or to increase the company's flexibility for future options.[49]

They then proceed incrementally to handle urgent matters, start longer term sequences with specific future branches and consequences that are perhaps murky, respond to unforeseen events as they occur, build on successes, and brace up or cut losses on failures. When properly managed, this is a proactive—rather than merely reactive—change process as some have suggested.[50] Successful strategists constantly reassess the future, find new congruencies as events unfurl, and blend the organization's skills and resources into new balances of dominance and risk aversion as various forces intersect to suggest better—but never perfect—alignments. The process is dynamic, with neither a real beginning nor an end. Pilkington Brothers, Ltd., provides an excellent example.

- After carefully formulating its broad float glass strategy in 1958, Pilkington Brothers, Ltd., quickly developed a technical dominance in flat glass throughout the world. With its patents and established businesses, it could control access to selected growth markets in specific countries. Float generated high growth and, after an initial investment period, high cash flows. These gave the company the resources to diversify geographically and into new product lines in order to decrease the risks inherent in the company's one product emphasis in a rapidly weakening British economy. It acquired, formed joint ventures, and expanded in selected product and geographical areas as opportunities became available. Meanwhile, socialism and modern communications combined to break down traditional dependencies among workers, employers, and communities. Growth and diversity required new professional managers and workers, and these executives created a new element in the lengthening gap between workers and owners. All these added to Pilkington's size and complexity.

By 1965, the company had become too complex to manage with its old centralized organization. When a key executive, Mr. Phelps, retired, this opened a chain of promotional possibilities; and after a number of formal and informal studies, the organization was decentralized. The process went too far, however, and the company had to be tightened up through further planning, reorganization, and new controls. Meanwhile, float technology led to entirely new product possibilities, even higher profits, and increased credibility for its successful (nonfamily) inventor, knighted as Sir Alastair Pilkington. All of these elements reinforced a decision made broadly in the early 1960s to go public near the end of the decade in order to help with the family owners' death duties and to provide a more flexible capital base for the company. In 1970, just before the company was to go public, a strike convinced the owners to ask Lord Pilkington, who was about to retire as chairman, to stay on for three more years before Sir Alastair became chairman. The strike also speeded moves away from Pilkington's paternalistic management style to a more professional one. In the mid-1970s, the company's strategy and posture were still being shaped by the key personalities and decisions of the 1950s.

Diagram 2 suggests some of the flow and interrelationships among these key events. When the original float strategy was formulated, no one could have forecast or foreseen the interaction of all these events. Any rigid posture would have been doomed. Logic, therefore, dictated the kind of constantly adjusted incrementalism one sees in this vignette. The history

Diagram 2
Simplified strategy flows
Diagram of Pilkington Brothers, Ltd., strategy development showing how separate subsystems develop independently, yet interrelate and flow together for final strategic posture as an innovative, decentralized, professionally managed, publicly held, worldwide, diversified glass products company. Cross-relations are vastly simplified for the diagram.

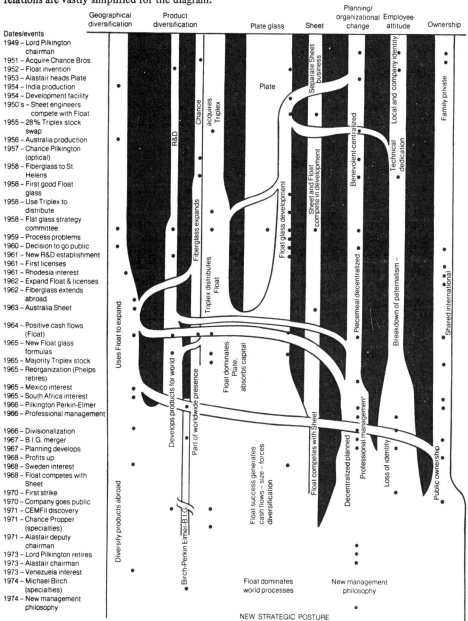

of all other companies studied would lead to similar conclusions. As noted in Chapter 5, strategy deals with the unknowable, not the uncertain. It involves forces of such great number, strength, and combinatory powers that one cannot predict events in a probabilistic sense. Hence it is logical that one proceed flexibly and experimentally from broad concepts toward specific commitments, making the latter concrete as late as possible in order to narrow the bands of uncertainty and to benefit from the best available information. This is the process of *logical incrementalism.*

Integrating the subsystems

How do top executives integrate these subsystem strategies into a cohesive whole? Since each major subsystem operates at a different pace, each is likely to be at an entirely different stage of problem definition, awareness building, preliminary conceptualization, experimentation, consensus creation, specificity, commitment, and control at any given moment. Consequently, except at the level of broad principles, it is impossible to set forth the total enterprise strategy in a way that instantaneously covers all areas. The overall strategy can never be truly complete in detail. Even if all the subsystems did accidentally come into place at any one moment, logic would dictate that the strategy begin to mutate and shift almost immediately as new data and events began to impinge on it. In fact, it may even be dangerous to believe that one should first formulate a detailed total strategy and then implement it. Too many examples suggest that this approach can build up rigidities, noncommitment, and opposition forces that are counterproductive.

Instead of seeking ultimate specificity in the total strategy, effective executives in my study accepted much ambiguity. They sought sufficient definition and balance to keep major subsystem thrusts from getting out of control and to keep the organization from working at cross-purposes. They tried to define the overall strategy in enough detail to encourage people to move in the right directions and to avoid disruptions. But they consciously avoided overspecifics that might impair the flexibility or commitment needed to exploit further information or new opportunities. Both subsystem and overall strategies remained broad enough to accommodate and deal with a wide range of possible futures. Yet to be effective, they had to form a cohesive whole. How did executives achieve the needed coordination?

At each stage of a strategy's development, effective executives constantly tried to visualize what new patterns might exist among the emerging strategies in various subsystems. As each subsystem strategy became more apparent, both its executive team and top-level groups consciously tried to project its implications for the total enterprise and to stimulate queries, support, and feedback from those involved in other interrelated strategies. Effective top executives saw that the various teams generating subsystem strategies had overlapping members. They required periodic updates and reviews before higher echelon groups that could bring a total corporate view to bear. They used formal planning processes to interrelate and evaluate the resources required, benefits sought, and risks undertaken vis-à-vis other elements of the enterprise's overall strategy. (See Chapter 5 for some suggestions in this regard.) Some used scenario techniques to help visualize potential impacts and relationships. Others utilized complex forecasting models to better understand basic interactions among subsystems, the total enterprise, and the environment. Still others consciously used specialized staffs, devil's advocates, or contention teams (see Chapter 4) to make sure that all important aspects of such strategies received a thorough evaluation.

All these more formal methodologies helped, but the real integration of all the components in a total enterprise's strategy eventually took place only in the minds of individual top executives. Each executive might legitimately perceive the intended balance of goals and thrusts somewhat differently. Some of these differences might be openly expressed as issues to be resolved when new information became available. Other differences might remain unstated, hidden agendas to emerge at later dates. Still others might be masked by accepting so broad a statement of intention that many different views could be brought toward a seeming consensus, whereas a more specific statement might be divisive. Nevertheless, effective strategies did achieve a level of consensus sufficient to focus action. And managed consensus tended to derive from the kinds of incremental interactive processes stressed here. But the kinds of strategic consensus one could observe appeared much like a giant river system, constantly in flux and flow with many more or less discrete tributaries contributing to its strength. The system's central thrusts might be quite clear, but its specific boundaries and currents would rarely be completely perceivable in their totality. Chapter 5 will examine some more formal methodologies for examining and evaluating critical strategic balances. Yet, however helpful such techniques might be, they did not provide the essence of effective strategy formulation. More incremental methodologies did. The next two chapters will develop these in depth.

CONCLUSION

The most effective strategies of major enterprises tend to emerge step by step from an iterative process in which the organization probes the future, experiments, and learns from a series of partial (incremental) commitments rather than through global formulations of total strategies. Good managers are aware of this process, and they consciously intervene in it. They use it to improve the information available for decisions and to build the psychological identification essential to successful strategies. The process is both logical and incremental. Such logical incrementalism is not "muddling," as most people understand that word. Properly managed, it is a conscious, purposeful, proactive, executive practice. Logical incrementalism honors and utilizes the global analyses inherent in formal strategy formulation models. It also embraces the central tenets of the political or power-behavioral approaches to such decision making. But it does not become subservient to any one model. Instead each approach becomes simply a component in a logical process that improves the quality of available information, establishes critical elements of political power and credibility, creates needed participation and psychological commitment, and thus enhances both the quality of strategic decisions and the likelihood of their successful implementation.

The rationality of this approach is supported by the organizational, psychological, and informational imperatives of most major enterprises. The total strategy in such enterprises is largely defined by the development and interaction of certain major subsystem strategies. Each of these subsystems to a large extent has its own peculiar timing, sequencing, informational, and power necessities. Different subsets of people are involved in each subsystem strategy—i.e., product positioning, diversification, organizational, government relations, and others. And each subsystem's strategy is best formulated by following a logic dictated by its own unique needs. Yet investigation suggests that the quality and impact of each of these subsystems' strategies are improved if executives move forward incrementally, modifying their conclusions from broad conceptions toward specifics as more information, confidence, and personal commitment are achieved. As each subsystem strategy pulses forward in this mode, it interacts with those of other subsystems, creating new opportunities, demands, or constraints for all subsystems at each stage of their development. Because so many uncertainties are involved, no manager or management team can predict the precise way in which any major subsystem will ultimately evolve, much less the way all will interact to create the enterprise's overall strategic posture. Diagram 2 provides a visual example of the complexity of such interactions over time.

Consequently, logic dictates that executives manage each subsystem incrementally in keeping with its own imperatives. And the subsystems' unpredictable interactions with each other and with multifarious outside environments require that the overall strategy be similarly managed. Effective strategic managers in large organizations recognize these realities and try to proactively shape the development of both subsystem and total-enterprise strategies in a logically incremental fashion. As they do so, they do not deal with information-analysis, power-political, and organizational-psychological processes in separate compartments. Instead they consciously and simultaneously integrate all three of these processes into their actions at various crucial states of strategy development. This chapter suggests why their actions are logically incremental. Others will amplify these conclusions and suggest how executives proactively manage strategy development in this mode.

NOTES

1. M. L. Mace, "The President and Corporate Planning," *Harvard Business Review* (January-February 1965), pp. 49-62; W. D. Guth, "Formulating Organizational Objectives and Strategy: A Systematic Approach," *Journal of Business Policy* (Autumn 1971), pp. 24-31; K. J. Cohen and R. M. Cyert, "Strategy: Formulation, Implementation, and Monitoring," *The Journal of Business* (July 1973), pp. 349-67; G. J. Skibbins, "Top Management Goal Appraisal," *International Management* (July 1974), pp. 41-42; F. Goronzy and E. Gray, "Factors in Corporate Growth," *Management International Review*, no. 4-5, 1974, pp. 75-90; and W. E. Rothschild, *Putting It All Together: A Guide to Strategic Thinking* (New York: AMACOM, 1976).

2. J. T. Cannon, *Business Strategy and Policy* (New York: Harcourt, Brace & World, 1968); G. A. Steiner, *Top Management Planning* (New York: Macmillan & Company, 1969); R. L. Katz, *Management of the Total Enterprise* (Englewood Cliffs, N.J.: Prentice-Hall, Inc., 1970); E. K. Warren, *Long-Range Planning, The Executive Viewpoint* (Englewood Cliffs, N.J.: Prentice-Hall, Inc., 1966); R. L. Ackoff, *A Concept of Corporate Planning* (New York: Wiley-Interscience, 1970); H. I. Ansoff, "Managerial Problem-Solving," *Journal of Business Policy* (Autumn 1971), pp. 3-20; E. C. Miller, *Advanced Techniques for Strategic Planning* (New York: American Management Association, 1971); R. F. Vancil and P. Lorange, "Strategic Planning in Diversified Companies," *Harvard Business Review* (January-February 1975), pp. 81-90; and R. F. Vancil, "Strategy Formulation in Complex Organizations," *Sloan Management Review* (Winter 1976), pp. 1-18.

3. For example: W. J. MacGinnitie, "How to Design a Strategic Planning System," *Best's Review, Property/Liability Insurance Edition* (May 1973), pp. 108-12; F. E. deCarbonnel and R. G. Dorrance, "Information Sources for Planning Decisions," *California Management Review* (Summer 1973), pp. 42-53; C. H. Springer, "Strategic Management in General Electric," *Operations Research* (November-December 1973), pp. 1177-82; M. E. Salveson, "The Management of Strategy," *Long Range Planning* (February 1974), pp. 19-26; and C. Holloway and G. T. Jones, "Planning at Gulf–A Case Study," *Long Range Planning* (April 1975), pp. 27-39.

4. Cohen and Cyert, in "Strategy: Formulation, Implementation and Monitoring," critique each step in a similar series in some detail.

5. W. K. Hall, in "Strategic Planning Models: Are Top Managers Really Finding Them Useful?" *Journal of Business Policy* (Winter 1972/73), pp. 33-42, develops the concept that formal planning models are just one element in a political commitment process.

6. H. Mintzberg, D. Raisinghani, and A. Théorêt, "The Structure of 'Unstructured' Decision Processes," *Administrative Science Quarterly* (June 1976), pp. 246-75.

7. H. A. Simon, "On the Concept of Organizational Goals," *Administrative Science Quarterly* (June 1964), pp. 1-22; P. Diesing, "Noneconomic Decision-Making," in M. Alexis and C. Z. Wilson, eds., *Organizational Decision Making* (Englewood Cliffs, N.J.: Prentice-Hall, Inc., 1967), pp. 185-200; C. Perrow, "The Analysis of Goals in Complex Organizations," *American Sociological Review* (February 1961), pp. 854-66; and P. Georgiou, "The Goal Paradigm and Notes Towards a Counter Paradigm," *Administrative Science Quarterly* (September 1973), pp. 291-310.

8. R. M. Cyert, H. A. Simon, and D. B. Trow, "Observation of a Business Decision," *The Journal of Business* (October 1956), pp. 237-48; J. M. Pfiffner, "Administrative Rationality," *Public Administration Review* (Summer 1960), pp. 125-32; W. J. Gore, *Administrative Decision-Making: A Heuristic Model* (New York: John Wiley & Sons, 1964); J. L. Bower, "Planning within the Firm," *The American Economic Review* (May 1970), pp. 186-94; A. Zaleznik, "Power and

Politics in Organizational Life," *Harvard Business Review* (May-June 1970), pp. 47-60; R. A. Bauer and K. J. Gergen, eds., *The Study of Policy Formation* (New York: Free Press, 1968); G. T. Allison, *Essence of Decision: Explaining the Cuban Missile Crisis* (Boston: Little, Brown & Co., 1971); and A. M. Pettigrew, "Information Control as a Power Resource," *Sociology* (May 1972), pp. 187-204.

9. R. M. Cyert and J. G. March, *A Behavioral Theory of the Firm* (Englewood Cliffs, N.J.: Prentice-Hall, Inc., 1963); L. R. Sayles, *Managerial Behavior: Administration in Complex Organizations* (New York: McGraw-Hill Book Co., 1964); Bower, "Planning within the Firm;" E. E. Carter, "The Behavioral Theory of the Firm and Top-Level Corporate Decisions," *Administrative Science Quarterly* (December 1971), pp. 413-28; Mintzberg, Raisinghani, and Théorêt, "Structure of 'Unstructured' Decision Processes;" J. Pfeffer, G. R. Salancik, and H. Leblebici, "The Effect of Uncertainty on the Use of Social Influence in Organizational Decision Making," *Administrative Science Quarterly* (June 1976), pp. 227-45; and R. E. Miles and C. C. Snow, *Organizational Strategy, Structure, and Process* (New York: McGraw-Hill Book Co., 1978).

10. J. G. March and H. A. Simon, *Organizations* (New York: John Wiley & Sons, 1958); Simon, "On the Concept of Organizational Goal;" and Cyert and March, *Behavioral Theory of the Firm.*

11. W. H. Riker, *The Theory of Political Coalition* (New Haven, Conn.: Yale University Press, 1962); Cyert and March, *Behavioral Theory of the Firm;* and W. D. Guth, "Toward a Social System Theory of Corporate Strategy," *The Journal of Business* (July 1976), pp. 374-88.

12. C. E. Lindblom, "The Science of 'Muddling Through,'" *Public Administration Review* (Spring 1959), pp. 79-88; D. Braybrooke and C. E. Lindblom, *A Strategy of Decision: Policy Evaluation as a Social Process* (New York: Free Press, 1963); and H. E. Wrapp, "Good Managers Don't Make Policy Decisions," *Harvard Business Review* (September-October 1967), pp. 91-99.

13. Lindblom, in "Science of 'Muddling Through,'" suggests that this disaggregation occurs in part because the administrator cannot be consistent in all aspects of policy or realize all the implications of even one policy thoroughly.

14. A. Newell and H. A. Simon, in *Human Problem Solving* (Englewood Cliffs, N.J.: Prentice-Hall, Inc., 1972), also note that when faced with complex unstructured decisions, executives tend to break them down into subdecisions to which more routinized or understood decision procedures can be applied.

15. March and Simon, in *Organizations,* p. 169, note the need to break large decisions into more familiar "action programs" that are "only loosely coupled together" in an "approximating fragmented" decision process.

16. March and Simon, in *Organizations,* and C. E. Lindblom, in *The Policy-Making Process* (Englewood Cliffs, N.J.: Prentice-Hall, Inc., 1968), note that the incremental manager is "a shrewd, resourceful, problem solver, wrestling bravely with a universe he is wise enough to know is too big for him."

17. Not the least of these is executive time, as H. Mintzberg, in *The Nature of Managerial Work* (New York: Harper & Row, 1973), notes; the top manager is a juggler who must constantly make small decisions whether or not he is ready for them.

18. This is not a reactive technique or "maintainer of equilibrium" as H. I. Ansoff suggested in "The Concept of Strategic Management," *Journal of Business Policy* (Summer 1972), pp. 2-7.

19. R. E. Neustadt, *Presidential Power: The Politics of Leadership* (New York: John Wiley & Sons, 1960); Braybrooke and Lindblom, *Strategy of Decision Policy Evaluation as a Social Process;* and Allison, *Essence of Decision.*

20. For example, H. I. Ansoff, *Corporate Strategy: An Analytic Approach to Business Policy for Growth and Expansion* (New York: McGraw-Hill Book Co., 1965); R. L. Katz, *Cases and Concepts in Corporate Strategy* (Englewood Cliffs, N.J.: Prentice-Hall, Inc. 1970); and S. Schoeffler, R. D. Buzzell, and D. F. Heany, "Impact of Strategic Planning on Profit Performance," *Harvard Business Review* (March-April 1974), pp. 137-45.

21. Guth, in "Formulating Organizational Objectives and Strategy," also notes this phenomenon.

22. J. B. Quinn, *General Motors Corporation: The Downsizing Decision,* copyrighted case, The Amos Tuck School of Business Administration, Dartmouth College, Hanover, N.H., 1978.

23. J. B. Quinn, *Xerox Corporation (A),* copyrighted case, The Amos Tuck School of Business Administration, Dartmouth College, Hanover, N.H., 1977.

24. J. B. Quinn, *Pilkington Brothers, Ltd.,* copyrighted case, The Amos Tuck School of Business Administration, Dartmouth College, Hanover, N.H., 1977.

25. J. B. Quinn and M. Jelinek, *General Mills, Inc.,* copyrighted case, The Amos Tuck School of Business Administration, Dartmouth College, Hanover, N.H., 1978; and J. B. Quinn and M. Jelinek, *Pillsbury Company,* manuscript in preparation.

26. Cyert and March, *Behavioral Theory of the Firm;* and J. Marschak, "Toward an Economic Theory of Organization and Information," in R. M. Thrall, C. H. Coombs, and R. L. Davis, eds., *Decision Processes* (New York: John Wiley & Sons, 1954).

27. *Head Ski Company, Inc.,* case © President and Fellows of Harvard College, 1967.

28. J. B. Quinn, in "Technological Innovation, Entrepreneurship, and Strategy," *Sloan Management Review* (Spring 1979), pp. 19-30, develops the rationale in more detail.

29. J. B. Quinn, *KMS Industries,* copyrighted case, The Amos Tuck School of Business Administration, Dartmouth College, Hanover, N.H., 1976.

30. M. L. Mace and G. G. Montgomery, Jr., *Management Problems of Corporate Acquisitions* (Boston: Division of Research, Graduate School of Business Administration, Harvard University, 1962); and J. B. Quinn and J. A. Mueller, "Transferring Research Results to Operations," *Harvard Business Review* (January-February 1963), pp. 49-66.

31. Vancil and Lorange, in "Strategic Planning in Diversified Companies," also note that formal strategic planning is inappropriate beyond setting broad guidelines for acquisition planning.

32. R. Normann, in *Management for Growth,* translated by N. Adler (New York: John Wiley & Sons, 1977), describes this as an interactive learning process, adjusting both goal perceptions and the relevancy of options incrementally as new information and psychological commitments develop.

33. J. G. March, J. P. Olsen, S. Christensen, et al., in *Ambiguity and Choice in Organizations* (Bergen, Norway: Universitetsforlaget, 1976), also note that the sequence in which decisions are made often determines the nature of this final outcome.

34. The *General Mills, Inc.* case provides an excellent example in its flour division divestitures.

35. J. B. Quinn, *Germanium Power Devices Corporation,* copyrighted case, The

Amos Tuck School of Business Administration, Dartmouth College, Hanover, N.H., 1979, provides an excellent example.

36. A. D. Chandler, *Strategy and Structure: Chapters in the History of the Industrial Enterprise* (Cambridge, Mass.: M.I.T. Press, 1962); and D. R. Daniel, "Reorganizing for Results," *Harvard Business Review* (November-December 1966), pp. 96-104.

37. J. B. Quinn, *Exxon Corporation,* case manuscript, The Amos Tuck School of Business Administration, Dartmouth College, Hanover, N.H., 1974.

38. The Pilkington experience was typical. Despite careful planning, the reorganization strategy overdecentralized and the "polo" at the center had to be recorrected. The addition of professional managers, while necessary, unintentionally changed the values of the company and encouraged the use of more formal plans and controls, and isolation of workers from owners, the willingness of workers to strike, the nature of reward systems, and so on.

39. S. H. Brown, "How One Man Can Move a Corporate Mountain," *Fortune* (July 1, 1966), pp. 81-83+; and Walter Guzzardi, Jr., "I.T.T. Gets the Message," *Fortune* (February 1961), pp. 112-18.

40. J. B. Quinn, *Chrysler Corporation,* copyrighted case, The Amos Tuck School of Business Administration, Dartmouth College, Hanover, N.H., 1977.

41. These are a bit different from the usual lists of benefits assessed for planning, such as in W. B. Schaffir, "What Have We Learned about Corporate Planning?" *Management Review* (August 1973), pp. 19-26, but they were repeatedly confirmed by top executives—rather than planners. They are amplified in Chapter 5.

42. J. B. Quinn, *Xerox Corporation (B),* copyrighted case, The Amos Tuck School of Business Administration, Dartmouth College, Hanover, N.H., 1977.

43. H. Mintzberg, "Strategy-Making in Three Modes," *California Management Review* (Winter 1973), pp. 44-53.

44. Ibid., p. 45.

45. March and Simon, *Organizations,* chap. 7, "Cognitive Limits on Rationality."

46. Cyert and March, in *Behavioral Theory of the Firm,* note that organizations break down complex problems into simpler subsets to obtain a "local rationality" that (while suboptimizing) sidesteps some issues of goal conflict and guides these toward consistency with "acceptable level" decision rules, i.e., policy limits.

47. Cyert and March, *Behavioral Theory of the Firm.*

48. F. F. Gilmore, in "Overcoming the Perils of Advocacy in Corporate Planning," *California Management Review* (Spring 1973), pp. 127-37, points out that this can also create some problems of its own.

49. Ansoff, in *Corporate Strategy, An Analytic Approach to Business Policy for Growth and Expansion,* details the need for internal and external flexibilities. Bower, in "Planning within the Firm," notes that executives place diversifying side bets to reduce their personal risk as well as the corporate risk.

50. Ansoff, "Concept of Strategic Management."

3
Strategic goals: Process and politics

I don't set goals for other people. That is one of their key jobs—to define their goals, to define success. I set goals for myself, but not for other people. I set the company goals in my own mind, and then they come out in discussions. But I don't sort of lay them down. . . . I've never taken a major decision without consulting my colleagues. It would be unimaginable to me, unimaginable. First, they help me make a better decision in most cases. Second, if they know about it and agree with it, they'll back it. Otherwise, they might challenge it, not openly, but subconsciously. . . .

Sir Alastair Pilkington
Chairman, Pilkington Brothers, Ltd.

STRATEGIC GOALS: PROCESS AND POLITICS

Setting goals is a special issue in strategy formulation. Many articles have described structured hierarchies of goals and rigorous methodologies for arriving at them analytically.[1] Although successful top managers in my sample organizations rarely followed such caveats when formulating their strategic goals, executives are constantly reminded of four almost biblical mandates:

1. Define specific goals and objectives for your organization.
2. State these goals clearly, explicitly, and preferably quantitatively.
3. Assign the goals to individuals or organizational units.
4. Establish quantitative performance measures to control the organization toward established goals.

Nevertheless, at the strategic level in my sample companies, I found that successful executives "announced" relatively few goals to their organizations. These few were frequently broad and general, and only rarely were they quantitative or measurably precise. Further, managements tended to arrive at their strategic goals through highly incremental processes, rather than through the kinds of structured analyses often prescribed or "required" according to management dogma. This chapter suggests why top managers acted as they did.* It also asserts that their practices were purposeful, politically astute, and effective. They did not represent breakdowns in management technique, sloppiness, or lack of top management sophistication—as some critics might suggest. Instead, managers at all levels can be more effective if they understand the logic and process considerations behind such broad goal setting and the incremental techniques used to develop these and more explicit goals.

WHY NOT ANNOUNCE GOALS?

Why don't top executives simply arrive at goals and announce them in the precise, integrated packages advocated

---

*Although conclusions apply to both public and private spheres, examples will be drawn dominantly from observations in large businesses.

by theoretical strategists and, indeed, expected by their organizational constituents? In fact, they may establish a few
broad goals by decree, but more often—and for good reason—
they avoid such pronouncements. Why?

Undesired centralization

Effective top managers understand that goal announcements can centralize their organizations. Such statements tell
subordinates that certain issues are closed and that their
thoughts about alternatives are irrelevant. Successful top
executives know they cannot have as much detailed information about products, technologies, and customer needs as
their line compatriots do. In formulating goals, they want
both to benefit from this knowledge and to obtain the
genuine participation and commitment of those who have
it.[2, 3] As suggested in an earlier example:

- James McFarland said that shortly after he became chief
  executive officer, "I asked myself what was expected of
  me as CEO. I decided that my role was really to build
  General Mills from a good into a great company. But I
  realized this was not just up to me. I wanted a collective
  viewpoint as to what makes a company great. Consequently, we took some 35 top people away for three days to
  decide what it took to move the company from goodness
  to greatness. Working in groups of six to eight, we defined
  the characteristics of a great company from various points
  of view, what our shortcomings were, and how we might
  overcome these." Over time these broad goals were translated into charters for specific divisions or groups. They
  became the initial guidelines that stimulated the company's
  very successful development over the next decade.

- Eugene Cafiero, then president of Chrysler Corporation,
  was trying to develop a posture to deal with ever-increasing
  government regulation in his field. He said, "I have started
  conversations with anyone inside or outside the company
  who can help me. I don't know yet what we should do.
  And I don't want to take a stand we can't all live with.
  Before we make any irrevocable decisions, I'll want a lot of

advice from those people in the company who understand the specific problems better than I do. And I'll want everyone pulling together when we do set our course."

Oddly enough, when lower levels demand clearer goals, they are often unwittingly working against their own desires for increased freedom and personal growth.[4] Far from stimulating such desirable results, goal announcements can centralize the organization, rigidify positions too soon, eliminate creative options, and even cause active resistance to the goals themselves.

Focus for opposition

Explicitly stated goals—especially on complex issues—can provide focal points against which an otherwise fragmented opposition will organize. Anyone with political sensibilities will understand this phenomenon. For example, President Carter's first publicly stated energy plan in 1978 immediately drew the adverse comments from many parochial interests who only opposed a specific part of the plan. Soon these highly fragmented forces appeared unified in their opposition to the total plan, and each fragment gained added credibility from this apparent unity. In a like manner, a land-use plan or a zoning ordinance quickly becomes a coalescing element for many disparate interests in a town. In industry, department or division heads who compete fiercely on most issues can become a formidable power bloc against some announced thrust that affects each only marginally. For example:

- In a textile fibers company strong marketing, production, and R&D managers—who fought each other constantly—formed a potent coalition to resist a product management scheme to coordinate the very things that caused their friction. And in decentralized companies powerful product division heads have forced new CEOs to give up, get out, or revert to acquisitions, rather than accept new interdivisional goals pushed from the top.

Because of such potential opposition, experienced executives are reluctant to put forward "goal packages," which could contain significant points of controversy. Instead, they progress by building consensus around one or a few important new goals at a time. Because the net direction of an organization's goals ultimately reflects a negotiated balance among the imperatives felt by the dominant executive coalition[5] and the most important power centers and stakeholders in the enterprise,[6] the last thing an executive wants is to weaken his or her position by creating an unintended counter-coalition. Again, this is a part of the incrementalism one sees in strategy development.

Rigidity

Once a top executive publicly announces a goal, it can become very difficult to change. Both the executive's ego and those of people in supporting programs become identified with the goal. Changing the goal broadcasts that the executive was in error and that all those pursuing the goal were on the wrong track. As a consequence, people often doggedly prolong outmoded—but publicly committed—goals, rather than swallow losses and move on. The government constantly continues obsolete military, energy, and social programs for just such reasons. And corporate bankruptcy lists are rampant with conglomerates, banks, transportation companies, and real estate ventures under duress because their officers tried frantically to fulfill announced—but unrealistic—growth goals.

- By contrast, George Weissman, chairman of Philip Morris, Inc., said, "We don't announce growth goals in *new* areas precisely because we don't want to be trapped into doing something stupid. We might be tempted to acquire a company when we shouldn't. Or we might hang on to an operation we really should sell off. Public statements can sometimes generate powerful expectations—internally and externally—that can pressure you to do the wrong thing."

- In a different vein, J. N. Stewart, director of GM's Marketing Staff, observed: "We don't go on line with our goals. That would make for too much rigidity. Around here, if it's written down, it's out of date. We certainly don't want to stop thinking about options because we've written something down. The people who have a commitment to writing things down find themselves very frustrated as to how the company really does operate."[7]

Top managers generally like to keep their options open as long as possible consistent with the information they have. One way to accomplish this is to define only broad directions and then respond to specific, well-documented proposals. There is an additional advantage to this approach. The proposers are more likely to identify with their propositions and see them through. Again, this contributes to incrementalism in goal setting and strategy formulation.

• John Gerlach, then Vice President—Corporate Growth at General Mills, said, "Our management doesn't state a specific diversification goal requiring so many millions in profits and sales within five years. Instead we say 'we want to be a competitive factor in a designated industry in five years.' This keeps us free to approach each field flexibly as opportunities develop. But we don't get committed until we have concrete numbers and proposals to look at."

Security

There are still other good reasons why effective top managers do not announce goals explicitly or widely. In any healthy organization, good people constantly bubble out to head other enterprises. Thus top executives are justifiably reluctant to provide potential competitors with specific information about their future moves.

• When talking to the investment community or his vice presidents, Litton Industries Chairman "Tex" Thornton was never very specific about the sequence and timing of "his plan" during Litton's rapid growth phase. Advance knowledge of Litton's interest could have inflated an acquisition's stock price, activated other potential acquirers, or caused third parties to intervene. With large numbers of Litton executives being sought by other companies, it would have been folly to disclose acquisition goals in detail. In addition, more general goals allowed Litton needed flexibilities to consider new opportunities as they became available.

Further, as one chief executive said, "the future can make fools of us all." There are many examples of former high executives ousted because unforeseen events made it impossible to fulfill their ambitious announced goals.

- During the booming late 1960s, the president of a large consumer products company announced to all his goal of 10 percent profit growth per year. But many in the company regarded this as "his goal"—not theirs. Despite some impressive successes, the president was hung for a failure to meet this goal in two successive years while he was trying to develop some entirely new ventures within the company. When these were slow in materializing, his vice presidents gleefully saw that his publicly announced goal was well remembered at the board level. The embarrassed board, which had earlier approved the goal, terminated the president's career.

In addition, there are other issues—like strategies for divestitures, consolidations, and plant closures—for which it makes sense not to announce goals at all until after they are accomplished facts.[8] One may also avoid prestated goals altogether in highly uncertain, gaming, negotiation, or preemptive situations. Optimistic early goal announcements can too easily convert reasonable results, which would have appeared perfectly adequate in retrospect, into perceived disasters. Such has been the fate of too many technical development programs (like controlled fusion R&D) or complex contract negotiations (like proposed sales to the People's Republic of China).

These are just some of many reasons why top managers do not follow the conventional wisdom about clearly announcing specific goals in advance. The few goals top managers do announce tend: (1) to reflect or help build a developing consensus, (2) to be broad enough in concept to allow flexibility and opportunism, and (3) to be sufficiently distant in time that several possible options could ensure their achievement.

WHEN SHOULD GOALS BE GENERAL?

Conventional wisdom also requires that effective goals be specific, measurable, and preferably quantitative. Many managers actually express embarrassment or frustration when they cannot reach this "ideal," but more sophisticated executives recognize that such highly precise goals are useful only in selected circumstances.[9]

● An executive vice president of one of the major automobile companies said: "The decisions where we can set specific numerical goals are the easy ones. Establishing the image of the overall car line, deciding what posture to take vis-à-vis developing legislation, determining what features the public will want in a car three years from now, setting goals for dealing with worker representation or host country demands abroad . . . those are the tough questions. And they don't have numerical answers."

One can attempt to be verbally precise in such areas, yet very often a broad goal statement is more effective than its narrower, more measurable counterpart might be. Why? Goals like "liveliness, completeness, timeliness, balance, objectivity, and accuracy" in the newspaper field would actually lose meaning in quantification. But there are other reasons as well why some goals should be general.

Cohesion

There will always be detailed conflicts in any organization's goals.[10] But at the strategic level a certain generality in selected goals can promote cohesion by ignoring detailed differences and emphasizing a widely held common value. Many can support continued growth, greater freedom, equal opportunity, full disclosure, or quality products as organizational goals. Oddly enough, however, adding more specific dimensions to these broad concepts may quickly complicate communications, lose some individuals' support, and even create contention.

If a community tries to agree on its precise goals in building a new school, it may never reach a sufficient consensus for action. People can differ irreconcilably on whether a traditional, experimental, precollege, classical, or vocational approach should predominate.[11] Yet they might easily agree on a program to build a new school. Then once the broad program is approved, they can resolve some fundamental goal and value differences by compromising on the much less emotionally charged architectural details.[12]

Similarly, top managers can often avoid serious rifts by focusing agreement on very broad objectives where substantial agreement exists,[13] and then treating more specific goal issues as decisions about concrete proposals or program details.[14] Again, incrementalism is logical.

• The new principal stockholder in a medium-sized ($200 million in sales) drilling equipment company wanted the company to grow relatively rapidly by selective acquisitions. One of the stockholder's board representatives prepared a detailed outline containing proposed areas for growth and diversification. Some other board members—based on limited experience—immediately took a rigid stance against one specific proposal, i.e., acquisitions of "service companies" supporting the company's line. Little progress could be made until the principal stockholder's representatives went back and sold the board on an idea they could all agree to, i.e., rapid growth through acquisition. As the board becomes more comfortable with this broad concept, the principal stockholder's representatives still hope to bring in some service company candidates and allay their fellow directors' fears with a specific example.

Cohesion, without stifling creativity, is essential in complicated design processes like the introduction of a new automobile line.

• President E. M. "Pete" Estes expressed GM's strategic approach this way: "We do not try to tell people how to get there from this level of the organization. We try to give them the broad concepts we are trying to achieve. . . . For example, yesterday we had 130 people at the Technical

Center where each division gave its plan through the 1980s. The only guidance we had given them was: the 27½ miles per gallon [mandated by the government] by 1985, six-person capacity, and luggage space and comfort for the consumer comparable to the present. Each product line could have a compact, subcompact, intermediate, and regular product in its line. And each of the supporting divisions had to have at least one major new product available each year. Now we have three or four creative strategies from each division . . . but still they are not all over the lot."

Identity and élan

Broad goals can create identity and élan. Effective organizational goals satisfy a basic human need.[15] They enable people to develop an identity larger than themselves, to participate in greater challenges, and to have influence or seek rewards they could not achieve alone.[16] Interestingly enough, many employees can identify better with broad goals like being the best or the first in an area than they can with more specific numerical goals.

- As the chief executive of a major consumer products company said: "We have slowly discovered that our most effective goal is *to be best* at certain things. We now try to get our people to help us work out what these should be, how to define *best* objectively, and how to *become best* in our selected spheres. You would be surprised how motivating that can be."

Most companies devote great attention to measurable output goals—like size, productivity, profits, costs, or returns—that lack charisma and provide no special identity for their people.[17] Yet they often fail to achieve these goals precisely because their people do not identify sufficiently with the company. To forge a common bond among individuals with widely diverse personal values, expectations, and capacities, such numerical goals must be teamed with goals that satisfy people's more basic psychological needs: to produce something worthwhile, to help others, to obtain recognition, to be free or innovative, to achieve security, to beat an opponent, or to earn community respect.[18]

● Repeatedly in truly innovative organizations, people will consider the goals of attainment so worthwhile that they will work all night with catnaps for weeks on end.[19] Or their project will become, as Alastair Pilkington said, "... almost a crusade. Chaps were literally taken off on stretchers from heat exhaustion, yet came back for more ... [they were proud that] St. Helens had become the center of the glass industry."[20] The amorphous concept of participating in something truly worthwhile drives many people to greater efforts than any monetary incentive could.

While such organizational goals must be general enough to achieve widespread support, they must also clearly delineate what distinguishes "us" (the identity group) from "them" (all others). This is the function of the basic concept definitions suggested in Chapter 5.

To improve their competitive postures, executives often consciously define the uniqueness or niche of their company's products, processes, technologies, services, or markets.[21] More thoughtful top managers also carefully analyze whether one strategic goal or another will better attract the skilled people and personal commitments they want.[22] Their people's talent and dedication then become the central strengths upon which the organization's success is built. An IBM salesperson, a Bell Labs researcher, a *New York Times* stringer, and a Steuben glassblower all enjoy a special élan—as do millions of others whose organizations achieve a unique identity. This élan provides a special psychic compensation for the people involved, and symbiotically it becomes their organization's most priceless asset. More often than not such élan develops around broad conceptual goals rather than precise mathematical targets.

WHEN SHOULD GOALS BE SPECIFIC?

Contrary to conventional wisdom, relatively few *strategic* goals need to be mathematically precise.[23] Properly derived,

those few can provide essential focal points and stimuli for
an organization. However, they should be generated with care
and used with balance.

Precipitating action

By making selected goals explicit at the proper moment,
managers can create a challenge, precipitate desired discussions or analyses, or crystallize defined thrusts.

- The president of a major packaging company wanted to
  move his organization in new directions. He first unleashed
  a series of management, staff, and consulting studies to
  help define the company's weaknesses and major opportunities for improvement. These were circulated as "white
  papers" for discussion by his top management team. After
  a while consensus began to emerge on critical issues and
  options. The president began to reinforce one: "the need
  to work existing assets much harder." In further discussions his organization crystallized this concept into a specific target return on net assets—vastly higher than the current return—as a principal goal for 1981. This goal established in 1976 triggered the shutdown of excess facilities, a
  new focus on profitability rather than volume, and a profit-
  centered decentralization of the whole organization.

Under these circumstances, after building consensus around
a broad goal, the top executive may merely approve its specific manifestation. Although the goal is a challenge, other
individuals in the organization have recommended it. The
executive knows that it is feasible and that key people understand and support the goal. And the time horizon is sufficiently distant to allow for alternative approaches that will
ensure a high probability of its achievement.

Major transitions

Specific new goals can also help signal a major change
from the past. Properly developed, they can challenge lower
levels to propose specific solutions yet not unduly constrain
their approaches. To be effective they must build on some

accepted values in the organization and leave time enough for proposed new programs to reach fruition.

● After much discussion, an aerospace company's top management established the goal of moving 50 percent into nongovernment business within a decade. This started a furor of creative proposals. Research put forward new technical concepts. Each division proposed how it could best realign its own business. Corporate staff units investigated industries and specific companies for acquisitions. The administrative vice president recommended a new control system to handle diversification. Revised banking relations were proposed. And so on. From all these thrusts top management slowly chose its desired pattern of internal versus external growth, market sectors, organizational form, and financial structure. Throughout, lower levels felt their ideas were appreciated, and they identified with changes made.

Pillsbury Company provides an even more dramatic example of setting goals for a major transition.

● When William Spoor became Chief Executive Officer of Pillsbury Company in 1972, he created a new set of specific goals to reenergize the company. He met with his general managers for several months to draw up a blueprint of what they thought needed to be done. Spoor asked each outside director and 12 outside analysts to assess the strengths and weaknesses of Pillsbury. All groups said basically the same things. The company had been floundering with an inconsistent Earnings per Share performance, a shotgun approach to Research and Development and backup investments for its various businesses, and too many individual divisions performing poorly or losing money. Based on these substantial inputs, Spoor and his management team drew up "The Pillsbury Dream" containing the five-year goals of the company. The overall process took almost a year of discussions.

Said Spoor, "When we finally arrived at our goals, there was no issue at all. All the key people had helped create them. . . . We said we wanted to create a five-year record of consistent growth in sales and earnings per share with a 10% average growth in sales and EPS, a Return on Equity of 16%, a Return on Investment on total capital of 20%, and Price/Earnings ratio in the top one third of the leading food companies. We wanted to be a quality company, first-class in all respects: in our people, our products, our facilities, and our business conduct. . . . We decided to really put ourselves on the spot. I suggested to the board that we go public with our objectives, really lay out for the public and the investment community what we intended to do. . . . [After several months] in July 1973 they let us set forth our growth objectives to the New York State Security Analysts."

After a crisis

After a crisis, disaster, or major trauma, an organization often needs distinct and clear new goals to focus action.

- Mr. Estes, president of General Motors, described his company's 1973-74 actions this way: "We had done a lot of talking and thinking about how to modify our line to meet developing fuel economy, environmental, and customer demands. In October 1973, the Middle East war broke out, the embargo came on the 22d, and the curtain came down on auto sales. This led us to discuss our reactions in somewhat more of a 'panic mode' than we would have liked. We concluded: (1) we should have a car smaller than Vega, (2) we needed a smaller luxury car . . . , and (3) we had to introduce these cars faster than ever before."

The Executive Committee agreed that the new subcompact car had to be number one in fuel economy, and the Executive Committee wanted an available car which would do the best job and be flexible for future changes. This led to the January 23, 1974, decision to go ahead and introduce the "T car"—soon to be Chevette—to the United States in an unprecedented 18 months. In April 1974, each division presented a ten-year plan to corporate top management. Estes continued, "The intermediate [A body] designs were new in 1973. But the larger cars [B and C bodies] were up for redesign in 1977. Fuel costs were rising and fuel economy appeared salable. So we set an initial target of reducing weight by 400 pounds. This figure had [several] merits: (1) we couldn't figure out how to get out more weight than that, (2) it would give us one more mile in fuel economy, [(3) it was a real challenge] without decreasing the comfort level, baggage capability, or six-person capacity of the cars."

Typically, specific new goals should combine a broad definition of longer-term success and some concrete, achievable, short-term goals to build confidence. Without visible intermediate goals, people can become frustrated and give up on the ultimate challenge. [24] Without a longer term vision, short-term actions quickly become tactical responses that lose their focus and meaning. Both must be integrated to achieve a true turnaround.

- Eugene Cafiero, president of Chrysler Corporation, said: "Establishing goals is the first thing I've always done in a new situation. I think about what we are trying to do. Does it have any focus? What is really needed? If I can convince people of the need, they can do remarkable things—it has always worked. I've always gotten people to participate. For example, when I took over the Newcastle plant, I got everyone to talk about what we were trying to do. Then I chose something that looked difficult, but I knew could be done. Once we got the organization to do something they thought was out of sight, they thought they could do almost anything. Our credibility and the credibility of the strategy went way up."[25]

- When Vincent Lombardi took over as head coach of the listless Green Bay Packers, he announced only that the team was going to be a winner. This was a broad goal that appealed to the values of players and owners alike but did not create false expectations. Then he went to work on fundamentals of blocking, tackling, conditioning. As the players step by step achieved specific, possible, but increasingly rigorous goals in these areas, their confidence rose. Then Lombardi concentrated on the. first preseason victory; then the next. Only as the players and the management gained confidence—and as the probability became reasonable—did Lombardi introduce the more challenging goal of an NFL championship. This specific goal, infused too soon, would have seemed unreal, and would have designated an otherwise fine season as a disaster.[26]

Only a few goals

At any given moment, an executive can push only a few specific new goals, giving them the attention and force they need to take hold.[27] Fortunately, a top executive rarely needs to press more than a few significant changes simultaneously. In fact, the essence of strategy is to identify this small number of truly essential thrusts or concepts and to marshal the organization's resources and capabilities consciously toward them. Then—to capture the organization's attention—the executive must consistently reinforce these strategic goals through his or her public statements, decision patterns, and personnel assignments. For these few goals, executives must be willing to put their credibility on the line and use the power and sanctions of their office to achieve results. Even so, the typical organization's ongoing momentum and resource commitments allow it to absorb only a few such major changes at once.

Two examples illustrate the complex interactions that lead to success or failure when setting specific goals at the top level:

• In 1969, RCA's chairman, Robert Sarnoff, initiated several major new thrusts simultaneously. While repositioning RCA in its traditional electronics-communications markets, he actively diversified the company through acquisitions. At the same time he also strove: (1) to build RCA's computer activities into an effective direct competitor of IBM, (2) to move the company's technological efforts from research toward applications, and (3) to strengthen the company's lagging marketing capabilities. He implemented much of this through an enlarged central corporate staff. It was difficult for the organization to absorb so much top-level-initiated change at once. Various aspects of the program met intense resistance from existing divisions. The computer venture failed, and Sarnoff's credibility with the organization became strained to the breaking point.[28]

● By contrast, shortly after Philip Hofmann became chairman of Johnson and Johnson, he announced a specific new goal of $1 billion in sales (with a 15 percent aftertax return on investment) before his retirement some seven years later. Annual sales were then approximately $350 million. Though the challenge was startling in scale, it built upon an established growth ethic in the company, and it did not constrain potential solutions. Instead it stimulated each division to define how it could best respond, thus maintaining the company's intended decentralization. It also allowed sufficient time for managers to propose, initiate, and carry out their new programs. Performance ultimately surpassed the goal by a comfortable margin.

At some point, as suggested, planning processes must refine goals into specific targets for operations or tactical units. But even here, successful goal setting is best achieved through incremental, iterative processes that intimately involve those who have to implement the proposed strategic thrusts.[29]

WHY ARE GOALS IMPORTANT?

Why should managers take such care in developing and expressing strategic goals? Proper goal formulation does much more than merely provide a basis for allocating resources and measuring performance for the organization. It also: (1) makes the best use of the organization's information sources by involving those who have the greatest specific knowledge, (2) obtains the genuine commitment of those who must implement the goals, and (3) maintains the opportunism and flexibility essential to effective strategies. Such are the purposes of the practices outlined previously. But well-developed goals can contribute even more; they are the essential ingredients leading to freedom, morale, and timely problem sensing throughout the entire organization. These benefits can accrue only when people at all levels genuinely internalize the goals and make them their own.

Freedom with control

If people share common purposes, they can self-direct their actions with minimal coordination from executive or staff groups.[30] This is especially critical for creative groups like research, advertising, or strategic planning. No individual's goals will completely match those of the enterprise; however, without basic goal congruence, control of these activities is impossible.[31] No amount of ex post facto performance measurement can ensure that creative people will imaginatively identify proper problems, generate imaginative alternatives, or invent new or responsive solutions. Such actions must be stimulated before the fact by ensuring that well-selected people understand and identify with the goals their activities support.

- The Bell Telephone Laboratories (studied in the late 1950s and early 1960s) offered an excellent example. To ensure that its programs were closely matched to customer needs, Bell Laboratories had developed a complex of information flows, planning processes, and program reviews that brought Advanced Systems, operating company, Western Electric, and individual customer preferences intimately into research, development, and design processes. To make sure these reached individual researchers, the laboratories had worked out the most careful goal communication process I had ever seen in an R&D setting. There was almost no distortion in the way people perceived the goals they were working toward—from the Laboratories president to the bench level. Consequently, each level could guide its own activities creatively, with minimum direction from above.[32]

Morale

Morale is a goal-oriented phenomenon. People in a high-morale organization almost by definition intensely share common performance goals. Although personal goals and organizational goals are never totally congruent,[33] people share some overriding purposes to the extent that they ignore internal irritations and adapt rapidly to external stimuli that will either help or potentially hinder goal accomplishment.[34] Entrepreneurial organizations, project teams on urgent tasks, dedicated medical groups, or even whole societies (like Israel or Japan) exhibit these characteristics.[35] A specific industrial example suggests how powerful the symbiotic effect of a stimulating goal and talented people can be.

● From 1970 to 1976 tiny KMS Industries had perhaps the world's most advanced laser fusion program for commercial energy production. As one executive said, "I don't know any of us who didn't agree that this was the most important task in the world. We thought we could lick the fight. If successful, we would have a new basis for creating energy, hydrogen, and hydrocarbons. It would make the United States and other nations independent of world energy markets. People on the fusion program had extremely high morale. They would work all night. They were thoroughly committed." On May 1, 1974—despite much larger Atomic Energy Commission and Russian expenditures in the field—a KMS team achieved the world's first "unambiguous" release of neutrons from laser fusion.[36]

A contrasting example makes the opposite point:

● The dominantly shared goal of many a government (or staff) department is the preservation of its members' positions and budgets. Lacking shared—or often even understood—performance goals, such organizations become "hotbeds of inertia." They focus extraordinary energies on minor internal irritants. When disturbed by external stimuli, they operate with awesome tenacity to reestablish accepted interpersonal and political equilibria—even to the point of negating their own output and jeopardizing their continuation.

Often managers spend enormous time trying to ease or resolve the interpersonal tensions in such organizations, but they accomplish little until they can get people to accept a new sense of common purpose. This can pose special problems during a downturn when people become very insecure about their jobs or the future of their entire enterprise. The following example shows how helpful stimulating new goal perceptions can be in these circumstances:

● In spring 1974 Messrs. Estes and Murphy of General Motors began to feel their downsizing program was very right. They thought they could be two years ahead of anyone else with their strategy. Said Estes, "In March or April, Tom Murphy and I began talking around the organization that things were getting better. At the same time people at Ford were saying 'things are in a hell of a mess.' But we went ahead with a ten-year plan for the downsizing of *intermediate* cars. In March 1975 we decided to remove 700 pounds from these to gain approximately 3 miles per gallon for their introduction in 1977 (1978 models). Our financial forecasts still said we couldn't meet even reduced dividend targets. Instead, we got $960 million. This took a lot of postponing projects and not fixing windows. But we got the job done. By late 1975 you could feel the morale coming up."

Many executives spoke of the benefits of creating a "dream" or "vision" that would provide a galvanizing, motivating drive for their organizations. This seemed extraordinarily difficult to accomplish for the total operations of the very large companies I studied. But one could repeatedly find such a vision at the heart of the most successful entrepreneurial small companies and major programs in larger enterprises.

● The founders of National Medical Care, Inc., two renal specialists, had tried in vain to work through federal programs, universities, and established hospitals to provide kidney dialysis services for people who might die without them. In desperation they started NMC, Inc., to deliver such services on a private basis. With a clear vision and purpose they were able in two years to assemble the capital, dedicated people, and facilities to establish ten major artificial kidney centers, delivering dialysis services at a fraction of the bureaucratically controlled government programs' costs. In the late 1970s the company had sales of over $100 million, while providing life-giving services to thousands.

● When Boeing and United Aircraft Corporation lost the bidding competition for the Air Force C-5A cargo plane, they decided to develop a better commercial jumbo jet on a private basis. "People called us crazy for saying we'd sell so many," said Thornton Wilson of Boeing. But the challenge of the 747 revitalized the engineering groups of Boeing and UAC—which had also recently lost the U.S. SST development competition. Within weeks one could see morale rebound in both companies. Although it was to be almost a decade before the commercial success of the 747 would be clear, both companies moved on to dominate their portions of the commercial jet market.

The potential morale benefits of a challenging and worthwhile vision of the future should be a central theme in all goal-setting processes. Too often this is subverted by overemphasis on solely financial goals.

Problem sensing

Finally, goals help define problems.[37] Organizations with no strong sense of broad purpose can precipitate their own demise by ignoring major problems or overlooking alternatives. Some companies define their services, concepts, and goals with such limited vision that they screen out major opportunities. Others have elaborate goal statements covering broad issues, but their control and reward systems reinforce—and cause people to internalize—only a few. When people do not internalize an adequate range of goals, the consequences can be extremely costly.

● In the late 1960s many conglomerates proudly concentrated on managing business as a financial enterprise. Their control and reward systems focused so much attention on continuously improving short-term financial performance that their managers often screened out other important issues as "nonproblems." This led them to undercut research and technology, product and personnel development, plant investments, international relations, and perhaps even ethics to an extent that sometimes jeopardized their companies' very viability.

• Recently, the chairman of a multibillion-dollar, diversified company publicly decried the $35 million his divisions would expend on depollution measures. It was clear that he perceived environmentalism only as a threat. Yet one division of his company (auto exhaust systems) was likely to sell an additional $600+ million of its product annually—with corresponding profits—because of the same environmental standards he resisted as "a total loss to the company."

WILL CONVENTIONAL PROCESSES WORK?

If goals are to stimulate freedom with control, high morale, and creative problem solving, people throughout the organization must understand and actively identify with them. Usually this requires the genuine participation of many individuals in setting and modifying the goals.[38] Yet those managing strategy development must not lose control over this vital process. Top managers must carefully blend consultation, participation, delegation, and guidance to achieve their purposes. How can they manage this complex art?

Bottom up?

The philosophers' ideal is to arrive at goal consensus through democratic discussion or through "bottom up" proposals. These views especially prevail within some small companies, Japanese enterprises, or managements that conscientiously try to practice McGregor's[39] Theory Y. They clearly have merit for some organizations. In fact, logical incrementalism requires the kind—though not necessarily the degree—of participation and commitment building that are the touchstones of such theories.

The managers in my sample did not follow the precepts of such theories in detail, however. Many commented that such approaches are very time-consuming and may be frustrating, wasteful, or even divisive. Opaque committee discussions can go on endlessly and still leave individuals with different views of what goals were agreed on. People may expend extraordinary amounts of time and energy on proposals that management later rejects as "irrelevant." And they may feel angry or manipulated when "their" carefully prepared proposals or goals are overruled for other organizational purposes only fully appreciated from on high.

Unwitting bureaucracy

Managers of larger enterprises rarely feel they can afford such purist approaches to democratic goal setting. At the same time, they sense the shortcomings of goals announced from above. Consequently, a pragmatic compromise emerges. Top managers often provide a framework of broad goals for their subordinate units. They then encourage lower level managers to make proposals that respond to these goals through planning, budgetary, and ad hoc processes. Before the proposals reach final approval, a series of staff interventions, personal discussions, and intermediate reviews tune them toward what various people think top management wants and will accept.[40]

This process brings a kind of collective wisdom to bear. There is some personal involvement at all levels, but often a bland, committee-like consensus emerges. This process works moderately well for routine modifications of existing thrusts, but it discourages significant changes in organizational goals. Thus, unwittingly, most large enterprises become conservatively bureaucratized. They continue existing momenta and overlook major external changes or new opportunities.[41]

HOW DO MANAGEMENTS EVOLVE EFFECTIVE STRATEGIC GOALS?

Dramatic new sets of strategic goals rarely emerge full blown from individual bottom-up proposals or from comprehensive corporate strategic planning. Instead, a series of individual, logical, and perhaps somewhat disruptive decisions interact to create a new structure and cohesion for the company. Top managers create a new consensus through a continuous, evolving, incremental, and often highly political process that has no precise beginning or end. A well-documented example—one with which many readers will be familiar—illustrates important dimensions of this logical incremental approach to strategic goal setting.

• IBM's strategic goal of "introducing its 360 computers simultaneously as a single line with compatibility, standard interface, business and scientific capability, hybrid circuitry, and the capacity to open new markets" probably started in 1959 when T. Vincent Learson became head of the Data Systems and General Products Divisions. The divisions' product lines had begun to overlap and proliferate, causing software, cost, and organizational problems. Top managers sensed this, but no clear solutions were at hand.

In 1960-61 various specific decisions began to eliminate alternatives and define key elements of the new goal. Proposals for two new computers, "Scamp" and the 8000 series, were killed to avoid further proliferation. In mid-1961 Learson and a subordinate, Bob O. Evans, arrived at a broad concept "to blanket the market with a single product line," and they initiated exploratory studies on a new product line called simply "NPL." During 1961 a special Logic Committee recommended that IBM use hybrid circuitry—rather than integrated circuits—in any major new line. In late 1961 NPL was foundering. Learson and Chairman Watson started a series of dialogues on strategy with division heads, but no clear concept emerged. Consequently, they formed the SPREAD Committee of key executives to hammer out basic concepts for a new line. In January 1962, the committee reported and top management approved its recommended concepts for a new integrative product line, now worked out in some detail. Broad top management support and a genuine organization momentum were building behind the new concept.

In 1962 development began in earnest, and IBM's board

approved a $100 million manufacturing facility for hybrid circuits. Still, technical difficulties and differences in viewpoint persisted. In late 1962 a special programming meeting was held at Stowe to discuss software development, but major programming problems remained unresolved. In 1963 various groups openly resisted the new line. The opposition was broken up or removed. In December 1963, Honeywell precipitated action by announcing a strong competitor for IBM's successful 1401 computer. Shortly thereafter, in January 1964, Learson conducted a performance "shoot out" between the 360/30 and the 1401/S solid logic computer. The 360/30 was judged good enough to go ahead. Final pricing, marketing, and production studies were now made. In March 1964, top management approved the line in a "final risk-assessment session" at Yorktown. And on April 7, 1964, Watson announced the 360 line. The decision now appeared irrevocable.

But in 1965 and later, new time-sharing features, smaller and larger computers, and peripheral equipment units were announced or "decommitted." IBM raised $361 million of new equity in 1965 to support the line—ultimately investing some $4.5 billion in the 360. Further changes occurred in the line and its supporting hardware and software. Finally, well into the 1970s, the 360 series provided IBM's essential strategic strength, its massive installed computer base. The decision and its impact extended over some 15 years.[42]

Logical incrementalism in goal setting

The pattern is common. At first there are simply too many unknowns to specify a cohesive set of new directions for the enterprise. More information is needed. Technical problems must be solved to determine feasibilities. Investments must be made in programs with long lead times. Trends in the marketplace must crystallize into sufficiently concrete demands or competitive responses to justify risk taking. Various resource bases must be acquired or developed. Different groups' psychological commitments must be diverted from ongoing thrusts toward a new consensus. Lead times for all these events are different, yet logic dictates that final re-source commitments be made as late as possible consistent with the information available—hence incrementalism.

Goals come into being only when they become intuitively understood and accepted guides for action.[43] Effective goal processes—like those in the preceding vignette—operate at three levels: (1) They define broadly what the organization intends to be and what it should accomplish. (2) They ensure that each key person's role goals are designed to support these conceptual thrusts.[44] (3) They obtain maximum iden-tity between people's personal goals and their role goals. Rarely can this be achieved through global goal-setting exer-cises, announcing goals to the assembled multitudes, or clear ringing statements of authority and responsibility. Instead, for the reasons cited, strategic goals tend to emerge par-tially, piecemeal, and in a continuous evolution. And effective change processes are managed accordingly. Various steps in the process incrementally sense emerging needs and chal-lenges, build a wider awareness concerning these needs, broaden and intensify political support so that action can occur, create pockets of support deep in the organization, crystallize developing foci at opportune moments, and final-ly give committed people the authority and resources to carry out the goals. Creating strategic goals in complex organi-zations is thus a delicate art, requiring a subtle balance of vision, entrepreneurship, and politics.[45]

To reshape an organization's accepted culture significantly, an executive must often overcome some potent psychological and political forces. Success may frequently depend on the very group whose perceptions the executive wants to change. Moving too precipitously can undermine essential strengths of the organization. All too easily the executive can alienate key people, lose personal credibility, and destroy the power base on which his or her future depends. Unless a crisis inter-venes, few executives can change an organization's ethos abruptly. Instead they usually must build commitment—and their own political support—incrementally around specific issues or proposals. The real art is to blend these thrusts to-gether thoughtfully, as opportunities permit, into patterns that slowly create a new logical cohesion.

Changing strategic goals typically involves managing a complex chain of interacting events and forces over a period of years. How do successful managers approach this challenge? For the reasons suggested, a kind of "logical incrementalism" usually dominates this most important strategic process. Some specific uses of this technique in goal setting have been described. In Chapter 4, I will develop in detail how various people proactively manage incrementalism through all stages of strategy formation.

CONCLUSION

In strategic goal setting, most managers in large companies follow this logical incremental process. Far from being haphazard, lazy, or expedient, the process is purposeful, politically astute, and effective. A major change in strategic goals may take years to effect as it did in IBM's case. Over this time horizon, the process is rarely completely orderly, rationally predictable, or consistent. Instead—if the strategy is well formulated—the executive responds flexibly and opportunistically to new threats, crises, and proposals, which could not have been foreseen at the time initial stimuli appeared to suggest the need for strategic change. The decision process constantly molds and modifies its own concerns, concepts, and priorities.[46]

Developing strategic goals for complex organizations is a delicate art, requiring a subtle balance of vision, entrepreneurship, and politics. The management techniques used at each stage are not quite the textbook variety. But seeing these in the context of the total informational and psychological processes of goal setting helps to explain their wide use and notable effectiveness. It also explains some of the seeming anomalies and real frustrations of management in large organizations.

Management styles vary, but effective top executives in major enterprises typically announce only a few broad goals from the top; they encourage their organizations to propose some; and they allow others to emerge from informal processes.[47] They eschew the gimmickry of simplistic formal planning or MBO approaches for setting their major goals.[48] Instead they tend to develop strategic goals through very complicated, largely political, consensus-building processes that are outside the structure of most formal management systems and frequently have no precise beginning or end—as in the IBM case cited in this chapter.

Those who understand these processes can contribute more effectively, whatever their position in the organization. Those who wish to make major changes in organizations should certainly comprehend these processes, their rationale, and their implications. Those who ignore them may find the costs very high.

NOTES

1. H. L. Tosi, J. R. Rizzo, and S. J. Carroll, "Setting Goals in Management by Objectives," *California Management Review* (Summer 1970), pp. 70-78; G. J. Skibbins, "Top Management Goal Appraisal," *International Management* (July 1974), pp. 41-42; and W. D. Guth, "Formulating Organizational Objectives and Strategy: A Systematic Approach," *Journal of Business Policy* (Autumn 1971), pp. 24-31.

2. In fact, E. A. Locke, in "Toward a Theory of Task Motivation and Incentives," *Organizational Behavior and Human Performance,* vol. 3, 1968, pp. 157-89, suggests that assigned goals have effect only to the extent that they are accepted and internalized by the subordinate.

3. Yet there are real problems of advocacy and screening of information which the executive must deal with as the proposer's ego gets involved in persuasion. See F. F. Gilmore, "Overcoming the Perils of Advocacy in Corporate Planning," *California Management Review* (Spring 1973), pp. 127-37.

4. E. Rhenman, in *Organization Theory for Long-Range Planning* (New York: John Wiley & Sons, 1973), p. 66, notes the frequently heard complaint.

5. C. Perrow, in "The Analysis of Goals in Complex Organizations," *American Sociological Review* (February 1961), pp. 854-66, stresses the central power of a dominant coalition which negotiates key goal relationships among itself and uses its combined power to enforce these as organization goals.

6. P. Georgiou, in "The Goal Paradigm and Notes Towards a Counter Paradigm," *Administrative Science Quarterly* (September 1973), pp. 291-310, suggests a wider negotiation involving lower level task groups as well.

7. J. B. Quinn, *General Motors Corporation: The Downsizing Decision,* copyrighted case, The Amos Tuck School of Business Administration, Dartmouth College, Hanover, N.H., 1978.

8. Although advocates of formal planning, R. F. Vancil and P. Lorange, in "Strategic Planning in Diversified Companies," *Harvard Business Review* (January-February 1975), pp. 81-90, also note the inappropriateness of formal goal setting for such operations.

9. H. Mintzberg, in "Strategy-Making in Three Modes," *California Management Review* (Winter 1973), pp. 44-53, notes that clear goals do not exist in the "adap-

tive organization," but he does not note how vague goals can proactively stimulate entrepreneurial search.

10. R. M. Cyert and J. G. March, *A Behavioral Theory of the Firm* (Englewood Cliffs, N.J.: Prentice-Hall, Inc., 1963).

11. M. Meyerson and E. C. Banfield, in *Politics, Planning, and the Public Interest: The Case of Public Housing in Chicago* (Glencoe, Ill.: Free Press, 1955), describe some of the problems of getting goal agreement on large projects.

12. This corresponds to the observation of Cyert and March, in *Behavioral Theory of the Firm*, that organizations never resolve the differences in preferences among key participants, but nonetheless can agree on specific actions.

13. J. D. Thompson, in *Organizations in Action* (New York: McGraw-Hill Book Co., 1967), notes that goals are essentially formed through coalition behavior.

14. C. E. Lindblom, in "The Science of 'Muddling Through,'" *Public Administration Review* (Spring 1959), pp. 79-88, notes that individuals with different ideologies or negotiating parties may never agree on goals but can agree on a specific policy or program that is less value laden for each.

15. C. I. Barnard, in *The Functions of the Executive* (Cambridge, Mass.: Harvard University Press, 1938), developed the basic perception of organizations as the medium through which individuals can pursue a diversity and higher order of personal goals.

16. Various theorists from M. P. Follett, in H. C. Metcalf and L. Urwick, eds., *Dynamic Administration: The Collected Papers of Mary Parker Follett* (New York: Harper & Brothers, Publishers, 1941) to D. McGregor, in *The Human Side of Enterprise* (New York: McGraw-Hill Book Co., 1960), and R. N. Anthony, in *Planning and Control Systems: A Framework for Analysis* (Boston: Division of Research, Graduate School of Business Administration, Harvard University, 1965), have extolled the benefits of goal congruence and identity, but have not mentioned broad goals as identity producing in this sense.

17. J. K. Shank, E. G. Niblock, and W. T. Sandalls, Jr., in "Balance 'Creativity' and 'Practicality' in Formal Planning," *Harvard Business Review* (January-February 1973), pp. 87-95, discuss the contrasting needs of challenge and performance measurement in formal planning.

18. A. Zaleznik, in "Power and Politics in Organizational Life," *Harvard Business Review* (May-June 1970), pp. 47-60, notes that people often support the good of the organization if its goals are meaningful even at a personal sacrifice.

19. R. E. Conot, *A Streak of Luck* (New York: Seaview Books, 1979).

20. J. B. Quinn, *Pilkington Brothers, Ltd.,* copyrighted case, The Amos Tuck School of Business Administration, Dartmouth College, Hanover, N.H., 1977.

21. Niching is merely a form of "dominance" as defined in Chapter 5. It is the core of the Boston Consulting Group's [B. D. Henderson, *Henderson on Corporate Strategy* (Cambridge, Mass.: Abt Books, 1979)] and PIM's [S. Schoeffler, R. D. Buzzell, and D. F. Heany, "Impact of Strategic Planning on Profit Performance," *Harvard Business Review* (March-April 1974), pp. 137-45] approach to strategic goal setting.

22. R. F. Vancil, in "Strategy Formulation in Complex Organizations," *Sloan Management Review* (Winter 1976), pp. 1-18, notes commitment as one of the prime criteria for successful strategies—and implicitly, therefore, strategic goals.

23. H. L. Tosi and S. J. Carroll, in "Managerial Reaction to Management by Objectives," *Academy of Management Journal* (December 1968), pp. 415-26, note the overuse of specific goals for efficiency measurement and the expressed need for different types of goals with varying degrees of specificity at different levels of the organization.

24. See Tosi and Carroll, "Managerial Reaction to Management by Objectives."

25. J. B. Quinn, *Chrysler Corporation,* copyrighted case, The Amos Tuck School of Business Administration, Dartmouth College, Hanover, N.H., 1977.

26. P. Bengston and T. Hunt, *Packer Dynasty* (Garden City, N.Y.: Doubleday & Company, Inc., 1969); and J. Kramer, *Instant Replay* (New York: New American Library, Inc., 1968).

27. H. E. Wrapp, "Good Managers Don't Make Policy Decisions," *Harvard Business Review* (September-October 1967), pp. 91-99.

28. A. T. Demaree, "RCA after the Bath," *Fortune* (September 1972), pp. 123-28+.

29. L. C. Lawrence and P. C. Smith, in "Group Decision and Employee Participation," *Journal of Applied Psychology,* vol. 39, 1955, pp. 334-37, showed that output increased significantly when employees participated in goal setting at production levels. Later studies [W. W. Ronan, G. P. Latham, and S. B. Kinne III, "Effects of Goal Setting and Supervision on Worker Behavior in an Industrial Situation," *Journal of Applied Psychology* (December 1973), pp. 302-307; G. P. Latham and J. J. Baldes, "The 'Practical Significance' of Locke's Theory of Goal Setting," *Journal of Applied Psychology* (February 1975), pp. 122-24] indicate that many other management factors must interact with participation to make it effective. But the balance of studies shows that specific goals improve operational performance; see G. P. Latham and G. A. Yukl, "A Review of Research on the Application of Goal Setting in Organizations," *Academy of Management Journal* (December 1975), pp. 824-45.

30. A. P. Raia, in "Goal Setting and Self-Control: An Empirical Study," *The Journal of Management Studies* (February 1965), pp. 34-53, looks at some key relationships in this regard for lower levels.

31. H. A. Simon, "On the Concept of Organizational Goals," *Administrative Science Quarterly* (June 1964), pp. 1-22.

32. J. B. Quinn, *Bell Laboratories,* copyrighted case, The Amos Tuck School of Business Administration, Dartmouth College, Hanover, N.H., 1965.

33. Cyert and March, *Behavioral Theory of the Firm,* p. 117.

34. For one assessment, see J. D. Hunger and L. W. Stern, "An Assessment of the Functionality of the Superordinate Goal in Reducing Conflict," *Academy of Management Journal* (December 1976), pp. 591-605.

35. Tosi and Carroll, in "Managerial Reaction to Management by Objectives," note the ego involvement and motivational effects goal participation and identity can have.

36. J. B. Quinn, *KMS Industries,* copyrighted case, The Amos Tuck School of Business Administration, Dartmouth College, Hanover, N.H., 1976.

37. Cyert and March, in *Behavioral Theory of the Firm,* suggest that problems evoke goals. My observations show that the converse is equally true in many cases.

38. J. M. Ivancevich, in "Changes in Performance in a Management by Objectives Program," *Administrative Science Quarterly* (December 1974), pp. 563-74, surveys the measures of gains through such participation.

39. D. McGregor, *Human Side of Enterprise* (New York: McGraw-Hill Book Co., 1960).

40. K. J. Cohen and R. M. Cyert, in "Strategy: Formulation, Implementation, and Monitoring," *The Journal of Business* (July 1973), pp. 349-67, note some of the information screening and negative effects on objectivity this process creates.

41. In this sense, the kind of bureaucratic incremental extensions of the status quo noted by C. E. Lindblom, in "Science of 'Muddling Through,' " also operate in private concerns.

42. T. A. Wise, "IBM's $5 Billion Gamble," *Fortune* (October-November 1966); and T. A Wise, "The Rocky Road to the Marketplace," *Fortune* (October-November 1966).

43. Even then the firm is likely to have a melange of goals, some clear, some ambiguous, some considered at one time, some at another, some perceived clearly in one organizational unit and not in others. See J. G. March, "Business Decision Making," in H. J. Leavitt and L. R. Pondy, eds., *Readings in Managerial Psychology* (Chicago: University of Chicago Press, 1964).

44. Power derives from the role of the individual and the support of his or her people; hence executives must represent their constituents to stay in power and to have influence in the coalition, unless their organizations are to be downgraded as a part of total strategy. See Zaleznik, "Power and Politics in Organizational Life."

45. R. A. Bauer and K. J. Gergen, eds., in *The Study of Policy Formation* (New York: Free Press, 1968), note that strategy formulation is "a social process in which intellectual processes [are] embedded" (p. 5). One cannot discount the importance of either aspect of the process.

46. This is the learning adaptive process referred to by R. Normann, in *Management for Growth,* translated by N. Adler (New York: John Wiley & Sons, 1977), and Cyert and March, in *Behavioral Theory of the Firm.*

47. One of the ways of avoiding goal conflicts in organizations is to sequence them, implicitly obtaining concerted action on one goal (productivity) while temporarily ignoring another (employment stability) for the time being. See Cyert and March, *Behavioral Theory of the Firm.*

48. J. B. Lasagna, in "Make Your MBO Pragmatic," *Harvard Business Review* (November-December 1971), pp. 64-69, suggests some of the real problems in implementing MBO in Wells Fargo. H. Levinson, in "Management by Whose Objectives?" *Harvard Business Review* (July-August 1970), pp. 125-34, suggests MBO may actually be little more than a manipulative device to impress the top managers' goals on the organization.

4
Managing logical incrementalism

Good managers have always been a scarce commodity, but today the supply is rapidly drying up, and many of those remaining are being organized into impotence. Just as bad money has always driven out good, so the talented general manager—the person who makes a company go—is being overwhelmed by a flood of so-called professionals, textbook executives more interested in the form of management than the content, more concerned about defining and categorizing and quantifying the job than in getting it done.... They have created false expectations and wasted untold man-hours by making a religion of formal long-range planning.

H. E. Wrapp
"A Plague of Professional Managers,"
New York Times, *April 8, 1979*

MANAGING LOGICAL INCREMENTALISM

Earlier chapters have tried to demonstrate why good managers should not—and do not—follow highly formalized textbook approaches in analyzing and selecting their major goals
and strategies. Instead they artfully blend formal-analytical,
behavioral, and power-political techniques to bring about
cohesion and step-by-step movement toward broadly conceived ends, which are then constantly refined and reshaped
as new information appears.[1] Their integrating methodology
can best be described as logical incrementalism.

But is this truly a process in itself, capable of being managed? Does it simply amount to applied intuition? Or are
there some conceptual structures, principles, or paradigms
that are generally useful? Some of the more complete published paradigms are briefly summarized in the following
section. Parts of others will be cited in the main body of this
chapter. Each of these makes important contributions, but
each only partially explains the kinds of strategic processes
observed in this study.

SOME INTEGRATIVE PARADIGMS

- Wrapp points out that good strategic managers do not
  make numerous specific policy decisions themselves.[2] They
  keep well informed through multiple channels of information. They concentrate on a few high-priority issues. They
  understand the power game and move through corridors of
  indifference where resistances are not too great. They introduce few specific thrusts from the top, instead stimulating proposals from lower levels. They make an art of
  imprecision and vagueness in their announced goals, although they may know very well where they really want
  the organization to go. Such executives "muddle with a
  purpose," accepting and committing to partial steps toward their goals and flexibly exploiting change opportunities as they occur. My samples support these as most important elements in the logical incremental processes of
  strategy formulation. But my observations also suggest
  that: (1) there are other significant behavioral elements in

the logical incremental process, (2) executives blend these *and* Wrapp's concepts together *proactively* to shape emerging strategies, (3) these appear in a somewhat identifiable sequence as strategies are formulated, and (4) executives consciously integrate such behavioral practices with the best available formal-analytical techniques to improve the intellectual quality and psychological attractiveness of their strategic decisions.

• Normann has correctly noted that the "goal orientation" implied in formal planning systems does not describe the way in which strategic growth decisions are really made.[3] His studies provide useful insights on how companies generate and respond to certain dominating ideas. He notes that changes in a firm's environment, technology, or the significant actors in its dominating coalition may create tensions or misfits that call for new visions—intuitive ideas of other reasonable future states for the enterprise. He states that planning toward these visions can proceed only step by step as a learning process involving: (1) the visions themselves and (2) the firm's capacities to reach them. He discusses some problems of too abstract or too precise visions and the politics of achieving consensus on and implementation of these visions. His "skillful executive" succeeds in exploiting the entrepreneurial potentials, creative drives, and ambitions of his or her people. And he describes some strategies for confrontation, cooptation, evasion, and converting obstacles into driving forces. But his well-researched studies concentrate primarily on product-cycle growth processes rather than the full range of strategies a major corporation faces. His formulations do not integrate the contributions of formal strategic analysis completely into the behavioral consensus-building process. Because his prescriptions tend to be oriented toward somewhat smaller, less complex enterprises than those in this study, they pose difficulties for practical management adoption in very large entities.

• Braybrooke[4] and Lindblom[5] pioneered the idea of "disjointed incrementalism" as the practical approach to strategy formulation in the public policy realm. Their important works suggest that, because of pragmatic constraints, public policy choices focus on incremental alteration of the status quo, rather than rational-deductive definitions of global goals followed by systematic choices among an array of complete programs to achieve selected goals in toto. Instead, they note that public decision makers often consider only a limited array of policies, which may cause partial movement in positive directions. Progress is made through "successive limited comparisons" of the options open to the decision maker. In the public sphere this results in a never-ending series of attacks on more or less permanent problems, with goals themselves often modified pragmatically to means available. In fact, they also note, there may not be agreement on ultimate goals at all because this might be divisive or even impossible to achieve. Instead the "best" policy or program may simply be the one that is acceptable enough to key players to achieve movement from one policy to the next.

These findings help explain the realities of public policy making and offer important specific insights into private-sector decision making. But the rational-deductive method of decision making is a bit more applicable in the latter, and observed behavior indicates that business managers consciously do integrate these and more disjointed incremental processes in their strategic decision making. Business executives consciously survey a wider departure from the status quo than bureaucrats apparently do, and my data suggest that business executives take a much more proactive approach toward change than Braybrooke and Lindblom describe for public-sector managers. Finally, executives in large companies seem to guide decision processes consciously and incrementally through a relatively definable series of steps designed to build support and commitment toward broadly conceived goals that may themselves be generated and refined through incremental processes.

- Bennis and others have analyzed the psychology of change and described the sequence of steps a "change agent" uses to catalyze change in organizations.[6] These steps might be

called: fact finding, developing personal awareness, training people in new interaction modes, creating an organizational "culture" to link the interests of various organizational groups, developing methods for more open joint
problem solving, obtaining agreement on goals for the
organization, anticipating and overcoming barriers to
implementation, agreeing on implementation steps, and
then stabilizing changes brought about. Bennis points out
that methodologies of various change agents vary in carry-
ing out these tasks. But certain common characteristics of
interest to line managers emerge from his observations:
(1) Major changes take three to five years. (2) Programs to
achieve significant change must be phased and largely
undertaken bottom up, but the legitimacy of alternatives
must be affirmed by the support of key people at the top.
(3) Successful change processes must deal with both intellectual content and emotional issues. (4) Effective change
processes must be adapted to the specific requirements of
the most important subsystems supporting the target system. (5) New goals tend to emerge toward the end of the
change process, not at its beginning.

My data suggest that these concepts apply rather well—
along with others noted—to effective line managers seeking
strategic changes in large organizations. But the "organization development" approach generally assumes an outside
change agent. Its goal is often a new management style for
an enterprise that might or might not be effective for specific line managers. And it does not make clear how such
managers effectively integrate proposed psychological
shifts with formal analytical techniques to help select,
calibrate, and maintain the content of new macro-strategies
amid the turmoil of ongoing shorter term decision processes.

As the notes throughout this chapter indicate, many other
behavioral and decision theorists have also provided useful
and profound insights into the workings of strategic processes. The preceding paradigms are merely samples of some
of the total systemic approaches most relevant here. Rather
than critiquing these and other systems in detail, the re-

mainder of the chapter will attempt to usefully structure the processes real managers used in establishing strategies for their large and complex enterprises. And it will compare and contrast their observed actions and their stated rationales to concepts developed elsewhere in the literature. No conceptual scheme is right or wrong in the abstract. It is only more or less useful than others.[7] I hope the following structure will be useful both to practical managers and to analysts of strategic decisions in large organizations.

INITIATING STRATEGIC CHANGE: PROACTIVE INCREMENTALISM

Following is perhaps the most articulate short statement on how executives feel they actually do manage incrementalism. It links many of the key elements later sections will discuss in detail.

- "How does one manage such a process? Typically you start with general concerns, vaguely felt. Next you roll an issue around in your mind till you think you have a conclusion that makes sense for the company. You then go out and sort of post the idea without being too wedded to its details. You then start hearing the arguments pro and con, and some very good refinements of the idea usually emerge. Then you pull the idea in and put some resources together to study it so it can be put forward as more of a formal presentation. You wait for 'stimuli occurrences' or 'crises,' and launch pieces of the idea to help in these situations. But they lead toward your ultimate aim. You know where you want to get. You'd like to get there in six months. But it may take three years, or you may not get there. And when you do get there, you don't know whether it was originally your own idea—or somebody else had reached the same conclusion before you and just got you on board for it. You never know. The president would follow the same basic process, but he could drive it much faster than an executive lower in the organization."[8]

Because of differences in organization forms, management styles, and the content of individual decisions, no single paradigm can hold for all strategic decisions.[9] But management of the most complex strategic decisions tends to involve the kind of broad process steps outlined below. The reader will recognize the parallels with various "phase theorems" about decision making,[10] but the actual process is much more multiphased and complicated in both analytical and political-behavioral terms than such theorems generally indicate.

Although various process phases—for both subsystem and overall enterprise strategies—flow generally in the sequence presented, the stages are by no means orderly or discrete (see Diagram 3). And it would be improper to assume that any manager consciously managed the process through all its phases linearly. Although executives did manage individual steps proactively, any single decision might well involve numerous loops back to earlier stages as unexpected issues were encountered. Or decision times might become extremely compressed and require short-circuiting leaps forward if major crises suddenly appeared. This book is concerned with observed attempts to manage strategic change in an orderly way. The management processes involved must inevitably deal with crises, but they are not dependent on them as causative agents. Crisis management of strategic change is a separate subject not addressed here.

Networks for sensing needs

How do top managers first sense needs for strategic change? Although most sample companies had elaborate environmental scanning procedures,[11] very often important strategic issues first emerged in quite vague or undefined terms,[12] like IBM's "organizational overlap" or "too much proliferation." These normally appeared as inconsistencies in internal action patterns or anomalies between the enterprise's current posture and some perception of its future environment.[13, 14] In the organizations studied the process of search could be both active and entrepreneurial when the executive was not operating in a crisis mode.[15] Early signals might come from almost anywhere, and they could initially be quite indistinct from the background noise of ordinary communications.[16] Crises, of course, could announce themselves with strident urgency in operations control systems. However, if the enterprise waited until signals reached high enough amplitude to be sensed by formal measurement systems,

Diagram 3. Some typical process steps in logical incrementalism (highly simplified to help visualize a few basic relationships)

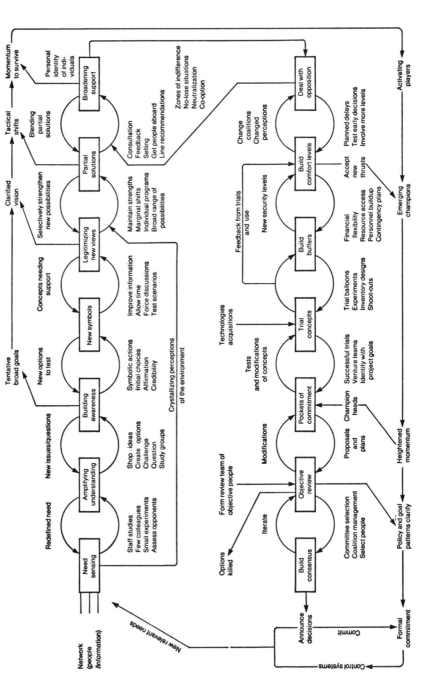

smooth efficient transitions might be impossible.[17] The organization might miss chances to exploit important opportunities in a timely way, or it could undergo traumatic losses as it dug out of crises perceived too late.

Consequently, effective change managers—like IBM's Vincent Learson in Chapter 3—consciously sought multiple contact points with other staff and line executives, workers, customers, suppliers, politicians, technologists, educators, outside professionals, government groups, and others.[18] As their careers advanced, they actively developed networks of people inside and outside the organization who served as potential sensors of change and credible contact points for objective information about the enterprise and its environments. They purposely used these networks to short-circuit all the careful screens their organizations built up to "tell the top only what it wanted to hear."[19] They constantly moved around, showed up at unexpected spots, sampled viewpoints, probed, and listened.

• Peter McColough, chairman and CEO of Xerox, reportedly spent only about half his time at corporate headquarters. He was active in high-level political and charitable activities—for example, as treasurer of the Democratic National Committee and chairman of the Urban League. He tried to "spend time on things that might affect society here and abroad because they affect Xerox and all our lives." He said, "I've tried to decentralize decision making. Still if something bothers me, I don't rely on reports or what other executives may want to tell me. I'll go down very deep into the organization, to certain issues and people, so I'll have a feeling for what they think. . . ." He refused to let his life be run by letters and memos. "Because I came up by that route, I know what a salesman can say. I also know that before I see [these memos] they go through 15 hands, and I know what that can do to them."[20]

To keep its top managers well informed, General Motors has institutionalized this kind of short-circuiting for informational purposes at all managerial levels. Numerous executives paraphrased the following viewpoint.

● "There is a lot of moving out of channels in this organization. Product Planning knows in advance what is acceptable. People are involved in a lot of presentations at multiple levels. Everybody knows everyone. And the top decision makers have actually had a chance to meet and deal
with a number of [lower echelon] people on a person-to-
person basis. We try to keep key decision makers informed
about the marketplace and whom to contact for detailed
information. They have input from formal presentations,
from continuous flows of informal information, and . . .
their own considerable experience garnered from a lifetime
career in the transportation business."[21]

Improving and leading the formal information system

To avoid undercutting intermediate managers, such bypassing must, of course, be limited to information gathering, with
no implication that orders or approvals are given directly to
lower levels. If handled properly, the practice actually improves formal information flows as well. Line managers are
less tempted to screen information when they know bypass
channels are operating. And they prefer to report impending
difficulties and actions taken themselves, rather than have
these crop up in questions from above. Lower levels are also
stimulated by the possibility that they may be able to "talk
to the very top" and that upper management really cares
about their views. The process—when most successful—was
a conscious part of a manager's total information system.
Some of his or her informal sources might even become
recognized as a "credibility organization" that corporate staff
members or planners checked with (or kept informed) to
make sure that their data were blessed by the people key
managers were likely to believe.[22]

Any person sifts signals about threats and opportunities
through a "perceptive screen" defined by his or her own
value system.[23] Consequently, an executive who is proactively
seeking new potential opportunities or threats will make sure
that this sensing network includes people who look at the
world a bit differently than does the dominating culture of
the enterprise. Some companies have even established small

groups of "wild birds" at corporate level to range throughout the organization stimulating offbeat approaches to issues.[24] Some—like Exxon and Pilkington—have structured devil's advocates into their planning processes. Others—like Xerox— have selected a group of independent thinkers to make special studies, extensively using independent consultants and outside authorities, to ensure that top managers view changing environments objectively. To allow scanning groups or networks to be dominated solely by senior executives imbued in the enterprise's own culture is to invite disaster.[25]

Successful enterprises, of course, have many formally structured horizon scanning, planning, and reporting systems to alert them to pending changes, but rarely in my observations did the earliest signals for strategic change come from these sources. Instead, they appeared in highly diffuse and informal ways. Seldom did a manager immediately know what precise action—if any—a complex issue called for. Rather, as one high level observer noted, "At this stage our top people spent a lot of time talking in the halls, asking questions for clarification, bringing in new information sources, and trying to sort out what was really relevant." Top executives themselves frequently described initial need sensing in the following terms: "something you felt uneasy about," "a general feeling that we needed to do something new," or "we could all see a problem developing, but didn't know what it meant or precisely what to do."

Effective strategic managers purposely tried to sense impending issues or opportunities before their organizations did. They actively engaged in a variety of different social and intellectual environments, read, listened, and searched beyond their formal reporting structures. Unlike some public-sector executives, they consciously sought options and threats beyond simple extrapolations from the status quo.[26] "If I'm not two to three years ahead of my organization, I'm not doing my job" was a common comment of such top managers. Although annual planning exercises formalized data inputs about selected futures and helped calibrate managers' intuitions, much of the sensing task was soft, informal, and interpersonal—but highly proactive—searching for new critical factors affecting opportunities and success.[27, 28]

Amplifying understanding

Next came the diagnostic process of amplifying understanding about vaguely sensed issues.[29] Extensive personal discussions, staff work, or consulting studies might be needed to define parameters or build essential data bases for any action. Very often the pressing initial symptom of a problem (demagogues attacking the auto industry) evolved under investigation into something more basic (a changing public expectation about auto performance). Careful managers recognized that a problem definition or response that was too rapid could create serious future problems—as did the automobile companies' early statements about the "impossibility" of meeting tight effluent and mileage standards—and be as costly as a response that was too late.

In some cases, however, executives might quickly perceive the broad dimensions of needed changes, but they still might want more convincing evidence or greater organizational support to stimulate effective action. Far from accepting the first satisfactory (satisficing) solution,[30] successful managers seemed to consciously generate and consider a broad array of alternatives.[31] Among other things, individual executives wanted to avoid being the prime supporter of a losing idea or having the organization attack or slavishly adopt "the boss's solution" and have to change it as more evidence became available. Typically at this stage, they wanted to have a few colleagues become more knowledgeable about an issue and help them think through its ramifications. They wanted to maintain the capacity to receive objective information and the flexibility to choose among the various solutions the best brains in the organization might offer.[32] And they wanted sufficient objective data to argue effectively against preconceived ideas or blindly followed past practices. Yet they did not want to threaten existing power centers prematurely in ways that might cause opponents to kill any change aborning.

- Chrysler Corporation had Dr. Hancock, an independent consultant, look into ways of predicting warranty costs and lowering its parts and subassembly costs. The report went through several iterations. Finally, however, it recommended: (1) a new way of calculating the overall marginal cost of parts and subassemblies including all quality costs before and in the marketplace, and (2) an integrated committee of engineering, marketing, production, sales, management, and systems people to work on product simplification and cost issues. These suggestions did not threaten the power structure, and people could easily see the benefits of reducing part numbers.

But the organization found it difficult to respond. No one knew how many "parts common" or "parts unique" were made for various cars. A whole new data system was needed to identify parts and specifications across all the car lines. But even more important were the human motivational problems involved. An engineer's or designer's ego was involved in each feature he or she had designed. Manufacturing people hated to change components they knew worked and fitted as they should. Sales people delighted in new features and unique designs which titillated the customer. And the art and fun of marketing and design lay in seeing new creations of one's mind mounted on thousands of cars. Without early staff studies like the Hancock report to provide a common basis for discussion and a concrete measure of benefit, these groups never could have been brought together in common cause.[33]

Even though individual executives might not have in mind a specific solution to an emerging problem, they could still proactively guide action in intuitively desired directions by defining the issues staffs would investigate, by selecting the people who made the investigations, and by controlling the process through which they reported. At the same time, such investigations allowed the guiding executive to broaden his or her information base, to assess and cope with potential opponents' actions, and to obtain initial organizational support for change without prematurely committing to any specific action. As in the Chrysler case, the executive might not release staff studies until they had gone through several iterations and posed solutions in desired directions. Even then executives might avoid too close an identification with a specific solution, preferring to keep it a staff recommendation until they were sure enough people would "get on board" to make it work.

Building awareness

To accomplish this, executives guiding strategic change often started to make a wider audience aware of the issue and its potential solutions.[34] They might "shop" the idea among a few trusted colleagues at first to test initial responses, or they might commission a few more studies to illuminate emerging options, contingencies, or opportunities. These could lead to a few specific incremental decisions. More often they simply generated broadened or intensified perceptions of future potentials. At this stage an executive might even have to offset the frustrations of study groups who felt they had failed because their earlier studies had not yet precipitated direct action. But the organization might still not be ready for specific decisions. Key players might not be aware enough about specific issues, variables, or options to change their past action patterns or even to investigate options creatively. Building awareness, concern, and an active interest in alternative solutions was often a vital link in the practical politics of change.

At this point top executives might not feel committed to any specific solution. Instead they might seek to tap the collective wit of the organization by making people aware of issues and forcing initial thinking about them. They frequently wanted a more thorough definition of problems and a sense of the options that might be feasible. But they did not want to cause irreconcilable opposition, emotional overcommitment, or organizational momenta they could not control.[35] The management processes involved were essentially those of challenging, questioning, listening, and perhaps generating options, but purposely avoiding commitments. An interesting example occurred in the General Motors downsizing decision:

• In the early 1970s there was still a glut in world oil supplies. Nevertheless, analyses in the GM Chief Economist's Office began to project a developing U.S. dependency on foreign oil and the likelihood of higher future oil prices.

These concerns led the board in 1972 to create an ad hoc energy task force headed by David C. Collier, then treasurer, later head of GM of Canada and then the Buick Division. Collier's group included people from manufacturing, research, design, finance, industry-government relations, and the economics staff. After a half-year's research, in May of 1973 the task force went to the board with three conclusions: (1) there was a developing energy problem, (2) the government had no particular plan to deal with it, and (3) energy costs would have a profound effect on GM's business. Collier's report created a good deal of discussion around the company in the ensuing months. "We were trying to get other people to think about the issue," said Richard C. Gerstenberg, then chairman of GM.

Changing symbols: Building credibility

As the awareness of the need for change grew, managers often wanted to signal the organization that certain types of changes were coming, even if specific solutions were not in hand. Top managers obviously could not communicate personally or even in written communiques with everyone who had to be influenced by a proposed strategy shift. But they could—and did—consciously use the informal grapevine to carry signals that the flux in the organization was changing. Without any verbal communications, they often made symbolic moves whose effects were amplified as they were relayed through word of mouth.[36] Recognizing the power of such silent communications, newly appointed top executives tended to be quite attentive to their early actions, expecting the organization to be waiting for the first signals of change. Some purposely undertook highly visible symbolic actions that wordlessly conveyed complex messages they could have never communicated as well or as credibly in verbal terms. One classic historical case and one modern business example can make the point vividly.

● When Lord Louis Mountbatten went to India to negotiate that country's release from the British Empire, he needed to change the confrontation atmosphere which had per-

vaded the discussions with previous British emissaries. He
began by inviting Indian leaders to dinners at the vice regal
palace in Delhi and—for the first time in history—offering
them their traditional foods, served Indian style. He re-
painted to soft muted shades the austere offices where he
would receive and negotiate with the Indian leaders individually. He reestablished the "shimmering scarlet and
gold" formal ceremonies of the vice regency as a platform
of pomp to attract the attention of the masses while he
made "magnificent descents of informality" in dealing
with individual leaders. He arrived unannounced at cock-
tail receptions, rode horseback unguarded with his wife
Edwina through the parks of Delhi, and invited each Indian
leader individually to get to know him personally before
discussing formal negotiations. The Indian reaction to
these symbolic changes was twofold: "Thank God we finally have a human being for viceroy and not a stuffed
shirt" and "You [Mountbatten] have become a very difficult person to negotiate with because [you] are drawing
larger crowds than anyone in India."[37]

• In 1975 Riccardo and Cafiero quickly sold off some of
their unprofitable nonautomobile divisions and went
through a dramatic staredown with the British government
to achieve concessions there. These moves were crucial to
the credibility of their U.S. austerity program. One executive said, "These moves said we were no longer on ego
trips in the United States or abroad. If a division couldn't
be made profitable, we would drop it. Riccardo and
Cafiero's credibility went way up after these actions. I
don't know what would have happened if they hadn't
pulled off the U.K. negotiation. It would have been hard
to believe the productivity and austerity programs here,
that's sure. The most important changes are often those
which signal a change in attitude at the top of an organization."

Similarly, other managers used symbolic moves to preview
or verify intended directions of change. These acts sometimes
occurred before the formal announcement of major new strategic thrusts. At other times they confirmed the intention of

top management to back a thrust already partially begun—as McColough's relocation of Xerox headquarters to Connecticut (away from its Rochester reprographics base) underscored the company's developing commitment to product diversification and organizational decentralization. An organization often needs such symbolic moves—or decisions it regards as symbolic—to build credibility behind a new strategy. Without such actions it may interpret even forceful verbiage as mere rhetoric and delay its commitment to intended new thrusts. An example with multibillion-dollar consequences illustrates the point.

- In GM's downsizing decision, engineers said one of top management's early decisions affected the credibility of the whole weight-reduction program: "Initially, we proposed a program using a lot of aluminum and substitute materials to meet the new mass targets. But this would have meant a very high cost, and would have strained the suppliers' aluminum capacity. However, when we presented this program to management, they said, 'Okay, if necessary, we'll do it.' They didn't back down. We began to understand then that they were dead serious. Feeling that the company would spend the money was critical to the success of the entire mass reduction effort."

Effective change managers: (1) recognized the impact their incremental decisions and action patterns had on the credibility and perceived directions of their new strategies and (2) tried to keep in mind the symbolic implications each individual act had as well as its capacity to resolve a particular issue immediately at hand.

Legitimizing new viewpoints

Often before going on to more specific strategic decisions, it was necessary to allow time to legitimize certain new options that had reached the awareness level but had an undue aura of uncertainty or concern about them. Early decisions, of course, tended toward solutions that arose out of executives' prior experiences. Because of familiarity, these were perceived as having lower risks (or potential costs) than newer alternatives. Therefore, top managers seeking change often consciously created discussion forums and allowed slack time for their organizations to talk through threatening issues, work out the implications of new solutions, or gain an improved information base that would permit new options to be evaluated objectively in comparison with more familiar alternatives.[38]

● When Joe Wilson thought Haloid Corporation should change its name to include Xerox, he first submitted a memorandum asking colleagues what they thought of the idea. They rejected it. Wilson then explained his concerns more fully, and his executives rejected the idea again. Finally Wilson formed a committee headed by Sol Linowitz who had thought a separate Xerox subsidiary might be the best solution. As this committee deliberated, negotiations were under way with the Rank Organization and the term Rank-Xerox was commonly heard and Haloid-Xerox no longer seemed so strange. "And so," according to John Dessauer, "a six-month delay having diluted most opposition, we of the committee agreed that the change to Haloid-Xerox might in the long run produce sound advantages."[39]

● General Mills' Executive Council became its sounding board for considering a strategy of diversification outside the foods area. Since most of this group had come out of the foods business, there was some concern that such a strategy might not be well received. The acquisition group therefore made a detailed review of the consumer products industries of the United States. From these they distilled six areas of major interest and a set of acquisition criteria top management could agree to. In essence, the criteria legitimized a more intense study of specific industries and candidates outside the foods field. And when the acquisitions group brought in carefully investigated nonfoods proposals, top management had already made a partial commitment "to move into new areas."[40]

By this stage the guiding executive might have a fairly firm vision of the most desirable general direction for movement.[41] Others might be beginning to share this view, but the best pathway forward still might not be clear. Once the broad concept began to achieve wider legitimacy, the executive could openly stimulate the organization to analyze its possibilities, develop new options, and test possible specific scenarios for action.

From tactical shifts to partial solutions

Rarely did the total solution to a major strategic problem suddenly appear full blown, like Minerva from the brow of Jupiter. Instead early resolutions were likely to be partial, tentative, or experimental.[42] The guiding executive tried to carefully maintain the enterprise's ongoing strengths while shifting its posture at the margin toward new needs. Beginning moves in a strategic shift often appeared almost tactical adjustments. As such they encountered little opposition, yet each partial solution added momentum in new directions. These directions might be only dimly or broadly perceived at first, awaiting further information from the external environment or experimental confirmation that more specific new options were feasible or desirable.[43]

• In the early 1970s GM executives said: "There was a distinct awareness of a developing fuel economy ethic. But our conclusions were really at the conversational level; that the big car trend was at an end. There was certainly no tendency to go whole hog in emphasizing economy-conservation factors. We were not at all sure sufficient numbers of large-car buyers were ready to move to dramatically lighter cars." Nevertheless, GM did start concept studies of what became the Cadillac Seville.

When the oil crisis hit in fall 1973, the company responded in further increments: at first by merely increasing production of its existing small car lines. Then as the crisis deepened, it added another partial solution, the subcompact "T car"—the Chevette, and accelerated the Seville's development cycle. Next, as economy appeared more salable, executives set an initial target of removing 400 pounds from big-car bodies by 1977. Then as fuel economy pressures persisted and engineering feasibilities offered greater confidence, this target was tightened further to 800-1,000 pounds (3 miles per gallon). No step by itself shifted the company's total strategic posture until the full downsizing of all lines was announced. But each partial solution built confidence and commitment toward a new direction.

During this period individual programs were usually undertaken on their own merit. Early statements of the strategic shift were often stated as "concerns" to which the enterprise was responding. The enterprise was not deemed ready yet to formally accept these as new goals overriding established organizational thrusts or psychological commitments. Executives themselves might not yet have perceived the full nature of the strategic shift they had begun.[44] Their early steps could still legitimately lead to a variety of different success scenarios, but they consciously delayed choosing which particular path to follow until further information was available. As events unfurled, the solutions to several seemingly unrelated problems might very well flow together in a not-yet-perceived synthesis. Strategic logic dictated only starting broad initiatives that could later be flexibly guided in any of several possible more explicit directions.[45]

Broadening support: Consultation, selling, and redundancy

Often even these broad thrusts needed expanded political support and understanding to achieve sufficient momentum to survive.[46] Consultative processes and discussion forums tended to be favored means for accomplishing this. If carefully managed, these did not become the "garbage can" of competing ideas some observers have noted.[47]

• In building support for its 1967 diversification programs, General Mills' acquisition group undertook what it called "sort of a popularity contest." After agreeing to the broad acquisition criteria (noted earlier), each member of the Executive Council was asked to rank the order in which various possible diversification areas should be considered. In essence this got a few top people behind selected projects or industries. As one might expect the winners were those closest to existing businesses. Cosmetics seemed closer than apparels. Broadcasting was closer than furniture because of the company's TV advertising experience. The one common denominator that got a good reception was the company's marketing capability. This deep-seated faith in the company's capacity to market to the homemaker and her family evolved into a widely accepted, but "loose," strategy over a period of time, through the continued interaction of key management personnel.

Other executives preferred to actively "sell" an emerging broad concept to their organizations, while letting their line personnel achieve personal identity with the idea by recommending their own solutions to specific subproblems.

- At Chrysler Corporation, Eugene Cafiero would use almost any forum to inculcate the ideas of participation and decentralization. Cafiero said, "I didn't know how to best do the jobs that needed to be done. I invited people to experiment, to keep what worked, and discard what didn't. . . . At every meeting with my managers, I discussed this involvement question. I've had 'rap seminars' with members of our Management Club. We've had 'trainee group' sessions to get people started. We had St. Clair Inn meetings with top manufacturing managers and vice presidents. Sometimes I stirred up minor revolutions, trying to get people out into the plants to talk to the people who had to do the job. Now some plants have substantial involvement. Others are still in the dark ages."

One executive said, "I don't know how many times Gene met with different groups to make his point. He would get the group together, roll up his sleeves and start to talk about a few crucial things: quality, reliability, doing the job better, getting people to participate. After a half hour or so, he'd lean back and say, 'What do you want to talk about? What do you think?' . . . Cafiero really made people feel like they were part of the action."

Such selling typically required more than a one-time "explanation" of the change. It required feedback, responses to questions, and very often massive redundancy and reinforcement of arguments favoring new views. Because of the on-going values of the organization, initial explanations or responses to questions might have little effect. It was impressive how many times successful change managers were willing to deliver the same message and listen to the same questions to achieve the support they wanted.

Management styles that ignored these concerns could pay a high price at implementation stages and could even find their strategies totally thwarted. As Cafiero said, "30,000 workers can foul up 300 managers any time." In addition to facilitating smooth implementation of planned changes, many managers reported that interactive consensus building could also improve the quality of the strategic decisions themselves and achieve positive and innovative assistance when things would otherwise go wrong. Such considerations have often been touted as central to Japanese-style participative decision making. But they are equally part of the American corporate style of getting the right people on board to consider decisions thoroughly before final commitments are made and to ensure their creative implementation. At this stage, management of coalitions began to dominate proactive strategic processes.[48]

FROM CONCEPT TO ACTIVE STRATEGY: INCREMENTALLY

Some broad lines of the new strategy might now be clear to a few key managers, and several others might have embraced particular emerging thrusts relevant to their operations. Some formal program commitments could even have been made and some movement achieved at lower levels. But the various initiatives might not yet add to a cohesive whole. And—even if they did—there were often sound political or informational reasons for not announcing a strategy in its full pristine glory at this early stage. Why not?

Opposition, zones of indifference, and no-lose situations

Executives in basically healthy companies realized that any attempt to introduce a new strategy would have to deal with the support its predecessor had. Barring a major crisis, a frontal attack on the old strategy could easily be interpreted as an attack on those who espoused it and brought the enterprise to its present levels of success. The former strategy and the judgments it involved may have been well adapted to a preceding time, and the people who made these judgments might still be in positions where their support would be critical to the success of any new strategy. In addition, there often were a variety of legitimate views as to what could and should be done in the circumstances the entity now faced, and a wise executive did not want to alienate people who would otherwise be supporters.

To bring the full force of the enterprise behind a new strategy, successful change managers carefully assessed and dealt with the most important centers of potential support or opposition to new thrusts. They tried to get key people behind their concepts whenever possible, coopt or neutralize serious opposition if necessary,[49] or find zones of indifference where the proposition would not be disastrously opposed.[50] Best of all, they sought no-lose situations that would activate all important players positively in their own self-interest.

• James McFarland took over at General Mills from his power base in the Grocery Products Division. Another serious contender for the top spot had been Louis B. "Bo" Polk, a very bright, aggressive young man, who headed the corporation's acquisition-diversification program. Both traditional lines and acquisitions groups wanted resources for their activities and had high-level supporters. McFarland's "goodness to greatness" conferences first obtained broad agreement on growth goals and criteria for all areas.

Out of this and the related acquisition proposal process (described earlier) came two thrusts: (1) to expand—internally and through acquisitions—in food-related sectors and (2) to acquire new growth centers based on General Mills' marketing skills. Although there was no formal statement, there was a strong feeling that the majority of resources should be used in food-related areas. But neither group was foreclosed, and no one could suggest the new management was vindictive. As it turned out, over the next five years about $450 million was invested in new businesses, and the majority were not closely related to foods.

Such tactics did not always work, however. Strong-minded executives sometimes disagreed to the point where they had to be moved to positions of less influence or stimulated to leave. But very often top executives simply saw such opposing views as healthy—a function of individual executives (because of their various backgrounds and experiences) perceiving the benefits and risks of new thrusts in a different light than they might. More information, careful handling, and the passage of time could often bring valued dissidents into the consensus group.

Building comfort levels: Changing perceived risks

One of the more common challenges in strategic change was improving managers' comfort levels concerning new ideas. Perceived risk is a function of how familiar a person is with an idea. Oil companies are used to $100 million investments in resource development, and their managements accept these as routine business risks. But lacking similar familiarity, the same investments in mining, nuclear, or non-energy diversifications may appear much more risky. Financial managers tend to perceive R&D risks in a different light than do technical entrepreneurs pushing new solutions. And diversifications outside of one's traditional fields generally appear more risky than ongoing thrusts. Most major changes in direction call for planned delays and action sequences to build at least some key people's comfort levels before going ahead. Again General Mills provides an interesting example:

- As General Rawlings shut down General Mills' unsuccessful (electronics, appliances, chemicals) diversifications of the 1950s, cash became available for new ventures. But these ventures had made the company suspicious of acquisitions and diversification outside the foods field. General Mills' R&D expenditures (1% of sales) had been low for its industry, so an early move was to invest the funds in R&D in diversified food products—snacks, beverages, and pet foods being primary targets. The key to a snacks strategy was finding a way to keep such oil-rich products shelf stable for a year. When research solved the problem, the company could introduce these products through familiar channels. With these entries successful, managers became willing to expand the line through snack acquisitions (Morton Foods, Tom Huston Peanuts, Cherry Levis, and others).

The company had also wanted to expand internationally, but little had happened. With increasing confidence in the company's ability to manage acquired snack operations, the corporate acquisition and finance head, "Bo" Polk, was able to move quickly in acquiring foreign snack producers (Smith's, Productos de Trigo, and others). Then, as its confidence in selecting and managing food-related acquisitions grew, top management was able to more easily accept nonfoods acquisitions (toys, crafts, clothing, and so on).

This pattern was common for successfully diversifying companies. Early acquisitions tended to be close to the company's expertise and experience and have a high probability of success. As a few successes occurred in the management of related new product lines or slightly diversified acquisitions, executives perceived further acquisitions as less risky. Finally the new lines and their acquired managements might begin to dominate the company's profit picture and culture. And old traditional lines—which once looked so sound and secure—might appear to the new coalition as risky remnants of the past. In all the diversifying companies studied, a crucial step in managing strategic change was incrementally developing the psychological comfort levels that allowed movement from one set of risk perceptions to the next.

Structuring flexibility: Buffers, slacks, and activists

As consensus built and confidence grew concerning possible new thrusts, successful change managers consciously began to develop their enterprises' capacities—in terms of flexibility and opportunism—to exploit them. There were too many unknowables in the total environment for managers to program or control the nature and timing of all the events the enterprise had to deal with in effecting a major change in direction. Logic dictated that managers purposely design needed flexibilities into their organizations and have reserve resources ready to deploy incrementally as events demanded. Three activities were essential in achieving planned flexibility: (1) establishing a horizon scanning activity to identify the general nature and extent of the most likely opportunities and threats the concern might encounter, (2) creating sufficient resource buffers—or "slacks"—to respond effectively as events actually unfurled, and (3) developing and positioning activists with a psychological commitment to move opportunistically and flexibly at the proper moment.

- "Although cringing a bit, in 1975 Xerox began to use the word 'commodity' to describe its product. . . . Technically we began to explore new options, and we made sure our R&D budgets grew to do this without shortcutting vital support work. We were trying to explore how much cost reduction was possible in the reprographics process. Would it be like computers with several rapidly progressing generations of technology and cost reduction? Or would we reach some limits quickly? We didn't know then. But we started the analyses. We canceled technical programs for diversification to put released resources in the heartland."

Formal planning programs usually provided mechanisms to scan future horizons for potential economic, social, and technological opportunities and threats. Some even generated contingency—or "what if"—plans. But these formal analyses often failed to achieve the essential touchstones of planned flexibility. Horizon scanning frequently became a routine designed primarily to justify ongoing plans, and contingency plans became precapsuled (and shelved) programs to respond in precise ways to stimuli that never quite occurred as expected. Seeing themselves as resource-constrained, some organizations—in the name of efficiency—budgeted for full resource utilization. Even R&D plans showed all people committed for a year in advance, thus assuming (often predictably) that nothing new would happen to require a change. Opportunistic organizations, by contrast, tended to use horizon scanning activities differently. They forced line and

top executives to answer two basic questions: (1) What actions *must* we take now (or in the next year) *to be ready* to
respond if this trend develops further? (2) What *resource
buffers* must we have to deal with the uncertainties these
events probably represent? They then consciously developed
improved levels of working capital, better access to outside
financial sources, more flexible organization structures,
greater personnel redundancy, more active information grape-
vines, better supplier and technological access systems, and
so on to allow rapid movement when necessary. The essence
of contingency planning is not in estimating which events will
occur and planning for those in detail, but in anticipating
what type and scale of resource buffers and organizational
flexibility are needed to exploit likely futures effectively.

The concept of resource buffers deserves special amplification. Designed flexibility requires quick access to resources to
cushion the sudden impact of forceful random events, to
offset opponents' sudden attacks, or to build rapid momentum for new strategic shifts. Some examples illustrate the
form these vital buffers can take:

- For critical purchased items General Motors maintains at
  least three suppliers, each with sufficient capacity to expand production should one of the others encounter a
  catastrophe. Thus the company has expandable capacity
  with no fixed investment. Exxon set up Esso Exploration
  to purposely undertake the higher risks and longer term
  investments necessary to search for oil in new areas,
  and thus reduce the potential impact on Exxon if there
  were sudden unpredictable changes in Middle East oil
  availability. Instead of hoarding cash, Pillsbury and General
  Mills sold off unprofitable businesses and cleaned up their
  financial statements to improve their access to external
  capital sources for acquisitions. Such access in essence provides the protection of a cash buffer without its investment. IBM's large R&D facility and its project-team approach to development assure that it has a pool of people
  it can quickly shift among various projects to exploit
  interesting new technologies. Pilkington used a "patent
  improvements clause" in its licensing strategy to ensure

that it had a free buffer of technology when its own patents expired and it would have to compete directly with its former licensees.

To utilize such flexibilities, the more entrepreneurial companies in my sample also developed "credible activists" whose role was to press proactively for movement as opportunities or threats developed around specific strategic thrusts. Product division heads (or product managers) served this function for existing product lines when motivation systems properly rewarded risk taking. But someone with credibility at the top also had to be empowered and motivated to press action on other major thrusts—like diversifications, new technologies, government regulatory responses, public image building, divestitures, or new raw materials access—when the time was ripe. When effective, this person always had direct access to the top and did not have to obtain approvals from multiple layers of organization, which required a unanimous yes for any positive decision but only a single no to kill an option. When these flexible response patterns were designed into the enterprise's strategy, it was proactively ready to move on those thrusts that by their very nature had to evolve incrementally.

Trial concepts: Systematic waiting

In some cases, the prepared strategist had to wait for events, as Roosevelt awaited a precipitating Pearl Harbor. The availability of desired acquisitions or real estate might depend on a death, divorce, fiscal crisis, management change, or erratic stock market break.[51] Technologies perversely awaited new knowledge, inventions, or lucky accidents. Despite otherwise complete preparations, a planned market entry might not be wise until new legislation, trade agreements, or competitive shake-outs occurred. Organizational moves had to be timed to retirements, promotions, or management failures. Very often the specific strategy adopted would depend on the timing or sequence in which such random events transpired.[52] For example:

• The timing of SDS Inc.'s availability was an important

cause of both the date and the result of Xerox's move into computers.

- Chrysler was *forced* to make a negative decision on sub-compacts before it was *forced* to dispose of its flagging European operations. This affected the timing (late), the design (European), and the initial strategic impact (disappointing) of its small-car line.

In other cases, the strategist proactively launched trial concepts—like Cafiero's "low vans" or McColough's "architecture of information"—to see what would fly in the organization or even in the marketplace. Sometimes guiding executives would state their intention of making a major commitment—like Spoor's "Super Box" or Continental Group's "fourth leg for the stool"—to attract options and concrete proposals. Without making a commitment to a specific solution, the executive activated the organization's creative abilities.[53] This approach kept the manager's options open until substantive alternatives could be evaluated. It prevented practical management people from rejecting a strategic shift because they were forced to compare what they saw as only "paper options" against well-defined and urgent current needs.

- Although Continental Group's top executives had thoroughly discussed and investigated the energy business, the natural resources industry, and insurance as possible "fourth legs" for the company, each major acquisition possibility was so different that the strategic choice really came down to the fit of a particular candidate within these possible industries—i.e., Peabody Coal or Richmond Insurance—and one would have precluded the other.

Companies that stockpiled product designs for later selection provided a fascinating variation of the "trial concept" approach. Because, for example, the full design cycle for an automobile or an advanced office machine might take five to seven years, companies like General Motors and Xerox tried to have a stockpile of tested concepts, components, and systems that they could introduce to the market quickly (in one to two years) as market preferences and competitive moves became more predictable. This strategic shortening of lead times increased flexibility, decreased risks, and gave the properly prepared larger company an almost overwhelming advantage over some smaller competitors in terms of improved quality potential and market response. Again, such practices enabled companies to structure their strategic choices proactively to take maximum advantage of incrementalism.

SOLIDIFYING COMMITMENT: INCREMENTALLY

By now individual executives might more clearly perceive the directions toward which the enterprise should progress. And they might begin the sometimes subtle processes of stimulating constructive movement and commitment toward their new perceptions, without undermining important ongoing thrusts or creating unnecessary counteractions against their purposes. Typically, new strategic goals would remain broad, unrefined, or perhaps even unstated at this time. More specific dimensions might be announced only when key pieces of information fell into place, unanswered issues approached resolution, or significant resources had to be formally committed.

Creating pockets of commitment: Experiments and "shoot-outs"

Exploratory projects—like IBM's NPL or Chrysler's consolidated distributorship experiments—sometimes were needed to refine or test potential options, create necessary skills or technologies, or build commitment deep within the organization. Initially such projects might be kept small, partial, and ad hoc, not forming a comprehensive program or seeming to be integrated into a cohesive strategy. Whenever possible, executives guiding the strategic process would let others suggest how best to shape these new thrusts. They generally tried to maintain the originator's identity with any idea that moved in the right direction. And they might shun being identified with specific projects to avoid escalating attention to one solution too soon or losing personal credibility if it failed. Careful executives wanted to keep their options open, control premature momentum, openly back only winners, and select the right moment to blend several successful thrusts into a broader program or concept.[54]

A useful technique for creating positive commitment in technical organizations was purposely to create multiple competing approaches—or parallel development projects—in various organizations toward the same broad goal. At the early stages of research or development, no one really knew which particular approach would turn out to be best. Having several teams compete against each other accomplished three things.

1. Technical people felt a sense of urgency to accomplish and be creative because they knew their results would be compared with those of others.
2. Each team provided an independent basis of expertise for critiquing other teams' results and thus improved the total information base for program evaluation.[55]
3. Competition helped develop each group's identity with its own results, with the effect that each team became a small pocket of committed people ready to move if its approach was selected.

This approach—which was illustrated so well in Pilkington's float glass development—was also characteristic of IBM, Bell Labs, and other highly creative organizations during their most productive periods. The same technique could be used for venture, acquisition, or productivity teams in other situations. The guiding executive merely provided broad goals, a proper climate, and flexible resource support. From there on, the real momentum came from below, with the executive making final choices based on a performance "shootout" between well-developed proposals.[56] This allowed top managers to delay their final decisions until the last moment and thus obtain the best possible match between the company's technological capabilities and changing market needs. By making ultimate choices more effectively, the process could actually increase the efficiency of the whole endeavor, despite the seeming added cost of parallel efforts. But it required the proactive building of resource buffers to support parallel projects. It called for a supportive, open atmosphere that encouraged people to bring forward and support their alternatives. And it demanded a system for reintegrating the "losing" team constructively into the organization.

Keeping political exposure low: Maintaining objectivity

In order to maintain their own objectivity and future flexibility, some executives might choose to keep their own political exposure low as they built a new consensus. This was especially likely if major power centers had to be broached.

- At General Mills, General Rawlings began to explore areas of the company's weakness that concerned many of the top management group in a general way. At first there were a series of informal presentations to a small top management group. Later these became Management Operating Reviews (MORs), consisting of all corporate officers, division managers, and controllers. As questions were raised, an individual would be asked to investigate it and report back at a specified time. Investigations and data gathering went on over a several-year period. As these studies came into place—all made by people down the line—they focused increased attention on the company's weak commodities businesses and hasty postwar diversifications.

  Following one of the MORs, the controller's staff was asked to study a possible exit strategy for the most obvious divestiture, formula feeds. Although the move was traumatic for some people, there was not a heavy psychological commitment to this business, and the corporate officers and board decided to terminate it. General Rawlings clearly orchestrated this and later divestitures, but the process diverted much of the political pressure onto the groups making specific studies—and Rawlings's flexibility was maintained for other issues.

A strong top executive who committed to a major change too soon could easily discourage others from asking the questions that should be raised.[57] Questioning the boss's conclusions, once announced, always risks putting oneself in the role of a recalcitrant or an adversary, rather than a friendly investigator of a developing idea. By having detailed investigations done several levels down, top executives could still shape the process and its results by reviewing interim reports and specifying the timing, format, and forums for release of data. Yet when the report came forward, they could direct the "flak" of antagonistic questioning to those who made the investigations and had the most detailed information to answer pointed queries. They could stand above the battle and genuinely review proposals more objectively—not being personally on the defensive for having committed their credibility behind a particular outcome. From this position, individual executives could more easily orchestrate a high-level consensus. Wise executives preferred, if possible, to have negative decisions come from a group consensus that they merely confirmed, reserving their personal vetoes for crucial moments. In a well-made decision, people at all levels contributed to the generation, amplification, and interpretation of the information used to the extent that it was often difficult to say who really made the decision.[58]

Eliminating options: Two levels down

In a similar vein, those guiding strategic change might have to quietly shape the many alternatives flowing upward in a healthy decentralized operation. Here individual executives often used what Wrapp refers to as "the hidden hand."[59] Persons at lower levels were encouraged to make proposals in response to broad goals understood or formally promulgated throughout the organization. Many proposals were simply routine extensions of existing activities, but some might begin to shape or support a major intended strategic shift. Through their information networks, individual top managers could follow a few important proposals and projects. They could encourage concepts they favored, let undesired or weakly supported options die through inaction, and establish hurdles or tests for strongly supported ideas they might not agree with but did not want to oppose openly.

To keep a low profile, an executive might encourage, discourage, or kill options through subordinates rather than directly. Since proposals generally developed somewhat randomly, specific timing was often highly opportunistic. A crisis, a rash of reassignments, a reorganization, or a key appointment might allow individual executives to focus attention on particular thrusts, add momentum to some, and perhaps quietly phase out others.[60] They were well aware of the adage: "If there are no other options, mine wins." But also, without being Machiavellian, they did not want undesirable options to gain a great political momentum that would have to be terminated in an open bloodbath. And they certainly did not want to send false signals that stimulated other segments of the organization to make further proposals in similar directions. They recognized that the patterns in which proposals were approved or denied would inevitably be perceived by lower echelons as precedents establishing future goals or policies.

Crystallizing focus and consensus: Managing coalitions

At critical points in the process, a guiding executive might feel that some developing patterns needed to be more formally crystallized or confirmed. Ad hoc committees—like IBM's SPREAD Committee or Xerox's Flavin Committee—were favorite devices for this. By selecting the committee's membership, charter, and timing, the guiding executive could, of course, largely influence and predict its results. The committee could be balanced to educate, evaluate, neutralize, or overwhelm opponents. It could legitimize new options, generate broad cohesion from fragmented thrusts, or be narrowly focused to build momentum. Attention to the committee's potential dynamics was essential. Properly selected and managed, it could broaden support and increase commitment significantly for new goals. Mismanaged, it could easily generate organized opposition—and a real trauma—should the executive later be forced to overrule its recommendations. An example suggests how the processes of guiding developing options and crystallizing an overall focus may flow together:

- IBM's chairman (Watson) and executive vice president (Learson) had become concerned over what to do about third-generation computer technology, a proliferation of designs from various divisions, increasing costs of developing software, internal competition among their lines, and the needed breadth of line for the new computer applications they began to foresee. Step by step, they oversaw the killing of the company's huge Stretch computer line (uneconomic), a proposed 8000 series of computers (incompatible software), and the prototype English Scamp computer (duplicative). They then initiated a series of strategic dialogues with divisional executives to define a new strategy. But none came into place.

Learson, therefore, set up the SPREAD Committee representing every major segment of the company. Its 12 members included the most likely opponent of any integrated line (Haanstra), the people who had earlier suggested the 8000 and Scamp designs, and Learson's hand-picked lieutenant (Evans). When progress became "hellishly slow," Haanstra was removed as chairman and Evans took over. Eventually the committee came forth with an integrating proposal for a single, compatible line of computers to blanket and open up the market for both scientific and business applications, with standard interface for peripheral equipment. At an all-day meeting of the 50 top executives of the company, the report was not received with enthusiasm, but there were no compelling objections. So Learson blessed the silence as consensus, saying "OK, we'll do it," that is, go ahead with a major development program.

The power interactions among key players were important at this time. Each player had a different level of formal authority, referent power, information control, and personal credibility.[61] Individuals might perceive the problem differently based on their particular experiences and vantage points. They could pull and haul using their influence toward both the solution they perceived as best for the whole organization and the one that most benefited themselves. In an organization with dispersed power, the central power figure was the one who could manage coalitions.[62] Since no one player had all the power, regardless of his or her personal skills or position, the action that occurred over time might differ from the intention of any one player.[63] Hence the guiding executive tried to sense whatever consensus might exist among the key parties on various aspects of an issue and get partial decisions and momentum on these. As comfort levels and politics within the group built around these decisions, the executive might begin consciously to seek out that combination of features in a more complete solution that the most influential could live with and support. The result was that the stream of partial decisions began to evolve toward a broader consensus acceptable to the critical power centers' changing coalitions on particular issues.[64]

As partial consensus emerged, the guiding executive might crystallize events by stating a few broad goals in more specific terms for internal consumption. Finally, when sufficient general acceptance existed and the timing was right, the "decision" might begin to appear in more public announcements. For example, as General Mills divested several of its major divisions in the early 1960s, its annual reports began to refer to these as conscious moves "to concentrate on the company's strengths" and "to intensify General Mills' efforts in the convenience foods field." Obviously such statements could not be made until many of the actual divestitures were complete and a new management coalition and consensus had emerged.

Formalizing commitment: Empowering champions

As each major thrust came into focus, the guiding executive might try to ensure that some individual(s) felt responsible for that goal. If it was an entirely new vector for the enterprise, top executives often wanted more than mere accountability for its success; they wanted genuine commitment from its leaders.[65] A really new major thrust, concept, product, or problem solution frequently needed the nurturing hand of someone who strongly identified with it and whose future depended on its success.

● Once General Mills' divestiture program was sufficiently under way, General Rawlings selected "Bo" Polk to head up an acquisition activity to use the cash thrown off. In this role Polk had nothing to lose. With strong senior management in the remaining consumer products divisions, the ambitious Polk would have had a long road to the top there. In acquisitions, he provided a small political target, only a $50,000 budget in a $500 million company. Yet he had high visibility and could build his own power base, if he was successful. With direct access to and the support of Rawlings, he would be protected through his early ventures. All he had to do was make sure his first few acquisitions were a success. Then as individual acquisitions succeeded, his power base could feed on itself—satisfying both Polk's ego needs and the company's strategic desires.

In a similar vein, Learson made Brooks, Evans, and Fairclough the champions for the IBM 360 program. In some cases, top executives might have to wait for a champion to appear before committing resources to a risky new thrust, but they might assign less dramatic goals as specific missions for ongoing groups. From this point on, the process was familiar. The organization's formal structure had to be adjusted to support the strategy.[66] Commitment to the most important thrusts began to be confirmed in formal plans. Detailed budgets, programs, controls, and reward systems had to reflect the defined major strategic thrusts, as outlined in Chapter 2. Finally, the guiding executive saw that recruiting and staffing plans were aligned with the new goals and then— when the situation permitted—reassigned supporters and persistent opponents of intended new thrusts to the most appropriate spots.

Continuing dynamics: Eroding consensus

Major strategic changes tended to take many years to accomplish. The process was continuous, with no clear beginning or end.[67] The decision process constantly molded and modified its own concerns and concepts. Old crusades became the new conventional wisdom, and over time, totally new issues emerged. Participants or observers might not even be aware of exactly when a particular decision was made or when a successor consensus superseded or modified it.[68] The process of consensus change was continuous and dynamic, and such purposefully managed continuity and dynamism helped avoid serious, perpetuated mistakes.[69] Some comments of a GM executive suggest the frequently imperceptible way in which strategic decisions incrementally evolved.[70]

- "We use an iterative process to make a series of tentative decisions on the way we think the market will go. As we get more data we modify these continuously. It is often difficult to say who decided something and when—or even who originated a decision. . . . Strategy really evolves as a series of incremental steps. . . . I frequently don't know when a decision is made in General Motors. I don't remember being in a committee meeting when things came to a vote. Usually someone will simply summarize a developing position. Everyone else either nods or states his particular terms of consensus."

A strategic change in Xerox was described in this way:

- "How was the overall organization decision made? I've often heard it said that after talking with a lot of people and having trouble with the number of decisions which were pending, Archie [McCardell] really reached his own conclusion and got Peter McColough's backing on it. But it really didn't happen quite that way. It was an absolutely evolutionary approach. It was a growing feeling. A number of people felt we ought to be moving toward some kind of matrix organization. We have always been a pretty democratic type of organization. In our culture you can't come down with mandates or ultimatums from the top on major changes like this. You almost have to work these things through and let them grow and evolve, keep them on the table so people are thinking about them and talking about them."

Yet once the organization arrived at its new consensus, the guiding executive had to move immediately to ensure that this too did not become inflexible. In trying to build commitment to a new concept, executives often surrounded themselves with people who saw the world in the same way. And such people could rapidly become systematic screens against

other views. The most effective executives therefore purposely continued the change process, constantly introducing
new faces and stimuli at the top. They consciously began to
erode the very strategic thrusts they might have just created—
a very difficult, but essential, psychological task. Thus strategy formulation in successful large enterprises became a
continuously evolving, political consensus process with
neither a finite beginning nor end (see Diagram 3).

CONTROLLING INCREMENTALISM

The kinds of incremental processes outlined previously are
not abrogations of good management practice, nor are they
Machiavellian or consciously manipulative maneuvers. Instead they recognize and deal with the pragmatic psychological and informational problems of getting a constantly
changing group of people with diverse talents and interests to
move effectively *together* in adapting to a continually dynamic environment. In fact, much of the impelling force
behind logical incrementalism comes from a desire to tap the
talents and psychological drives of the whole organization,
to create cohesion, and to generate identity with the emerging strategy. The remainder derives from the interacting
nature of the relatively random factors and lead times affecting the several independent subsystems that constitute any
complex overall strategy.

Incremental, not piecemeal

Nevertheless, the total pattern of action—though highly
incremental—must not remain piecemeal. This requires constant, conscious reassessment of the organization, its capacities, and its needs as related to the surrounding environments.
And it requires continual attempts by top managers to integrate these actions into an understandable, cohesive whole.
How does this integrative function operate? What do managers themselves describe as the key factors?

- Mr. Estes, president of General Motors, said, "We try to
  give them the broad concepts we are trying to achieve. We

operate through questioning and fact gathering. Strategy is a state of mind you go through. When you think about a little problem, your mind begins to think how it will affect all the different elements in the total situation. Once you have had all the jobs you need to qualify for this position, you can see the problem from a variety of viewpoints. But you don't try to ram your conclusions down people's throats. You try to persuade people what has to be done and provide confidence and leadership for them."

Offering another perspective from the same organization, J. N. Stewart, director of the marketing staff, said:

- "No one has written down strategic objectives, for example: 'to produce a product that will meet as wide an array of needs as possible.' But these are well understood throughout the organization. The decision process tends to work within these broad concepts, and the concept itself is molded by a series of incremental decisions made in response to particular opportunities or problems. The inputs and weightings used in these decisions vary widely, but the sum of these decisions and ideas represents the strategy. It is not a one-man, one-vote system. Certain people with greater expertise will wield a heavier vote on an issue, and people will defer to the most persuasive person. The strategy of GM may not even exist in the mind of one man. I certainly don't know where it is written down. It is simply transmitted in the series of decisions made."

A continuous, pulsing dynamic

The process of incremental strategy formation may be likened to planning for a fleet of ships to make a coordinated attack on a river delta city.

- One first needs agreement on the city as a target and the general timetable for its conquest. Some reasonable, but not pinpoint, estimates are probably available of one's own resources, the city's defenses, and those in the various river channels leading to it. The wise strategist first gathers more intelligence, then with his or her most knowledgeable staff people and squadron commanders, determines the best probable channels for approaching the city and the likely strength needed to force each. The strategist then selects the most talented and committed field leadership that can be found for each squadron, prepares provisions and reserve supplies based on the most probable contingencies the units will meet, and develops an intelligence and communication system to help realign the forces as events unfold. Together the strategist and the squadron leaders establish goals, checkpoints, some agreed-upon rules of action, and a coordinated timetable. Within these each squadron leader prepares his or her own strategy—subject to the grand strategist's approval—for advance up each assigned channel.

Once launched, each squadron pulses forward separately depending on the natural and enemy resistances it meets.[71] At each stage up the river, information about resources, terrain, and enemy forces becomes firmer. Both the strategist and the squadron leaders wisely adjust their plans to new realities until neither the sum of the individual approach thrusts nor the final assault plan may resemble the original plan. Each thrust is a major strategic subsystem—like those in a business—with its own imperatives. Each may experience delays or dynamic spurts forward due to unforeseen events. And each requires feedback loops to other decisions affecting the same resources.[72, 73] The interaction of these decisions becomes the actual strategy used.

The validity of the original strategy lies not in whether it is maintained intact, but in its capacity to adapt successfully to unknowable realities, reshape itself, and ultimately use resources most effectively toward selected goals. Because of improved information and a more experienced leadership as time progresses, the final coordinated approach and assault strategies should, in fact, be of higher quality than their originals—if the total process is properly managed.

The decision process for each strategic subsystem is similar to Ansoff's "cascade" of decisions moving from the selection of broad targets, to general routes, to specific pathways, to initial commitments, to short tactical adaptations until the subsystem strategy is complete or reshaped toward new goals.[74] The total strategic process is anything but linear. Integrating all the subsystem strategies is a groping, cyclical process that often circles back on itself, encounters interruptions and delays, and rarely arrives at clear-cut decisions at any one time. The strategy's ultimate development involves a series of nested partial decisions (in each subsystem) interacting with other partial decisions in all subsystems and the total resource base available. Pfiffner aptly described the process as like "fermentation in biochemistry, rather than an industrial assembly line."[75]

CROSS-SECTIONAL MANAGEMENT

How do executives manage such pulsing, dynamic, organic processes, when by definition they cannot know in advance all the contingencies that must be met? The answer can only be "incrementally." How do executives cross-sectionally coordinate the various interacting subsystems in the decision dynamic? Some key elements—like planned intelligence activities, logistics systems, checkpoints on subordinate strategies, and responsive communication systems—are outlined in the vignette on the attack up the river. But when asked this question in interviews, top executives never offered very clear or structurally precise responses, perhaps indicating the imprecision of the art. Their most insightful comments and effective actions seemed centered on certain concepts.

People and philosophy

Selection of key people was clearly the most important single ingredient in most executives' minds. Just as Roosevelt's choice of Marshall as chief of staff was probably his most critical decision affecting the U.S. performance in World War II, so is the choice and development of the top 10 to 50 people who run most major enterprises.

• Said Robert Hatfield, chairman and CEO of Continental Group: "How do you manage the strategic process? It all comes down to people: selecting people. First, you look for people with certain general characteristics. They have to be bright, energetic, flexible, with high integrity or they won't be adaptive and last in the long run. Among these, you look for the best people with the kinds of experience and interests likely to lead the company in directions you want it to go. But you have to be careful with this. You don't want just 'yes men' on the directions you believe in. You want people who can help you think out new approaches too. Finally, you purposely team people with somewhat different interests, skills, and management styles. You let them push and tug a bit to make sure different approaches get considered. And you do a lot of chatting and informal questioning to make sure you stay informed and can intervene if you have to."

In addition to selecting people with the technical skills most likely to be relevant over the time horizon of the strategy, most top executives tried consciously to team different management styles together: a "tough" manager with a "people-oriented" manager, a conceptualizer with an implementer, an entrepreneur with a controller, and so on. When such teaming was not apparent, strategies tended to fall on hard times. Making shifts in the composition, balance, and relative roles of key people in the top management coalition was perhaps the most crucial way chief executives controlled and coordinated strategic directions.[76]

Developing a shared corporate philosophy or common set of values was perhaps second in importance among the coordinative techniques cited.

● One CEO said: "If good people share the same values, they will instinctively act together. We must know how people will respond intuitively when they are thousands of miles away. . . . We work hard and consciously to understand each other and where we are going. If we know these things and communicate openly, our actions will be sensible and cohesive. Yet we'll have the flexibility to deal with changing environments. These—and the choice of top-flight people—are our real controls for coordinating strategy development."

Formal plans and questions

Formal planning activities fulfilled certain vital functions in coordinating strategies. They annually forced all high-level executives to look cross-sectionally at where their piecemeal decisions were leading the enterprise relative to changing environments. When most effective, such activities were integral components of incremental need-sensing, awareness-building, consensus-generating, and commitment-affirming processes. So developed, they ensured that integration of strategic thrusts went beyond mere intuitive calibration of the incremental decisions that formed the strategy. They developed data that otherwise would not be available; they forced managers to communicate systematically about strategic issues in the presence of this richer data base; and they brought lower level executives into strategic processes on a more comprehensive basis.

- One General Motors executive said, "Formal meetings [on subsystem strategies] make sure that everything gets looked at. One is forced to listen to a complete rationale. We get clear cost estimates and a thoroughly worked out plan for a given [subject]. Everyone feels more comfortable about decisions after they have been discussed in a [broadly based] forum. More importantly, the line people know how we are planning to get where we are going. The more they understand this, the more they know what to do on their own as the program progresses."

Formal planning sessions helped aggregate data about subsystem commitments and their potential overall impact. They also provided a basis for visualizing the balance of these commitments across organizational lines and the probable sum of their impacts on the company's resources. In strategy *formulation,* however, annual formal plans seemed primarily another mechanism in resource bargaining between operating groups and the corporate center. No company had really achieved Alastair Pilkington's goal:

- "[The company] is moving much more consciously to feeling it can think out the future it wishes to have, define what it means by success in the future, and then lay out a route toward it. The company has moved from feeling it would essentially deal with situations and opportunities as they arose. Now we feel we should create the future, rather than react to external circumstances."

The two core methodologies used by top managers for coordinating strategic development and proactively guiding key executives toward a consensus about their company's future were wide-ranging personal interactions and skillful questioning. As noted, top executives tended to give few orders and announce few specific decisions. Instead, most operated very informally, largely through questioning processes, clarifying issues and alternatives until a kind of consensus emerged.

● Another General Motors executive said, "For the most part policy simply evolves. In meetings, people say things that do or don't hold up to argument. Slowly everyone begins to sort out a sensible position from all of this. . . . We may write this position into testimony or a speech writer will put it into a draft speech for one of our corporate officers. After an initial review by the principal, we will then circulate the draft to all the appropriate staffs for comment. . . . The top people are very open to critiques of this sort. The ideas tend to flush upward so the top level can adopt them as they see a consensus emerging. If there is a major policy question, the executive may take the statement to the Executive Committee for comment or approval. Mr. Murphy will nearly always comment on any important issue."

Successful top executives developed a positive style of questioning and commentary that implicitly complimented the person responding yet maintained an aura of the executive's own understanding and control over the situation. This simultaneously allowed them to tap the organization's full talents, improve their own knowledge beyond that of any subordinate, and intuitively lead the strategy without dictating it. It avoided the potential rigidities of order giving, maintained the identity of each person with his or her response, and honored the decentralization most large organizations intend. Yet in the hands of a skilled executive, such questioning could be as guiding and coordinative as any more formal planning analysis or order—and generally much more motivating.

Controls for balance, objectivity, and continuity

Other writers have observed that formal organization is really a strategy for control.[77] My data clearly confirm its use and utility in controlling the balance, objectivity, and continuity of strategies being developed. Formal organization moves did not just follow strategy changes. Executives used them to cause strategic shifts, to influence movement in general (but not yet explicitly determined) directions, and to affirm or implement specific strategic commitments as they were made. By placing people with known individual goals and talents in roles that would reward their expected behavior patterns, top executives could control the direction, pace, and momentum of a strategy before they themselves might fully understand what its precise dimensions should be. Significant congruence among individual executives' personal goals, their assigned leadership roles, and the organization's perceived needs was crucial in maintaining intended strategic flexibilities yet achieving consistent direction.[78] The opportunity identification, creative problem solving, and early implementation stages of strategy generation especially required that subordinates self-direct their activities in congruent patterns.[79] Consequently, executives managed organizational and goal development processes much more closely at these junctures, letting more traditional control systems take over at other times.

Maintaining objectivity during a prolonged period of strategy development posed special problems. Gould, Inc., has developed one of the more interesting ways of coping with this issue.

● Daniel Carroll, then president of Gould, Inc., said, "The longer an acquisitions group looks at a candidate, the more individuals can become mesmerized by its potentials. To offset this tendency, for major acquisitions we often form a Red Team and a Green Team to investigate a potential takeover. The Green Team will take a basically positive viewpoint, trying to figure out the best way to bring in and develop the candidate company. And the Red Team will try to come up with all the arguments why we shouldn't go ahead or problems we might encounter if we do. Their joint presentations sometimes get hot and heavy, but both sides see to it that we look at all aspects of an acquisition with as few blinders on as possible."

For similar reasons, skilled executives carefully arranged to have new people constantly moving into the decision stream and challenging past assumptions with new ideas and potentials. These people helped to police the strategy's overall balance and kept it lively and dynamic. This ongoing management renewal provided essential elements of internal reassessment and objectivity during a strategy's long evolution. Likewise, a properly structured and utilized board of directors—perhaps the only coherent executive body continuously in existence during an entire strategy change—helped ensure top management's own objectivity. A good board saw that management (1) stayed tuned to all important changing environments, (2) sensitively reviewed the enterprise's overall performance in light of these trends, and (3) consciously balanced organizational and resource commitment patterns to achieve all intended long- and short-term goals.[80]

Coalition management

Coalition management was at the heart of most controlled strategy development.[81] Top managers recognized they were at the confluence of innumerable pressures from stockholders, environmentalists, government bodies, customers, suppliers, distributors, producing units, marketing groups, technologists, unions, special-issue activists, employees, ambitious executives, and so on, where knowledgeable people of goodwill could easily disagree on proper actions. In response to changing pressures and coalitions among these groups, the top management team constantly formed and reformed its own coalitions on various decisions in accordance with different members' values concerning the particular issues at hand.[82]

Most major strategic moves would tend to assist some interests—and some executives' careers—at the expense of others. Consequently, each set of interests could serve as a check on the others and thus help maintain the breadth and balance of the strategy.[83] To avoid significant errors, some managements tried to ensure that all important polities had representation or access at the top.[84] And the guiding executive group might continuously adjust the number, power, or proximity of these access points as needed to maintain a desired balance and focus.[85] These delicate adjustments represented a source of constant negotiations and implied bargains among the leadership group. Control over the balance of forces these interests could bring to bear was perhaps the ultimate control top executives must have to guide and coordinate their companies' strategies.[86]

Establishing, measuring, and rewarding key thrusts

Few individual executive or top management teams could keep the full dimensions of a complex strategy in mind as they dealt with the continuously changing flux of urgent issues they faced. Consequently, effective strategic managers constantly sought to distill out a few (six to ten) central themes that would help draw several diverse efforts together into a common cause.[87] Once identified, these helped to maintain focus and consistency in the strategy. They made it easier to both discuss and monitor intended directions. Ideally, these themes could be converted into a "matrix of strategic thrusts" across divisions to bring cohesion to formal plans. These in turn could serve as a basis for strategic performance measurement, control, and reward systems. Unfortunately, few companies were able to implement such a complex planning and control pattern as well as might be desired. Texas Instruments came as close as any company observed. Chapter 5 makes some suggestions that may be helpful in this regard.

Ultimately a strategy must be reduced to specific action plans. Commitment controls and reserved decisions must coordinate the use of resources toward the strategy's intended central thrusts and keep individual subordinate units from risking the viability of the total enterprise.[88] And both formal and informal information systems must be designed to sense needs, measure progress, and offer rewards in terms of the balanced set of thrusts the strategy intends.[89] The most glaring errors (for example, the U.S. entry into Vietnam or General Dynamics' 880-990 aircraft decisions) have occurred when key decisions were not reserved to proper levels or when information systems became attenuated or purposely skewed. Chapter 5 will suggest some formal planning and control mechanisms that can help integrate incremental decisions, align resources more effectively, and perhaps avoid such disasters.

CONCLUSIONS

In recent years there has been an increasing chorus of discontent concerning corporate strategic planning. Many managers are concerned that despite elaborate strategic planning systems, costly staffs for this purpose, and major commitments of their own time, their most elaborate strategies never get implemented. These executives and their companies have generally fallen into the classic trap of thinking of strategy formulation and implementation as separate sequential processes. They have relied on the awesome rationality of their formally derived strategies and the inherent power of their positions to cause their organizations to respond. When this does not occur, they become bewildered, if not frustrated and angry. Instead, successful managers who operate with logical incrementalism build the seeds of understanding, identity, and commitment into the very processes that create their strategies. By the time the strategy begins to crystallize in focus, pieces of it are already being implemented. Through their strategic formulation processes, they have built a momentum and psychological commitment to the strategy, which causes it to flow toward flexible implementation. Constantly integrating the simultaneous incremental processes of strategy formulation and implementation is the central art of effective strategic management.

Significant strategic shifts in large enterprises take years, if not decades, to accomplish. Consequently, it is rare for a single person to mastermind a complete change in a major organization's total strategy—although this can occur in a time of crisis or when an individual's tenure is exceptionally long. What one sees in the short run as an important strategic shift very often turns out under investigation to be part of a much longer continuity that has been building for some years and will later gently mutate and evolve into a quite different form than it now possesses. Those who wish to shape strategy in large organizations must learn to live with and manage this continuously evolving consensus-creating process.

Although each strategic issue will have its own peculiarities, a somewhat common series of management processes seems required for most major strategic changes (see Diagram 3). Most important among these are: sensing needs, amplifying understanding, building awareness, creating credibility, legitimizing viewpoints, generating partial solutions, broadening support, identifying zones of opposition and indifference, changing perceived risks, structuring needed flexibilities, putting foward trial concepts, creating pockets of commitment, eliminating undesired options, crystallizing focus and consensus, managing coalitions, and finally formalizing agreed-upon commitments. These are by their nature incremental processes, constantly interacting with each other and with outside events. But all stages can be managed logically and proactively to stimulate and guide major strategic changes both in subsystems and at the overall enterprise level. Effective change managers do this using the kinds of techniques and philosophies illustrated in this chapter.

Many such continuous, pulsing dynamic processes tend to be occurring simultaneously—often in entirely different phases of fulfillment—in any major enterprise. Together they defy formal integration at any given moment into a single all-embracing strategic plan or document, yet they must be coordinated laterally to maintain reasonable consistency and cohesion. Much of this coordination process is intuitive, but top managers did suggest certain common foci of coordination that tended to fall back on somewhat more formal management techniques. Although the essence of managing incrementalism lies in the sequential consensus-building processes outlined earlier, these can be assisted, calibrated, focused, and even stimulated by these more formal strategic analysis and control techniques. This chapter and the next suggest how these formal and informal processes can be blended effectively into the incremental processes of strategy generation.

NOTES

1. R. M. Cyert and J. G. March, in *A Behavioral Theory of the Firm* (Englewood Cliffs, N.J.: Prentice-Hall, Inc., 1963), p. 123, note this learning-feedback-adaptiveness of goals and feasible alternatives over time as organizational learning.

2. H. E. Wrapp, "Good Managers Don't Make Policy Decisions," *Harvard Business Review* (September-October 1967), pp. 91-99.

3. R. Normann, *Management for Growth,* translated by N. Adler (New York: John Wiley & Sons, 1977).

4. D. Braybrooke and C. E. Lindblom, *A Strategy of Decision: Policy Evaluation as a Social Process* (New York: Free Press, 1963).

5. C. E. Lindblom, *The Policy-Making Process* (Englewood Cliffs, N.J.: Prentice-Hall, Inc., 1968).

6. W. G. Bennis, *Changing Organizations: Essays on the Development and Evolution of Human Organizations* (New York: McGraw-Hill Book Co., 1966).

7. Quoted from R. C. Snyder and G. D. Paige, "The United States Decision to Resist Aggression in Korea: The Application of an Analytical Scheme," *Administrative Science Quarterly* (December 1958-59), pp. 340-78.

8. J. B. Quinn, *Xerox Corporation (B),* copyrighted case, The Amos Tuck School of Business Administration, Dartmouth College, Hanover, N.H., 1977.

9. O. G. Brim et al., *Personality and Decision Processes; Studies in the Social Psychology of Thinking* (Stanford, Calif.: Stanford University Press, 1962).

10. E. Witte, "Field Research on Complex Decision-Making Processes–The Phase Theorem," *International Studies of Management and Organization* (Summer 1972), pp. 156-82.

11. W. D. Guth, in "Formulating Organizational Objectives and Strategy: A Systematic Approach," *Journal of Business Policy* (Autumn 1971), pp. 24-31, and F. J. Aguilar, in *Scanning the Business Environment* (New York: Macmillan, 1967), suggest some formal approaches and philosophies.

12. H. Mintzberg, D. Raisinghani, and A. Théorêt, in "The Structure of 'Unstructured' Decision Processes," *Administrative Science Quarterly* (June 1976), pp. 246-75, confirm this early vagueness and ambiguity in problem form and identification.

13. H. Mintzberg, in *The Nature of Managerial Work* (New York: Harper & Row, 1973); and H. I. Ansoff, in "Managerial Problem-Solving," *Journal of Business Policy* (Autumn 1971), pp. 3-20, discuss this aspect of problem identification.

14. Normann, in *Management for Growth,* p. 19, also discusses various types of "misfits" between the organization and its environment as a basis for identifying problems.

15. H. Mintzberg, "Strategy-Making in Three Modes," *California Management Review* (Winter 1973), pp. 44-53; and W. D. Guth, "Toward a Social System Theory of Corporate Strategy," *The Journal of Business* (July 1976), pp. 374-88.

16. Mintzberg, Raisinghani, and Théorêt, in "Structure of Unstructured Decision Processes," note that there may be long dormant times for opportunity signals received diffusely at very low amplitudes, while crisis signals tend to be sharp and urgent often triggered by a single stimulus.

17. This is why organizations engage in the "problem search" patterns suggested by R. M. Cyert, H. A. Simon, and D. B. Trow, in "Observation of a Business Decision," *The Journal of Business* (October 1956), pp. 237-48. Also see L. R. Sayles, *Managerial Behavior: Administration in Complex Organizations* (New York: McGraw-Hill Book Co., 1964), for the problems of timing in transitions.

18. E. E. Carter, in "The Behavioral Theory of the Firm and Top-Level Corporate Decisions," *Administrative Science Quarterly* (December 1971), pp. 413-28, describes active search processes by executives to define new problems, not just to respond to problems as Cyert and March suggest. H. Mintzberg, in *Nature of Managerial Work,* p. 78, also describes this informal scanning activity.

19. For a classic view of how these screens operate, see C. Argyris, "Double Loop Learning in Organizations," *Harvard Business Review* (September-October 1977), pp. 115-25.

20. "Personal Management Styles," *Business Week* (May 4, 1974), p. 43.

21. J. B. Quinn, *General Motors Corporation: The Downsizing Decision,* copyrighted case, The Amos Tuck School of Business Administration, Dartmouth College, Hanover, N.H., 1978.

22. J. L. Bower, in "Planning within the Firm," *The American Economic Review* (May 1970), pp. 186-94, notes that such people can kill or expand a project based solely on the confidence top management has in their judgment. Management looks at the data source for "credible quantitative data," not just the data themselves.

23. R. Normann, "Organizational Innovativeness: Product Variation and Reorientation," *Administrative Science Quarterly* (June 1971), pp. 203-15; and W. D. Guth and R. Tagiuri, "Personal Values and Corporate Strategy," *Harvard Business Review* (September-October 1965), pp. 123-32.

24. T. Alexander, "The Wild Birds Find a Corporate Roost," *Fortune* (August 1964), pp. 130-34+.

25. Argyris, in "Double Loop Learning," suggests the difficulty of breaking down these systematic information screens, once developed, without a conscious structure of variable open access to the top. Cyert and March, in *Behavioral Theory of the Firm,* note the training and experience of searchers as a bias in their capacity to perceive opportunities or threats.

26. Described by Braybrooke and Lindblom in *Strategy of Decision: Policy Evaluation as a Social Process.*

27. Unlike managers observed by J. G. March and H. A. Simon, in *Organizations* (New York: John Wiley & Sons, 1958), effective strategic managers in my sample did not wait for a stimulus; they actively sought such stimuli in their networks.

28. Braybrooke and Lindblom, in *Strategy of Decision: Policy Evaluation as a Social Process,* refer to these as "critical unknowns."

29. This stage corresponds to Mintzberg's "diagnostic routine." See Mintzberg, Raisinghani, and Théorêt, "Structure of Unstructured Decision Processes."

30. Cyert and March, in *Behavioral Theory of the Firm,* p. 120, also suggest that executives choose from a number of satisfactory solutions; later observers suggest they choose the first truly satisfactory solution discovered.

31. Wrapp, in "Good Managers Don't Make Policy Decisions," also noted that this was true of top management search procedures.

32. As a member of the top management coalition begins to sponsor a proposal, a process of "uncertainty absorption" takes place; see March and Simon, *Organizations.* People begin to judge the competency of the person who is sponsoring the idea rather than the evidence presented, and the individual's credibility and power suffer if he or she is wrong.

33. J. B. Quinn, *Chrysler Corporation,* copyrighted case, The Amos Tuck School of Business Administration, Dartmouth College, Hanover, N.H., 1977.

34. Carter, in "Behavioral Theory of the Firm and Top Level Corporate Decisions," suggests that for effective strategies multiple levels and people with a wide array of backgrounds should be involved in strategic decisions.

35. F. F. Gilmore, "Overcoming the Perils of Advocacy in Corporate Planning," *California Management Review* (Spring 1973), pp. 127-37.

36. E. Rhenman, in *Organization Theory for Long-Range Planning* (New York: John Wiley & Sons, 1973), p. 63, notes a similar phenomenon.

37. L. Collins and D. Lapierre, *Freedom at Midnight* (New York: Simon & Schuster, 1975).

38. R. M. Cyert, W. R. Dill, and J. G. March, in "The Role of Expectations in Business Decision Making," *Administrative Science Quarterly* (December 1958), pp. 307-40, point out the perils of top-management advocacy because existing polities may unconsciously bias information to support views they value.

39. J. H. Dessauer, *My Years with Xerox: The Billions Nobody Wanted* (Garden City, N.Y.: Doubleday, 1971).

40. J. B. Quinn and M. Jelinek, *General Mills, Inc.,* copyrighted case, The Amos Tuck School of Business Administration, Dartmouth College, Hanover, N.H., 1978.

41. Note that this "vision" is not necessarily the beginning point of the process; see Mintzberg, *Nature of Managerial Work.* Instead it emerges interactively as new data and viewpoints become available; see Norman, *Management for Growth.*

42. J. G. March, J. P. Olsen, S. Christensen, et al., *Ambiguity and Choice in Organizations* (Bergen, Norway: Universitetsforlaget, 1976).

43. This is part of the process of "uncertainty avoidance" as noted by Cyert and March in *Behavioral Theory of the Firm.*

44. An initial consensus on goals by the dominant coalition is by no means a common element in the strategic decision process. See E. E. Carter, "A Behavioral Theory Approach to Firm Investment and Acquisition Decisions," unpublished doctoral dissertation, Graduate School of Industrial Administration, Carnegie-Mellon University, 1970.

45. Mintzberg, Raisinghani, and Théorêt, in "Structure of Unstructured Decision Processes," liken the process to a decision tree where decisions at each node become more narrow, with failure at any node allowing recycling back to the broader tree trunk.

46. Wrapp, in "Good Managers Don't Make Policy Decisions," notes that a conditioning process which may stretch over months or years is necessary to prepare the organization for radical departures from what it is already striving to attain.

47. March, Olsen, Christensen, et al., *Ambiguity and Choice in Organizations.*

48. See R. E. Miles and C. C. Snow, *Organizational Strategy, Structure, and Process* (New York: McGraw-Hill Book Co., 1978); and W. H. Riker, *The Theory of Political Coalition* (New Haven, Conn.: Yale University Press, 1962). Cyert and March, in *Behavioral Theory of the Firm,* also suggest that coalition management dominates this phase of goal formulation to be succeeded by later "stabilization" and "adaptive" phases where coalitions are less important.

49. Sayles, *Managerial Behavior: Administration in Complex Organizations*, provides an excellent overview of the processes involved.

50. Cyert and March, in *Behavioral Theory of the Firm*, and J. G. March, in "Business Decision Making," in H. J. Leavitt and L. R. Pondy, eds., *Readings in Managerial Psychology* (Chicago: University of Chicago Press, 1964), both note the need of executives for coalition behavior to reduce the organizational conflict due to differing interests and goal preferences in large organizations. C. I. Barnard, in *The Functions of the Executive* (Cambridge, Mass.: Harvard University Press, 1938), provides perhaps the first reference to the concept of the "zone of indifference."

51. Cyert and March, in *Behavioral Theory of the Firm*, also note that not only do organizations seek alternatives, but also "alternatives seek organizations" as when finders, scientists, bankers, and others bring in new solutions.

52. March, Olsen, Christensen, et al., *Ambiguity and Choice in Organizations*.

53. This is a variant of P. O. Soelberg's "trap search" in "Unprogrammed Decision Making," *Industrial Management Review* (Spring 1967), pp. 19-29.

54. Witte, in "Field Research on Complex Decision-Making Processes–The Phase Theorem," notes a number–up to 51–of specific decisions in observed strategic processes which had to be blended in a several-year series to attain the final strategic outcome.

55. Cyert, Dill, and March, in "Role of Expectations in Business Decision Making," note that forecasts are often developed to justify decisions desired, hence the need of the executive to personally maintain his or her objectivity and obtain checks on forecasts at this early stage.

56. In a sense this approach counters the concept (Mintzberg, Raisinghani, and Théorêt, "Structure of Unstructured Decision Processes") that only one fully developed, custom-made solution comes forward–unless one considers that only one option survives the final selection or that completed developmental systems do not amount to a full option.

57. C. Argyris, in "Interpersonal Barriers to Decision Making," *Harvard Business Review* (March-April 1966), pp. 84-97, notes that when the president introduced major decisions from the top, discussion was "less than open" and commitment was "less than complete," although executives might assure the president to the contrary.

58. March, "Business Decision Making," p. 454.

59. Wrapp, "Good Managers Don't Make Policy Decisions."

60. The process tends to be more of eliminating the less feasible options rather than determining a target or objective. The process typically reduces the number of alternatives through successive limited comparisons to a point where understood analytical techniques can apply and the organization structure can function to make a choice. See Cyert and March, *Behavioral Theory of the Firm*.

61. H. C. Metcalf and L. Urwick, eds., in *Dynamic Administration: The Collected Papers of Mary Parker Follett* (New York: Harper & Brothers, Publishers, 1941), and A. Zaleznik, in "Power and Politics in Organizational Life," *Harvard Business Review* (May-June 1970), pp. 47-60, develop these aspects of authority and power in detail.

62. J. D. Thompson, "The Control of Complex Organizations," in *Organizations in Action* (New York: McGraw-Hill Book Co., 1967).

63. G. T. Allison, *Essence of Decision: Explaining the Cuban Missile Crisis* (Boston: Little, Brown & Co., 1971).

64. C. E. Lindblom, in "The Science of 'Muddling Through,'" *Public Administra-*

tion Review (Spring 1949), pp. 79-88, notes that the relative values weighting of individuals and the intensity of their feelings will vary sequentially from decision to decision, hence the dominant coalition itself varies with each decision somewhat.

65. Zaleznik, in "Power and Politics in Organizational Life," notes that confusing compliance with commitment is one of the most common and difficult problems of strategic implementation. He notes that often organizational commitment may override personal interest if the former is carefully developed.

66. A. D. Chandler, *Strategy and Structure: Chapters in the History of the Industrial Enterprise* (Cambridge, Mass.: M.I.T. Press, 1962).

67. K. J. Cohen and R. M. Cyert, "Strategy: Formulation, Implementation, and Monitoring," *The Journal of Business* (July 1973), pp. 349-67.

68. March, in "Business Decision Making," notes that major decisions are "processes of gradual commitment."

69. As noted by Lindblom in "Science of 'Muddling Through.'"

70. Sayles, in *Managerial Behavior, Administration in Complex Organizations,* notes that such decisions are a "flow process" with no one person ever really making the decision.

71. H. Boettinger, AT&T's corporate planning director, refers to this as the process of "pulsing your way into the future" in "Corporate Planning: Piercing Future Fog in the Executive Suite," *Business Week* (April 28, 1975), pp. 46-54.

72. Cyert, Simon, and Trow, in "Observation of a Business Decision," describe the "nesting" of decisions within each of these loops.

73. P. Diesing, "Noneconomic Decision Making," in M. Alexis and C. Z. Wilson, eds., *Organizational Decision Making* (Englewood Cliffs, N.J.: Prentice-Hall, Inc., 1967).

74. H. I. Ansoff, in *Corporate Strategy: An Analytic Approach to Business Policy for Growth and Expansion* (New York: McGraw-Hill Book Co., 1965), describes a similar process as a cascade of decisions.

75. J. M. Pfiffner, "Administrative Rationality," *Public Administration Review* (Summer 1960), pp. 125-32.

76. D. McGregor, in *The Human Side of Enterprise* (New York: McGraw-Hill Book Co., 1960), and C. Argyris, in *Organization and Innovation* (Homewood, Ill.: Richard D. Irwin, 1965), have pointed out the need for goal consonance and human environments where managers can influence the goal-setting process and hence be energized or self-actualized in achieving them.

77. Chandler, *Strategy and Structure: Chapters in the History of the Industrial Enterprise.*

78. Pfiffner, in "Administrative Rationality," and H. A. Simon, in "On the Concept of Organizational Goals," *Administrative Science Quarterly* (June 1964), pp. 1-22, note the complexities and interrelationships of these three concepts.

79. Bower, "Planning within the Firm," p. 190.

80. Sayles, *Managerial Behavior: Administration in Complex Organizations.*

81. R. M. James, in "Corporate Strategy and Change—The Management of People," monograph, University of Chicago, 1978, does an excellent job of pulling together the threads of coalition management at top organizational levels.

82. Cyert and March, *Behavioral Theory of the Firm,* p. 115.

83. Lindblom, in "Science of 'Muddling Through,'" notes that every interest has a "watchdog" and that purposely allowing these watchdogs to participate in and influence decisions creates consensus decisions all can live with. Similar conscious access to the top for different interests can now be found in corporate structures.

84. Zaleznik, "Power and Politics in Organizational Life."

85. Sayles, in *Managerial Behavior: Administration in Complex Organizations,* pp. 207-17, provides an excellent view of the bargaining processes involved in coalition management.

86. Thompson, in *Organizations in Action* suggests that the central power figure in decentralized organizations must be the person who manages its dominant coalition, the size of which will depend on the issues involved and the number of areas in which the organization must rely on judgmental decisions.

87. Wrapp, in "Good Managers Don't Make Policy Decisions," notes the futility of a top manager trying to push a full package of goals.

88. W. K. Hall, in "Strategic Planning Models: Are Top Managers Really Finding Them Useful?" *Journal of Business Policy* (Winter 1972/73), pp. 33-42, notes that top managers approve strategy in decentralized organizations. They rarely present it top down.

89. For examples of how mismatches occur, see R. L. Ackoff, "Management Misinformation Systems," *Management Science* (December 1967), pp. B147-56.

5
Formal planning systems and incrementalism

The whole of directing should be concerned just with the future. The danger is that you do everything in the "eternal now.". . . The difficult thing is creating a proper future. And it is a creative activity. Dealing with problems which already exist merely requires that sensible people respond sensibly to a situation. That is a much easier activity altogether. You've got to get everybody involved in creating the future and keep them consistently focused on it. The day is past when an organization could be peaked to one man who issues directives that go down the pyramid unquestioned.

Sir Alastair Pilkington
Chairman, Pilkington Brothers, Ltd.

FORMAL PLANNING SYSTEMS AND INCREMENTALISM

Well-developed formal planning systems should play an important and integral role in the incremental processes of generating, calibrating, and implementing creative strategies. Yet too often they do not carry out this role effectively. Why? Unfortunately, formal planning as frequently practiced:

1. Results primarily in either formless wordy statements of principle or detailed budgetary plans, neither of which meets the most basic criteria—like concentration of forces, concession of positions, and planned flexibility—that effective strategies demand.
2. Deals inadequately with the multiple goals and psychological commitments the organization truly represents and hence becomes a sterile, bureaucratic exercise removed from the coalition behavior and consensus-generating maneuvers necessary to create change in major organizations.
3. Uses formal analytical techniques and "bottom up" formulation approaches which militate against generating the coordinated cross-divisional thrusts and commitment patterns that are the essence of strategy.
4. Overemphasizes financial analysis methodologies that: foreclose meaningful strategic options, encourage short-term attitudes and behavior, drive out potential major innovations, misdirect resource allocations, and actively undercut the enterprise's intended strategies.
5. Converts planning departments into bureaucratized agencies grinding out annual plans rather than catalyst groups intervening properly in the incremental processes that determine strategy.

Yet these need not be the characteristics of formal planning systems. This chapter will attack each of the preceding issues in sequence and suggest how companies can (1) better adapt their planning structures to the realities of logical incrementalism, and (2) overcome some of the shortcomings so often encountered in formal planning. As a starting point, much can be learned by analyzing certain classical streams of formal strategic thought. Perhaps the most powerful, best documented, and most directly relevant literature is that on military-diplomatic strategy formulation. This offers many potentially important insights for modern business leaders and provides a useful meta-framework around which many of the observed shortcomings of formal business planning can be resolved.

THE CLASSICAL APPROACH

Military-diplomatic strategies have existed since prehistoric times. In fact, one function of the earliest historians and poets was to collect the accumulated lore of these successful and unsuccessful life-and-death strategies and convert them into wisdom and guidance for the future. As societies grew larger and conflicts more complex, generals, statesmen, and captains studied, codified, and tested essential strategic concepts until a coherent body of principles seemed to emerge. In various forms these were ultimately distilled into the maxims of Sun Tzu,[1] Machiavelli,[2] Napoleon,[3] Von Clausewitz,[4] Foch,[5] Lenin,[6] Hart,[7] Montgomery,[8] or Mao Tse-Tung.[9] Yet with a few exceptions—largely introduced by modern technology—the most basic principles of strategy were in place and recorded long before the Christian era. More modern institutions primarily adapted and modified these to their own special environments.

Although one could choose any number of classical military-diplomatic strategies as examples, Philip and Alexander's actions at Chaeronea (in 338 B.C.) contain many currently relevant concepts.[10] This strategy changed the course of early civilized history and became the foundation upon which Alexander later conquered the known world. For those who are not familiar with these events, their grand strategy, battle strategy, and implementation are summarized in the accompanying box. The most critical strategic elements are italicized for emphasis as are those paralleled by later strategists.

Modern analogies

Similar concepts have continued to dominate the modern era of formal strategic thought. As this period begins, Scharnhorst still points to the need to *analyze social forces and*

A CLASSICAL STRATEGY

A grand strategy

Philip and his young son, Alexander, had very *clear goals.* They sought to rid Macedonia of influence by the Greek city-states and to *establish dominance* over what was then essentially northern Greece. They also wanted Athens to *join a coalition* with them against Persia on their eastern flank. *Assessing their resources,* they *decided to avoid* the overwhelming superiority of the Athenian fleet and *chose to forego* attack on the powerful walled cities of Athens and Thebes where their superbly trained phalanxes and cavalry would not *have distinct advantages.*

Philip and Alexander *used an indirect approach* when an invitation by the Amphictyonic Council brought their army south to punish Amphissa. In a *planned sequence of actions* and *deceptive maneuvers,* they cut away from a direct line of march to Amphissa, *bypassed the enemy,* and *fortified a key base,* Elatea. They then took steps to *weaken their opponents politically and morally* by pressing restoration of the Phocian communities earlier dispersed by the Thebans and by having Philip declared a champion of the Delphic gods. Then *using misleading messages* to make the enemy believe they had moved north to Thrace and also *using developed intelligence sources,* the Macedonians in a *surprise attack* annihilated the Greeks' positions near Amphissa. This *lured their opponents away from their defensive positions* in the nearby mountain passes to *consolidate their forces* near the town of Chaeronea.

There, *assessing the relative strengths* of their opponents, the Macedonians first *attempted to negotiate* to achieve their goals. When this was unsuccessful they had a *well-developed contingency plan* on how to *attack and overwhelm* the Greeks. Prior to this time, of course, the Macedonians had *organized* their troops into the famed phalanxes, and had *developed the full logistics* needed for their field support including a longer spear, which helped the Macedonian phalanxes penetrate the solid shield wall of the heavily massed Greek formations. *Using the natural advantages* of their grassy terrain, the Macedonians had developed cavalry support for their phalanxes' movements far beyond the Greek capability. Finally, using a *relative advantage*—the *command structure* their hierarchical *social system* allowed—against the more democratic Greeks, the Macedonian nobles had *trained their personnel* into one of the most *disciplined and highly motivated forces* in the world.

The battle strategy

Supporting this was the battle strategy at Chaeronea, which emerged as follows. Philip and Alexander first *analyzed their specific strengths and weaknesses and their opponents' current alignments and probable moves.*

A CLASSICAL STRATEGY *(continued)*

The Macedonian strength lay in their new spear technology, the *mobility* of their superbly disciplined phalanxes, and the powerful cavalry units led by Alexander. Their weaknesses were that they were badly outnumbered and faced—in the Athenians and the Theban Band—some of the finest foot troops in the world. However, their opponents had two weak points. One was the Greek left flank with lightly armed local troops placed near the Chaeronean Acropolis and next to some more heavily armed—but hastily assembled—hoplites bridging to the strong center held by the Athenians. The famed Theban Band anchored the Greek right wing near a swamp on the Cephissus River. (See map.)

Philip and Alexander *organized their leadership* to *command key positions;* Philip took over the right wing and Alexander the cavalry. They *aligned their forces* into *a unique posture* which *used their strengths* and *offset their weaknesses.* They decided on those spots at which they would *concentrate their forces,* what *positions to concede,* and what *key points* they *must take and hold.* Starting with their units angled back from the Greek lines (see map), they developed a *focused major thrust* against the Greek left wing and *attacked their opponents' weakness*—the troops near Chaeronea—with the most disciplined of the Macedonian units, the guards' brigade. After building up pressure and stretching the Greek line to its left, the guards' brigade abruptly began a *planned withdrawal.* This *feint* caused the Greek left to break ranks and rush forward, believing the Macedonians to be in full retreat. This *stretched the opponents' resources* as the Greek center moved left to *maintain contact* with its flank and to attack the "fleeing" Macedonians.

Then *with predetermined timing,* Alexander's cavalry *attacked the exposure* of the stretched line at the same moment Philip's phalanxes *re-formed as planned* on the high ground at the edge of the Heamon River. Alexander *broke through* and *formed a bridgehead* behind the Greeks. He *refocused his forces against a segment* of the opponents' line; his cavalry *surrounded and destroyed* the Theban Band as the *overwhelming power* of the phalanxes poured through the gap he had created. From its *secured position,* the Macedonian left flank then turned and *attacked the flank* of the Athenians. With the help of Philip's *planned counterattack,* the Macedonians *expanded their dominance* and *overwhelmed the critical target,* i.e., the Greek center.

Implementation

Then came final implementation. Realizing their defeat, the Greeks surrendered. Keeping their *goals in mind* and with a *sense of time horizon* rare in those days, Philip and Alexander called off their rampaging troops

A CLASSICAL STRATEGY *(concluded)*

and used the victory to *achieve their broader aims.* In a magnanimous settlement (for those times), they allowed the Athenian prisoners to return home and agreed to return the ashes of the Athenian dead. In return Athens was to abandon all territorial claims in Macedonia, dissolve the Athenian Maritime League, and become Macedonia's ally. As noted, this great victory was the touchstone and model for Macedonia's later conquest of the known world. Although its authors doubtless did not conceive and prescribe its actions and relationships with such immaculate precision prior to the battle, its precepts were enduring and have constantly reappeared both in other successful "grand" and "battle" strategies and in the mainstreams of strategic thought over the next 2,300 years.

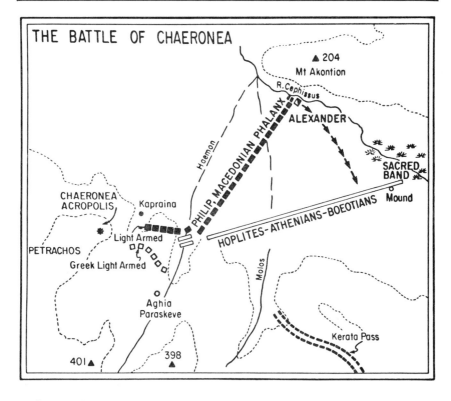

Source: Modified with permission from P. Green, *Alexander the Great,* Praeger Publishers, New York, 1970.

structures as a basis for *understanding effective command styles* and *motivational stimuli.*[11] Frederick the Great proved this point in the field. Presumably based on such analyses, he adopted *training, discipline,* and *fast maneuvers* as the central concepts for a tightly disciplined German culture that had to be constantly ready to fight on two fronts.[12] Von Bülow continued to emphasize the dominant strategic roles of *geographical positioning* and *logistical support systems* in strategy.[13] Both Jomini and Von Bülow stressed the concepts of *concentration, points of domination,* and *rapidity of movement* as central strategic themes and even tried to develop them into mathematically precise principles for their time.[14]

Still later Von Clausewitz expounded on the paramountcy of *clear major objectives* in war and on developing war strategies as a component of the nation's *broader goals* with *time horizons* extending beyond the war itself.[15] Within this context he postulated that an effective strategy should be focused around a relatively *few central principles,* which can *create, guide, and maintain dominance* despite the enormous frictions that occur as one tries to position or maneuver large forces in war. Among these he included many of the concepts operant in Macedonian times: *spirit or morale, surprise, cunning, concentration in space, dominance of selected positions, use of strategic reserves, unification over time, tension and release,* and so on. He showed how these broad principles applied to a number of specific attack, defense, flanking, and retreat situations; but he always stressed the intangible of *leadership.* His basic positioning and organizational principles were to be mixed with boldness, perseverance, and genius. He constantly emphasized—as did Napoleon[16]—the need for *planned flexibility* once the battle was joined.[17]

Later strategic analysts adapted these classic themes for larger scale conflicts. Von Schlieffen linked together the huge numerical and production *strengths* of Germany and the vast *maneuvering capabilities* of Flanders fields to pull the nation's might together conceptually behind a *unique alignment of forces* ("a giant hayrake"), which would *outflank* his French opponents, *attack weaknesses* (their supply lines and rear), capture and *hold key political centers* of France, and *dominate or destroy* its weakened army in the field.[18] On the other side, Foch[19] and Grandmaison[20] saw *morale* ("élan"), *nerve* ("cran"), and continuous *concentrated attack* ("attaque à outrance") as *matching the values* of a volatile, recently defeated, and vengeful French nation, which had decided (for both moral and *coalition* reasons) to *set important limits* on its own actions in World War I—that is, not to attack first or through Belgium.[21]

As these two strategies lost shape and became the head-on slaughter of trench warfare, Hart revitalized the *indirect approach,* and this became a central theme of British strategic thinking between the wars.[22] Later in the United States, Matloff and Snell began to stress planning for *large-scale coalitions* as the giant forces of World War II developed.[23] The Enigma group *moved secretly* to *develop the intelligence network* that was so crucial in the war's outcome.[24] But once engaged in war, George Marshall still saw the only hope for Allied victory in *concentrating overwhelming forces* against one enemy (Germany) first, then after *conceding early losses* in the Pacific, *refocusing Allied forces* in a gigantic *sequential coordinated movement* against Japan.[25] In the eastern theater, MacArthur first *fell back, consolidated a base* for operations, *built up his logistics, avoided his opponent's strengths, bypassed* Japan's established defensive positions, and in a *gigantic flanking maneuver* was ready to invade Japan after *softening its political and psychological will* through saturation bombing.[26] The biggest failures in Allied strategy had to do with *time horizons*—in the effects of the atomic bomb and in *planning for governance* in the postwar world.

All these modern thinkers and practitioners utilized classical principles of strategy dating back to the Greek era, but perhaps the most startling analogies of World War II lay in Patton's[27] and Rommel's[28] battle strategies, which were almost carbon copies of the Macedonians' concepts of planned concentration, rapid breakthrough, encirclement, and attack on the enemy's rear.

Similar concepts still pervade well-conceived strategies—whether they are government, diplomatic, military, sports, or business strategies. What could be more direct than the parallel between Chaeronea and a well-developed business strategy that first probes and withdraws to determine opponents' strengths, forces opponents to stretch their commitments, then concentrates resources, attacks a clear exposure, overwhelms a selected market segment, builds a bridgehead in that market, and then regroups and expands from that base to dominate a wider field? Many companies have followed just such strategies with great success. Control Data Corporation provides a well-documented example:

- Control Data Corporation's (CDC's) early strategy was centered around two key personalities, its CEO, William Norris, and its technical genius, Seymour Cray. Their goals were clear: to build a major computer company around Cray's capacities to design giant computers. But their first product, the 1604 solid-state computer, was essentially a feint to make initial market contact and generate revenues. Major resources were concentrated behind Cray's development of the complex 6600 computer, at that time the biggest, most powerful, and most sophisticated computer in the world. With this entry CDC attacked IBM's weakness, i.e., the high end of its line. Carefully matching its strengths (design) and offsetting its resource weaknesses (cash and marketing capability), CDC marshaled its resources into a unique posture (limited product line breadth, software support, leasing availability, and business applicability) to overwhelm its selected segment (large, scientific central processors) of the computer market.

  Once it breached IBM's market at the high end, CDC hoped its success there would release enough resources for it to turn and attack other aspects of IBM's broad line position (namely business applications and peripherals). The strategy which emerged was well designed in terms of timing, having clear goals, exploiting opportunities in the external environment, utilizing key personnel in proper command relationships, matching the values of its leaders, providing motivation and focus for its personnel, using deception and surprise, bypassing opponents' strong points, moving flexibly, conceding secondary positions, concentrating on key points to hold, sequencing actions to use resources most effectively, etc. Using the resources, reputation, and stock market leverage developed by its early successes, CDC formed coalitions (acquiring through stock) with a number of small companies which built new strengths (peripherals, commercial credit, software) for its longer term horizons. These were the key strategic moves affecting the company's basic posture and long-term viability.

DIMENSIONS OF STRATEGY

Analysis of military-diplomatic strategies and similar analogies in other fields provides some essential insights into the basic dimensions, nature, and design of formal strategies.

First, effective formal strategies contain three essential elements: (*a*) the most important *goals* (or objectives) to be achieved, (*b*) the most significant *policies* guiding or limiting action, and (*c*) the major *action sequences* (or programs) that are to accomplish the defined goals within the limits set. Since strategy determines the overall direction and action focus of the organization, its formulation cannot be regarded as the mere generation and alignment of programs to meet predetermined goals. Goal development is an integral part of strategy formulation.[29]

- Clearly, the goals of regional hegemony and coalition with Athens were inseparable components of Macedonia's grand strategy—as was the Allies' choice of unconditional surrender or Control Data's selection of an entrepreneurial, high-risk attack on the large computer field. In a similar vein, establishing specific policies ("Don't attack Athens' fleet" or "Avoid IBM's central line, leasing support, and software availability") and determining major action sequences ("Germany first and Japan later" or "Large scientific computers first, business applications later") are integral parts of strategy formulation because they provide the ultimate basis for focusing resources.

Second, effective strategies develop around a *few key concepts and thrusts,* which give them cohesion, balance, and focus. Some thrusts are temporary; others are carried through to the end of the strategy. Some cost more per unit gain than others. Yet resources must be *allocated in patterns* that provide sufficient resources for each thrust to succeed regardless of its relative cost/gain ratio. And organizational units must be coordinated and actions controlled to support the intended thrust pattern or else the total strategy will fail.

- For example, Philip's feint may have cost more lives per yard of advance than Alexander's cavalry charge. The Allies' slow advance into West Germany cost more in men and material per unit of advance than their spectacular island hopping in the Pacific. And Control Data's 1604 was never expected to have the same impact as its 6600. But each was a crucial component of a total strategy designed for maximum net benefit of the whole enterprise. The imperatives of the total strategy had to override the relative cost considerations of its components; and resources, organizations, and actions had to be controlled in intended patterns.

Third, strategy deals not just with the unpredictable but also with the *unknowable.* For major enterprise strategies, no analyst could predict the precise ways in which all impinging forces could interact with each other, be distorted by nature or human emotions, or be modified by the imaginations and purposeful counteractions of intelligent opponents.[30] Many have noted how large-scale systems can respond quite counter-intuitively to apparently rational actions or how a seemingly bizarre series of events can conspire to prevent or assist success.[31]

- For example, despite some absolutely superb intelligence work, there was no way the Allies invading Europe in 1943 could estimate accurately how the German shore defenses, reserved armored units, special SS units, individual generals and political leaders, French underground, Russian military and political actors, untested Allied troops, mixed-lingual field commanders, new offensive and defensive weapons, weather, road conditions, Axis counterintelligence, German population and productivity, and German air force would actually interact when the time came. As it turned out, some of the determining events were that: acceptable weather did hold for a few crucial days, Hitler's psychophants refused to wake him and tell him of the invasion, SS and Wermacht unit commands did not cooperate adequately, key field officers like Rommel were away from the front, German reserve units were not released in time for maximum impact, Allied troops performed superbly, and German coastal defenses had not been given the resources to make them as effective as they could have been. Without these events the invasion would have been much more costly—and might even have been thrown back—with the strategy looking much less successful in retrospect.

Consequently, the essence of strategy—whether military, diplomatic, business, sports, political, or eleemosynary—is to *build a posture* that is so strong (and potentially flexible) in selective ways that the organization can achieve its goals despite the unforeseeable ways external forces may actually interact when the time comes.

Fourth, just as military organizations have multiple echelons of grand, theater, area, battle, infantry, and artillery strategies, so should other complex organizations have a number of hierarchically related and mutually supporting strategies.[32] Each such strategy must be more or less complete in itself, congruent with the level of decentralization intended. Yet each must be shaped as a cohesive element of higher level strategies. Although, for reasons cited, achieving total cohesion among all of a major organization's strategies would be a superhuman task for any chief executive officer, it is important that there be a systematic means for testing each component strategy and seeing that it fulfills the major tenets of a well-formed strategy.

The criteria derived from military-diplomatic strategies provide an excellent framework for this, yet too often one sees purported formal strategies at all organizational levels that are not strategies at all. Because they ignore or violate even the most basic strategic principles, they are little more than aggregates of philosophies or agglomerations of programs. They lack the cohesiveness, flexibility, thrust, sense of positioning against intelligent opposition, and other criteria that historical analysis suggests effective strategies must contain. Whether formally or incrementally derived, strategies should be at least intellectually tested against the proper criteria.

Criteria for effective strategy

In devising a strategy to deal with the unknowable, what factors should one consider? Although each strategic situation is unique, are there some common criteria that tend to define a good strategy? The fact that a strategy worked in retrospect is not a sufficient criterion for judging any strategy. Was Grant really a greater strategist than Lee? Was Foch's strategy better than Von Schlieffen's? Was Xerxes's strategy superior to that of Leonidas? Was it the Russians' strategy that allowed them to roll over the Czechoslovaks in 1968? Clearly other factors than strategy—including luck, overwhelming resources, superb or stupid implementation, and enemy errors—help determine ultimate results. Besides, at the time one formulates a strategy, he or she cannot use the criterion of ultimate success because the outcome is still in doubt. Yet one clearly needs some guidelines to define an effective strategic structure.

A few studies have suggested some initial criteria for evaluating a strategy.[33] These include its clarity, motivational impact, internal consistency, compatibility with the environment, appropriateness in light of resources, degree of risk, match to the personal values of key figures, time horizon, and workability. These have been well explained in the sources cited, and they are useful starting points. But in addition, historical examples—from both business and military-diplomatic settings—suggest that effective strategies should at a minimum encompass certain other critical factors and structural elements. These are briefly summarized here.*

● **Clear, decisive objectives:** Are all efforts directed toward

---

*For an interesting parallel, see VeLoy J. Varner and John I. Alger, eds., *History of the Military Art: Notes for the Course* (West Point, N.Y.: U.S. Military Academy, Department of History, 1978). Their criteria are stated respectively as: the principle of the objective, the principle of the offensive, the principle of mass, the principle of economy of force, the principle of maneuver, the principle of unity of command, the principle of surprise, the principle of security, and the principle of simplicity.

clearly understood, decisive, and attainable overall goals? Specific goals of subordinate units may change in the heat of campaigns or competition, but the overriding goals of the strategy for all units must remain clear enough to provide continuity and cohesion for tactical choices during the time horizon of the strategy. All goals need not be written down or numerically precise, but they must be understood and be decisive—i.e., if they are achieved they should ensure the continued viability and vitality of the entity vis-à-vis its opponents.

- **Maintaining the initiative:** Does the strategy preserve freedom of action and enhance commitment? Does it set the pace and determine the course of events rather than reacting to them? A prolonged reactive posture breeds unrest, lowers morale, and surrenders the advantage of timing and intangibles to opponents. Ultimately such a posture increases costs, decreases the number of options available, and lowers the probability of achieving sufficient success to ensure independence and continuity.

- **Concentration:** Does the strategy concentrate superior power at the place and time likely to be decisive? Has the strategy defined precisely what will make the enterprise superior in power—i.e., "best" in critical dimensions—in relation to its opponents. A distinctive competency yields greater success with fewer resources and is the essential basis for higher gains (or profits) than competitors.

- **Conceding selected positions:** Does the strategy purposely choose positions to concede to its opponents? This is the corollary to concentration. No entity has sufficient resources to overwhelm all its opponents at all points. Hence the strategy must not only consciously determine what points to concede but should also allocate only the minimum necessary resources to achieve secondary purposes. Only by such patterning—in both time and place—can available resources be deployed for the most effective and efficient use.

- **Flexibility:** Has the strategy purposely built in resource buffers and dimensions for flexibility and maneuver? Re-

served capabilities, planned maneuverability, and repositioning allow one to use minimum resources while keeping
opponents at a relative disadvantage. As corollaries of concentration and concession, they permit the strategist to
reuse the same forces to overwhelm selected positions at
different times. They also force less flexible opponents to
use more resources to hold predetermined positions, while
simultaneously requiring minimum fixed commitment of
one's own resources for defensive purposes.

- **Coordinated and committed leadership:** Does the strategy
  provide responsible, committed leadership for each of its
  major goals? Individuals must be assigned roles that create
  the unity of command necessary to carry out each key
  thrust in the strategy. In these roles they must be able to
  coordinate the full available resources of the enterprise
  toward the desired outcome. More important, they must
  be so chosen and motivated that their own interests and
  values match the needs of their roles. Successful strategies
  require commitment, not just acceptance.

- **Surprise:** Has the strategy made use of speed, secrecy, and
  intelligence to attack exposed or unprepared opponents at
  unexpected times? With surprise and correct timing, success can be achieved out of all proportion to the energy
  exerted and can decisively change strategic positions. However, surprise and mobility are rarely achievable without
  the loyalty and discipline which come from high morale
  and personal identity with goals.

- **Security:** Does the strategy secure resource bases and all
  vital operating points for the enterprise? Does it develop
  an effective intelligence system sufficient to prevent sur-
  prises by opponents? Does it develop the full logistics to
  support each of its major thrusts? Does it use coalitions
  effectively to extend the resource base and zones of
  friendly acceptance for the enterprise? Intelligence systems, logistics planning, and coalitions can significantly
  extend resource bases and security zones at minimum real
  costs for an enterprise.

- **Communications:** Has the strategy developed clear, uncomplicated, broad plans and the communications networks to adjust these effectively? In retrospect many strategies have failed not because they lacked structural merit but because: (1) they were not sufficiently well understood, (2) they experienced catastrophic human errors which were not perceived or corrected in time, (3) they could not be adequately coordinated for implementation, or (4) they could not be rapidly enough adjusted to respond to opponents' unexpected actions. Effective communication systems are essential to each of the key strategic components above.

These are obviously not rigid, dogmatic postulates, rather they are reference or checkpoints for strategists. As Von Clausewitz says, "All that theory can do is give the artist or soldier points of reference and standards of evaluation . . . with the ultimate purpose not of telling him how to act but of developing his judgment." [34] Yet very often even such basic principles are almost totally submerged or forgotten, both in the incremental processes described above and in the mechanics of formally derived strategies for large organizations. In both processes, the strategist should periodically step back and make sure the emerging patterns of his or her enterprise's strategy meet the tenets outlined here.

LIMITS OF FORMAL PLANNING

Formal planning models are theoretically designed to ensure that many of the preceding considerations are built into the strategies they present. As noted in Chapter 2, such planning includes certain steps. For convenience these are repeated:

1. *Analyzing one's own internal situation:* strengths, weaknesses, competencies, problems.
2. *Projecting current product lines'* profits, sales, investment needs, etc., into the future.
3. *Analyzing selected external environments* and opponents' actions for opportunities and threats.
4. *Establishing broad goals* as targets for subordinate groups' plans.

5. *Identifying the gaps* between expected and desired results.
6. *Communicating* planning assumptions, goals, and policies to lower echelons.
7. *Requesting proposed plans* from subordinate groups with more specific target goals, resource needs, and supporting action plans.
8. Occasionally *asking for special studies* of alternatives, contingencies, or longer term opportunities.
9. *Reviewing and approving* divisional plans and summing these for corporate needs.
10. *Developing long-term budgets* presumably related to plans.
11. *Assigning implementation* plans.
12. *Monitoring and evaluating* performance for emphasis presumably against plans, but usually against budgets.

Diagram 4 describes how these steps relate to each other at any given level of management. The loops recognize that each stage is part of a continuous iterative process. Because these steps have been so thoroughly described in the literature and because almost all sophisticated business organizations now use some variation of this approach in their annual planning exercises, it is not necessary to dwell on details here.

One would expect that adherence to such procedures would lead to a finely honed strategy, but this rarely happens. As earlier chapters suggest, logic, politics, and events do not lend themselves well to the process in detail. But more insidiously, within the structure itself, mechanics often begin to overwhelm thought processes. And unconsciously, certain analytical procedures undermine the very strategies they are supposed to create.

Some anomalies in formal planning

This is particularly true of the financial techniques that tend to dominate the analysis, proposal, and review cycles of formal planning in both business and government units. As currently used, they contribute to four strategic anomalies.

1. Along with other factors, they shorten the effective time

Diagram 4
Critical steps in long-range planning

1. Situation analysis
   Competencies
   Faults
   Challenges
   Strengths/weaknesses

2. Projective analysis
   Continue policies?

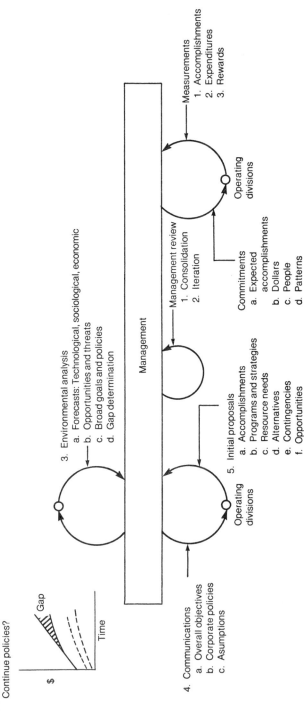

3. Environmental analysis
   a. Forecasts: Technological, sociological, economic
   b. Opportunities and threats
   c. Broad goals and policies
   d. Gap determination

4. Communications
   a. Overall objectives
   b. Corporate policies
   c. Asumptions

5. Initial proposals
   a. Accomplishments
   b. Programs and strategies
   c. Resource needs
   d. Alternatives
   e. Contingencies
   f. Opportunities
   g. Creativity

Management

Management review
1. Consolidation
2. Iteration

Commitments
a. Expected accomplishments
b. Dollars
c. People
d. Patterns

Measurements
1. Accomplishments
2. Expenditures
3. Rewards

Operating divisions

Gap

Time

$

horizon of planning to such an extent that they eliminate from consideration whole classes of opportunities and threats with potentially significant strategic consequences.
2. They interdict the balancing of operating units' commitments into a cohesive pattern across all divisions.
3. They essentially foreclose radical internal innovation.
4. They tend to drive out important goals and programs whose effects cannot be easily quantified.

How does all this happen?

Options driven out. Typically, high-level staff groups make situational, projective, or environmental analyses that identify long- and short-range options, opportunities, and threats. At first, these tend to be broadly stated and contain a provocative mix of quantitative and qualitative challenges. But to make various options analytically comparable, planners often convert the impact of potential choices into mutually consistent present value (PV) or internal rate of return (ROR) terms. If followed rigorously, this practice quickly drives out of consideration most options with payoffs or costs that: (1) are beyond a time horizon of four to five years or (2) defy reasonable quantification in financial terms. Examples include such things as programs for: basic research, alternate resources, reforestation, radical technology changes, improved worker attitudes, environmental control, public image building, or similar options—even though these may be vital to the future health of the organization or its entire industry. Too frequently these analytical practices cause organizations to ignore important opportunities and threats until it is too late to take any effective action.

Nonalignment toward strategic thrusts. Let us assume, however, that top-level strategic analyses purposely avoid the biases introduced by financial techniques and that top management chooses a balanced mix of quantitative, qualitative, long-term, and short-term thrusts as its intended strategy. Conventional wisdom still requires that each operating unit— whether it be a functional unit (marketing, production, service, R&D, etc.) or a decentralized product division—rank its proposed actions to support the strategy against the same PV or ROR criteria that would have distorted the original analy-

ses.[35] In screening proposals, the logic seems impeccable. To
have each division contribute the most profit, accept those
divisional proposals with the highest measured PV or ROR
and reject those in the lower ranges—especially those below
system-wide "capital cutoff points" or "hurdle rates." Unfortunately, this practice will usually destroy any strategic
patterns top management may have selected from its earlier
situational, projective, or environmental analyses How does
this happen?

Consider a case in which broader strategic analyses suggest
that R&D should support a balanced mix of: (1) further extensions of existing product lines, (2) new product thrusts
not currently in the corporation's exploitation portfolio,
(3) new technologies for an expanded presence in newly
developing geographical markets, (4) new knowledge to allow
choices for future options, (5) scientific or technical contributions to improve the image of the corporation, (6) environmental solutions to government demands, (7) development of
scientists, technicians, and support systems to maintain the
corporation's future flexibility, and (8) listening-post activities to prevent preemption by unforeseen new technologies.
Yet if analysts rank all the R&D programs proposed to meet
these various goals against a single PV or ROR standard, they
will invariably find that only certain programs—those that
extend current products' positions, improve present processes, or support "near-future, risk-free" new product
entries—make the top of the list. In most cases, these limited
goals will absorb the entire R&D budget of the company,
leaving the other seven goals untouched and the corporation's
intended strategy basically exterminated.

Coordination across divisions

This effect is compounded as each of the subordinate
operating units submits its individual proposals.[36] Projects
ranked by PV, ROI (return on investment), or ROR in production are unlikely to be congruent with those supporting
the same criteria in marketing or R&D, and vice versa. The
same is true of the proposals from the individual product
divisions. Rigorously used, financial criteria will direct capital
toward present product or "cash-cow" divisions, while starv-

ing other activities with valid strategic goals in inherently longer payout situations or lower return industries.

- For example, during the 1960s such criteria would have disastrously driven Exxon to invest ever more funds in Middle East oil where prospects were high and short-term returns were great. Its coal, nuclear, alternate energy, oil reserve diversification, and new (nonoil) product activities could never muster the same kinds of returns. Nor could its marketing or refining units show operating returns (based on market-level transfer prices) that could compete with Middle East exploration and production returns. Yet it was vital that the company develop standby coal reserves, make "insurance" investments in new oil sources outside the Middle East, build up its refinery and distribution networks to use the crude it had, and start product diversifications outside of oil as a hedge against loss of its overseas resource base or undue government regulation. Fortunately for the company's later health, its top management overrode the strict application of financial criteria and made longer term, lower PV investments in Esso Exploration (for diversified oil holdings), coal options (as a resource hedge), Exxon Enterprises (for product and risk diversification), and distribution and refinery networks (for flexibility, political leverage, and long-term stability). Implicitly, it accepted lower financial returns in each of these divisions to achieve the desired strategic result of greater resource flexibility.

Without serious intervention by corporate powers, financially ranked projects in individual divisions are extremely unlikely to add up to a cohesive pattern supporting major strategic thrusts like those in Exxon's situation—or those supporting new geographical market developments, environmental demands, future technology needs, resource developments, or similar thrusts that must cut across divisional lines. They also create other serious strategic problems.

No radical innovations. Overreliance on formal financial evaluations and measurements also systematically drives out radical innovation in most entities. The typical lead time for such innovations is 7 to 13 years from first discovery to profitability.[37] Given the cost-of-capital and probability assessments usually imposed by large enterprises, few radical innovations could survive formal screening practices.

- As Sir Alastair Pilkington, inventor and developer of the float glass process and later chairman of Pilkington Brothers, Ltd., said: "In the case of float, the figures are intriguing. It eventually took float 12 years to break even on cash flows. At one time it had a negative cash flow of £7 million ($19.6 million). Yet float was a commercial success immediately after we had solved its process problems. That's just how long it takes. If you went to an accountant and said, 'I've got a great idea to create a massive negative cash flow for certain, and it may—if it's a great success—break even on its cash flows in 12 years,' you wouldn't find many accountants who'd say 'that's exactly what I want.'"[38]

If the key players had acted on the rational financial information available at the time, there would have been no xerography, no metal skis, no aircraft, no jet engines, no television, no computers, no wireless communications, no float glass, and so on ad infinitum. In each case, standard financial calculations (including estimated markets, probabilities of technical success, lead times, and investment returns) would have directed funds toward less risky or more profitable options. And important strategic choices would have been automatically foreclosed for most larger entities. Such formalities are an important reason why most revolutionary innovations originate outside the industry they upset, and why so many radical innovations come from smaller companies. Only the so-called irrationality of fanatic individual entrepreneurs or force-fed government markets have allowed many of the most important innovations to move from the discovery stage into practical realities.

An operational extrapolative mode

Such factors force many companies' formal planning from a strategic toward an "operational-extrapolative" mode. And this tendency is generally further exacerbated by their measurement and reward systems. The people who draw up most of the specific proposals to fulfill strategic goals are from the operating echelons. These operating managers know that their long-term plans will soon be converted into tight operating budgets, one- to six-month program commitments, and financial performance measurement systems that emphasize the present, the current month, or the current quarter.[39] They know they are unlikely to be penalized if they take no risks or even avoid risks they should have taken. But they must not take a risk and fail.

Line managers receive few rewards for investments that pay off only after three to five years, when they have moved to another division or post. And still fewer rewards accrue from doing a superior job on qualitative programs whose effects cannot be measured immediately, if ever, quantitatively. By far the most visible and pervading standards in business are the current profitability and ROI of each unit. These tend to downgrade or drive out the longer term and more subtle aspects of strategy at all levels. Many operating managers, being constantly driven by current performance measures, find it hard to discern top management's broader strategic intentions. Consequently they cannot initiate effective proposals to support the strategy or maintain the patterned thrusts a true strategy requires. Overuse of financial criteria— so commonly encountered in formal planning and control systems—virtually assures that any cross divisional strategies, no matter how carefully formulated at the top, will be subverted in practice.

PLANNING FOR MULTIPLE GOALS

Carefully conceived formal strategic planning can override much of this suboptimizing behavior. It can and should be an integral element in the logical incremental processes described previously. Properly developed, formal planning activities can be of enormous help in:

1. Providing an improved data base, communication system, and set of analytical skills for forecasting and planning.
2. Teaching managers about the future, changing their receptiveness to new ideas, and creating a proactive attitude about future opportunities and threats.

3. Acknowledging and endorsing the full array of broad goals the enterprise is to serve.

4. Causing managers to think consciously about the central or unifying concepts that bring cohesion to their concern's diverse activities.

5. Refining these central concepts into a relatively few principal thrusts around which the organization can pattern its resource commitments and measure its managers' performance.

6. Periodically forcing managers to balance and assess their commitment patterns and strategic postures in terms of the strategic criteria defined above.

7. Specifically building into resource bases and commitments provisions for flexibility, imagination, and opportunism.

8. Establishing performance measurement, recognition, and reward systems that recognize all the concern's major goals and support its most important intended thrust patterns.

These elements of formal planning can be of significant help in calibrating and integrating the incremental processes that effective strategy formulation demands. Without these features, formal planning can quickly become a procedural straitjacket extrapolating current commitment patterns, dogmas, and practices toward disaster—as did the rigid, day-by-day, detailed attack plan of the German army in World War I.[40] Unfortunately, many formal government, institutional, and corporate planning systems accomplish just that.[41] Earlier chapters have shown how formal planning can contribute at specific stages of the logical incremental strategic process. The remaining sections of this chapter will suggest some basic ways in which the *overall* formal planning process can better support the flexible, consensus-building processes at the heart of logical incrementalism.

Satisficing, not maximizing

At the most elemental level, the process must begin by designing into its premises the fact that organizations inherently satisfice output toward a multiplicity of goals.[42] My data argue that business organizations do not satisfice toward the "first satisfactory solution" as some authors have suggested.[43] Nor do they pursue the single goal of maximum profitability which basic economics courses so often prescribe[44]—and some business heads mistakenly and unfortunately promulgate as their sole raison d'être. There are many good reasons for multiple goals and the satisficing behavior of organizations. Some authorities have pointed out that, because they have limited cognitive capacities, information access, or forecasting abilities, managers could not "maximize" a single output function (like profit) even if they wanted to.[45] Others have suggested that organizations satisfice because: (1) their managers must form coalitions in order to rule, (2) the coalitions' members each demand a price for their cooperation, and (3) the organization's meeting this price causes suboptimization or satisficing.[46] Such observations clearly have merit.

More basically, however, organizations satisfice because they are made up of human beings. No human being—except an essentially insane person or one in dire circumstances—can consistently pursue only one goal.[47] Each individual in an organization requires that it meet several of his or her most important goals to some degree.[48] These individuals make demands against the organization in negotiating their own positions in it.[49] These reflect, for example, their desired levels of satisfaction on the job, stability of employment, social atmosphere, facilities, comfort, cleanliness, location, and other factors. These are not just constraints to profitability; they are goals in their own right. And people make trade-offs in their management decisions according to their own internalized priorities among the goals they perceive as relevant to the enterprise and to themselves.[50] One of the real arts of strategy formulation lies in recognizing this multiplicity of interests, finding an acceptable zone within which people can cooperate effectively, and stimulating them to coordinate their many diverse drives toward cohesive purposes.

Multiple goals and coalitions

Any organization's ultimate direction is the result of many such choices and trade-offs. They all cause satisficing among customer benefits, supplier relations, profits, stability, costs, social atmosphere, professionalism, physical comfort, growth, innovativeness, process familiarity, market penetration, resources risked, power, public acceptance, size, and so on.[51] As one goal seems satisfied to a greater extent, individuals subjectively discount its marginal utility relative to other goals, and it is satisficed a bit more. Ultimately top management—or the "dominant coalition" running the enterprise[52]— also implements in its major decisions a set of goals representing its own personal and interpersonal trade-offs among many such competing objectives.[53] And even these are modified to reflect the demands of lower echelons and thus achieve their support.[54] The attempt to find an acceptable and motivating compromise among multiple competing goals is what forces much of the coalition behavior observed in large organizations, including major businesses.[55]

Very rationally, such entities try to optimize utility (not maximize profits) among the key interests, stakeholders, and players that determine their future.[56] Sound strategic planning, therefore, must start by recognizing the existence of the organization's multiple goals, the need for coalition behavior, and the requirement that all pertinent parties' interests be served in a balanced way.[57] Otherwise, any resulting strategy will not have the support of those needed to make it effective. Or by marshaling resources toward the wrong, or limited, ends, the strategy will ensure its own failure. This is precisely what happens when organizations allow single-criterion systems (like PV, ROI, or ROR) to dominate their resource allocations. The result is the equivalent of what would have happened if the Macedonians had sent all their forces behind Alexander's cavalry charge because such units could make the greatest advances with the fewest possible losses in the short run. The total balance of forces needed for success would be destroyed, and the overall strategy would be subverted.

How can one conceptualize developing a strategy that both honors economic rationality—or the essential business ethic of using the least resources for the maximum gain—and develops the kind of strategic thrusts that (1) meet a full range of intended goals, (2) avoid the anomalies that the misuse of formal analytical and planning techniques can create, and (3) provide the needed focal points for consensus building in a logical incremental mode?

ESTABLISHING BROAD CONCEPTS

A most important stage is understanding and formulating the broad concepts and goals the strategy is to embrace and serve. In many cases, such as national strategies, there can be no single stated consensus on this point. As various National Goals Commissions have found out to their dismay, the country's real national goals defy articulation in any one cohesive document short of a Constitution. They are merely a temporary vector resulting from the actions and views of all interested public and private forces. With great pain and persuasion, the President, the Cabinet, and the Office of Management and Budget may occasionally force a few strategic goals into being across all executive departments.[58] But only in times of great crisis does one see a truly cohesive strategy at the national level, and even then suboptimizing behavior is likely to be high.[59]

What to be? What to accomplish?

In private enterprise the constraints are less severe, but nevertheless real. Here a chief executive can—if he or she conscientiously chooses—guide an entity toward formulation of some broad central concepts that provide a useful framework for its strategies. To do so, the executive must create an operable consensus on certain basic issues. What is the intended *nature* of the enterprise; what is it *to be* in the world?[60] In what *directions* should the organization move; what is it *to accomplish?* What *special competencies* will make the organization *unique* and *better* able to perform its functions than its competitors?[61] Answers to these questions provide the basic structure that the enterprise's overall allocation patterns and action programs must ultimately support. Yet very few companies' strategic planning systems are geared to resolve even these basic issues effectively. Instead their outputs leap from uselessly general "credo" statements of basic values to overly specific budgetary targets and plans. They lack that rich intermediate set of largely qualitative goals that define the intended uniqueness, focus, special competencies, and major positioning thrusts of the strategy.

To ensure that conceptual goals capture such essential relationships and are not merely simplistic generalities or summaries of divisional goals, one classic book recommends that for a business—in addition to the elements described above—such goals should consider at least its desired:[62]

1. *Product/market scope* and the particular nature of services to be provided there.
2. *Relative market position* (or penetration) in selected sectors.
3. *Level and mode of innovation.*
4. *Profitability and other financial results.*
5. *Degree of organization decentralization.*
6. *Employee attitudes* to be generated.
7. *Managerial outlook and skills* to be developed.
8. *Levels of productivity* (in terms of value added).
9. *Physical and financial resource* capabilities.

Such definitions have the merit of cutting across divisional lines and getting beyond simplistic unidimensional concept definitions. Thus it would be insufficient to consider Exxon's central concept to be "an energy company" or Pilkington Brothers' simply to be a "glass company." Instead, the latter might be justly described in 1974 as seeking to become:

> A worldwide, diversified, innovative, high technology, glass company dominantly positioned in flat glass in selected developing countries and the British Empire, operating in a highly decentralized mode, with strong centralized creative planning, developing a new professionalism in its management and in its employee-human relationships, intending to grow at 15 percent per year with pretax returns on investment at least in the upper one third of the industry worldwide.

Analysis and intuition

How does a company arrive at such guiding concepts? Quantitative analysis is only partially effective at best. Because the alternatives are so numerous and considerations are so diverse, decisions about these ultimate ends tend to be highly unstructured and largely political choices.[63] What constitutes an optimal decision depends largely on each observer's values and particular perceptions of what is possible, desirable, and most worthwhile to do with the resources available.[64] Reasonable people looking at the same data can—and often do—arrive at quite different conclusions, any number of which could be justified and made to appear correct in retrospect. Since there is no objectively right answer concerning the proper ultimate ends for an organization, sensible practice dictates giving top priority to the *processes* through which such choices are made. Chapter 3 reviewed some of the most important considerations in detail.

Within these processes, of course, analytical content should be as high as is reasonable to decrease uncertainties, to eliminate some demonstrably wrong answers, to stimulate imaginative new concepts, and to give people maximum confidence in the choices they do make.[65]

- For example, Boston Consulting Group (BCG) is famous for its analyses which contribute to one part of this decision. BCG people first analyze the company's existing resources and capabilities in depth, developing extensive quantitative data about the company and its various markets. They then determine what limits this resource base sets on the company's potential growth and how fast the company could grow in key fiscal dimensions if it were properly positioned. Then they "try on" a series of product/market scenarios—iteratively segmenting the company's own potentials and those of its possible markets—until they find a product/market niche in which: (1) the company can be a "dominant force," and hence earn greater returns and have greater control over its destiny than its competitors, and (2) the company's internal capabilities (R&D, marketing effort, economies of scale, etc.) can be made strong enough to meet BCG's minimum criteria for success in the selected niche.

For maximum effectiveness, such analyses must be linked to management processes like those discussed in Chapter 4, which allow key people to talk out imponderables and arrive at an intuitive balance they can live with concerning both quantitative factors and those qualitative issues and unknowns they are likely to find even more disturbing or potentially challenging. A primary focus of the entire process should be to energize the organization to achieve as much as possible toward whichever of the potential "right answers" is selected. High-level commitment to a somewhat less quantitatively optimized set of concepts will often achieve more progress in desired directions than lesser commitment to more analytically refined goals.

Gestalt in concept selection

In making final choices, managers often must deal with a number of conflicting political pressures, internal and external matters with varying amounts of hard data, substantial uncertainties, and complete unknowns. In such decisions, many observers have noted that management's gestalt—that is, its subconscious feel for all the factors, their importance, and relationships—is marvelously tuned by intuition.

• After the oil embargo and the December 23, 1973, Executive Committee meeting, which so critically reshaped General Motors' car lines, one executive present said: "So much of the discussion was really instinct. There were strong feelings, rather than studies or data, that said every division should have a small car in its line. Some board members had been very vocal in pressing [CEO] Gerstenberg for small cars. The Olds and Buick groups were influenced primarily by a concern for the competitive position of their dealers. The Cadillac division staff saw they needed a smaller car. And Chevrolet felt it needed a car still smaller than its Vega to offer its dealers. The decision process was highly unstructured." But as a result of this meeting the Executive Committee instructed the engineers to make the final modifications on small cars for each line and to complete the pending plans for substantial reductions in the 1977 big cars. This was the signal for the biggest structural shift in General Motors' strategic posture since Alfred P. Sloan.[66]

In such cases, without being able to quantify many relationships, top managers can often come remarkably close to
what a careful theorist might have concluded if the theorist
had a great deal of time, possessed more information than
was available at the moment, and shared management's
intended weighting of factors.[67] Because of the subtle quantitative and qualitative balances it can embrace, this gestalt
—properly calibrated by sensibly made situational, projective, environmental, and special ad hoc studies—is probably superior to any rigorous model as a basis for defining the overall concept of an enterprise. An example suggests
how one management sought to integrate such formal
analyses step by step into other consensus-building processes:

- A $200 million textile specialties company—within a high-
ly decentralized multibillion-dollar larger corporation—had
been marginally profitable for some years. When a new
management team took over in the mid-1970s, it decided
to reposition the company. Executives first analyzed their
division's performance versus other parent company divisions and against other textile companies. With these data
the president and his chief of operations sat down with a
consultant and worked through how they would "define
success for their division five to seven years hence" and
some of the main barriers to achieving that success. Using
these broad goals as criteria, they "triaged" their existing
divisions. They found some of their divisions could easily
support the desired success patterns, others would clearly
be a perpetual drain, and a third grouping's potential was
unclear. With corporate consent, the two sold off or shut
down the "drain" divisions, generating some $25 million in
cash.

With this resource as a focal point they then got together
their internal executive board and again asked the question: "How would we define success five to seven years
from now?" In a series of meetings, using previously prepared data and special studies as background, executives
decided they wanted: "to be the leading company in
health, specialty, and related textile products; to be among
the top 5 percent in financial performance in the textile

industry in terms of both profits and stability; to be attractive to capable new talent; to be able to compete effectively against other units for corporate capital funds; to provide a real sense of achievement for their people; to produce products recognized by their customers for their distinctiveness and high quality; to be a major innovator in new processes for the industry; and to be recognized wherever they operated as a standard setter in terms of facilities, employee relations, and external relations." Using these parameters, the executive committee played through a series of scenarios until it achieved wide consensus on the more specific dimensions of what the company was to be and to accomplish. A few more operations now appeared marginal in terms of this definition and—after further investigation in depth—they were divested. The definitions also provided a basis for internal reallocations of resources and trial criteria for potential acquisitions. As the company's financial results improved, it selectively released its new statements of concept to a wider executive group.

PRINCIPAL THRUSTS

As these broad conceptions of purpose come into focus, an iterative process must begin to compare them against the present situation and to decide what major resource reallocations and structural changes are needed to convert the entity's existing posture into the closest acceptable approximation of the desired future stance. Typically, broad concepts—rather than crystalline numerical goals—are the most important elements in these realignments. For example:

• After several abortive tries at developing leading-edge technology, the management of a large aerospace company realized that the company's "true expertise lay in arriving late and overwhelming opponents with a huge development effort." Consequently, the company's research program was designed only to "listen" for developing new technologies. Management slowly built up resource reserves in several areas, which prepared the company to move rapidly and with great effect into selected markets when the time came. To maintain the company's competitive edge, its management established very advanced model and production test facilities in selected areas of expertise, excess capacity in various development model shops and engineering groups, and access to large-scale borrowing infusions from local banks and insurance companies. As interesting new fields emerged, the company entered selected areas as a "strong second" with a massive personnel and capital commitment supported directly by corporate headquarters. It licensed or forced cross-licensing of crucial technologies, was able to price somewhat lower because it did not have to recoup extensive research and development costs, and entered any new field with full-scale producing facilities to keep unit costs to a minimum.

More than two, less than ten

To be effective, the strategy's main dimensions must be distilled into a few—more than two, less than ten—principal thrusts critical to the new posture. Some of these may logically become a mission of only one division or unit. More often—just as in major military strategies—several divisions will have to commit portions of their total resources and act in concert to carry out the most important missions. At this point, strategy, as expressed in these principal thrusts or missions,[68] must clearly override other allocation or structural considerations within individual divisions or units.[69] A successful example suggests the kind of coordination that is often needed:

• A relatively small ($50 million in sales) company's management wished "to grow in a series of protected small niches in the chemical specialties industry." The company's traditional strengths had been in innovating new chemical solutions to problems of OEM producers. To carry out its concept, the management group established its own R&D programs as extensions of its customers' (dominantly mechanical) research activities. It developed very close relationships with customer technical groups through its own marketing and technical service endeavors. It organized its production-technical activities around fast-response development groups, constantly reshaped into special program teams which created new technologies for specific customer needs. It avoided high-volume chemicals or those which would not require sophisticated technical capabilities. It protected its market positions both through patents and through a careful pricing strategy, which demanded very high initial margins on new technical solutions but dropped prices to prevent competitive entries as the technology became more widely understood. It maintained high returns on investment by producing in small "semiworks" facilities at high gross margins. The company often sold off a product line when it became large enough for bigger companies with full-scale plants to enter the market.

A matrix of thrusts

How can such strategic coordination be achieved in a larger enterprise? Conceptually one can envision these principal thrusts—comprising the major elements of the strategy—as a matrix of coordinating plans laid across the functional and operating units that must carry them out[70] (see Diagram 5). Within its own plans and budgets, each division must provide *sufficient* support for each strategic thrust and make sure that the thrust is effectively implemented. As anyone knows who has tried it, this is a most difficult task in both an intellectual and a political sense.

The process is eased if each principal thrust is assigned a fiscal "cutoff point," "hurdle rate," or "imputed cost of capital" appropriate to its strategic mission. These, of course, must override the normal internal program evaluation criteria of each cooperating group, or else resources will flow only to those activities most financially attractive in the short run and starve other elements in the strategy. For example, programs supporting "cash-cow" activities might have to exceed a 30 percent ROR; new products diversifying corporate risks might need only a 15 percent ROR; next-generation technology investments could be acceptable down to break-even

Diagram 5

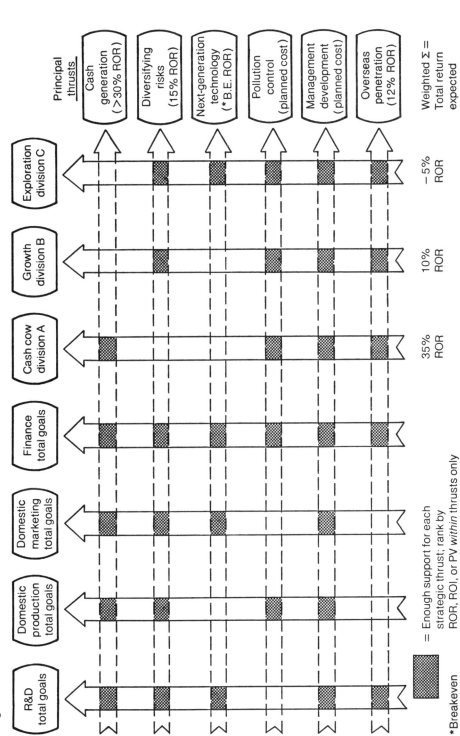

Principal thrusts

Cash generation (>30% ROR)

Diversifying risks (15% ROR)

Next-generation technology (* B.E. ROR)

Pollution control (planned cost)

Management development (planned cost)

Overseas penetration (12% ROR)

Weighted Σ = Total return expected

Exploration division C — -5% ROR

Growth division B — 10% ROR

Cash cow division A — 35% ROR

Finance total goals

Domestic marketing total goals

Domestic production total goals

R&D total goals

◼ = Enough support for each strategic thrust; rank by ROR, ROI, or PV *within* thrusts only

◼ Breakeven

*Breakeven

RORs in their inception stages; depollution technologies might not have positive financial returns at all; and managerial development might have to be budgeted as a planned cost, with no attempt to measure current financial benefits. An example suggests how an overall strategic decision should affect such internal allocation criteria:

- One of the more successful aerospace companies, because of large production contracts for existing aircraft, arrived late in the 1960s space market. Its management team decided purposely to ignore the then-popular entry into booster technology. Instead, it chose to "jump over" competition and develop a leading edge in those payload technologies which would be needed later than boosters. This choice clearly shaped the structure and skills of the company's technical programs and its commitment patterns and expectations in all divisions. The management group used its aircraft contracts as "cash cows" to see the company through a prolonged development period. It was able to make needed long-term capital commitments, without current payoff, for payload space technologies in part because one individual controlled so much of its stock and was CEO. When space vehicles were finally required, the company met competitors (who had been working on other aspects of space) with a proved capability they could not easily match.

To evaluate financial preferences *within* each thrust, analysts may reasonably rank individual programs—coordinated across all divisions—against each other using whatever criterion (ROR, PV, or ROI) seems appropriate. But programs supporting different thrusts should not be ranked directly against each other.[71] *Enough* effort must be placed behind each major thrust in each division to ensure its accomplishment. This always leads to some negotiation during planning and commitment cycles. Some costs might be absorbed at corporate levels to avoid significant distortions in comparing individual divisions' measured performance. Or the profit or return targets for individual divisions can be adjusted downward to recognize costs undertaken primarily for corporate purposes. It is essential that each division's expected total returns be adjusted to reflect its intended role in the corporate strategy and/or the nature of the particular industry in which it operates. For example, consumer product divisions might have to earn a 30 percent ROI, sheet steel divisions acquired to stabilize supplies may earn only 10 percent at market transfer prices, and some "prestige" or "image-producing" lines (like drugs to cure rare diseases) might be worthwhile even at a planned loss.

A planned portfolio

When completed, formal strategic planning activities should lead to a portfolio of cross-divisional thrusts and differentiated targets for individual divisions, which *in the aggregate meet all corporate financial and nonfinancial goals*. This is totally rational in economic terms. Few large investors buy only one class of high-yield or growth stocks. Instead they typically honor the full range of their values by investing in some very secure bonds; some high-dividend, cash-cow stocks; some low-yield, high-growth stocks; some steadily growing, nondividend stocks; some insurance policies; a pension plan; a small, high-risk venture; a prestige company with products they admire; a park development that may lose money but make the community more pleasant; and some low-yield stocks that create a water company or other support service their community needs. Although not maximizing financial returns, different variations of this portfolio clearly could optimize utility for different private investors. If one grants that real enterprises legitimately have multiple economic and qualitative goals, a portfolio of investments is equally justified to fulfill their various purposes.

• Texas Instruments, Inc., had developed the nearest parallel to this approach of any complete system encountered. As the company grew in size, it decentralized operations into small profit centers to maintain customer responsiveness, innovation, and entrepreneurial spirit. But it became concerned that these units would become short-term oriented and fail to see and solve problems on a scale appropriate to the total organization. It therefore designed its Objectives, Strategies, and Tactics (OST) system as a basis for those formal planning, review, and control activities which cut across the complete operating structure. At the corporate level, a stated set of corporate objectives put forth the company's broad economic purposes, the reasons for the company's existence, and its responsibilities to various stakeholders.

For each major objective in this set there were one to several complete strategies cutting across the various groups, divisions, and product centers of the company. Each strategy had designated milestones for accomplishment, and a series of Tactical Action Programs (TAPs) was established containing the detailed steps necessary to accomplish these milestones. Specific managers were assigned to head each objective, strategy, and TAP. These managers might simultaneously head a complete operating unit, but they would have a separate budget for their strategic program, distinct from their operating budgets.

Total resources were allocated to ensure that each objective, strategy, and TAP had sufficient resources to accomplish its mission. At the corporate level, an OST Committee made these strategic resource allocations and reviewed progress on strategic activities, while a Management Committee oversaw operating units' budgets and performance. Operating divisions had to meet different short-term standards based on the nature of their particular business. OST funds were allocated across divisions as necessary to obtain the desired cross-divisional thrust. At least 10 percent of OST funds were kept uncommitted early in the year to be deployed flexibly as new needs arose. Separate incentive plans rewarded managers for operating performance and for strategic performance. Although a corporate-wide model could pull together all elements of various budgets at any one time, no "corporate plan" book was issued since the total plan was in constant flux.[72]

The essence of formal strategic planning is (1) to establish the enterprise's goals at a level that provides the greatest satisfaction to all critical stakeholders and (2) to create a pattern of commitments and psychological rewards that will achieve the greatest advance toward these goals at the least expected cost. The preceding sections provide the needed formal framework for doing this in a way that maintains the focus, lateral coordination, multiple goal orientation, and overriding priorities a well-developed strategy should have. The concepts are relatively simple, but, as the vignettes suggest, their implementation is not. Implementation is easiest when single organizational units can be made responsible for entire thrusts. Unfortunately, despite the most careful attempts to design individual organizational units that embrace discrete sets of strategic thrusts, two- and three-level matrices are common in most complex organizations.[73] Even General Electric Corporation, with its highly rationalized group, strategic business unit, and product division structures, found it must use additional matrices in its strategic planning.[74]

The overall balance among the portfolio's various thrusts determines the net direction of the total enterprise. Yet there is no single objective criterion to say what the "right balance" should be. Different executives reviewing the overall balance—because of their different personal values and weightings of key factors—may legitimately disagree on this point. However, if proper processes were used in generating and evaluating the various thrusts, all relevant factors should have been considered in the buildup of each element. Continuous negotiations should have defined broad zones of consensus and the outside limits where that consensus would fall apart. Earlier power interplays should have refined the final choices among matrix elements into a relatively few marginal choices before the final matrix comes into place. Consequently, top managers who wish to control the overall direction of these negotiations carry a mental image of their intended portfolio in mind, and they consciously manage earlier strategic processes and negotiations in keeping with their perceptions of desirable directions. Periodic formal analyses and reviews of their intended and emerging portfolios genuinely help executives calibrate their intentions and maintain their focus. But these are ancillary, not determining, processes.

THE STRATEGIC PROCESS

Most effective top executives consciously go through the rigorous intellectual processes of formal planning, but they are also constantly aware that real strategies rarely come about solely through such formal analytical processes. These managers keep a clear vision in mind of where they would like to go and use all the valid analytical data they can as they guide their organizations toward a new strategy. However, they also consciously manage the several-year, iterative, political, consensus-building process that is necessary to convert their broad visions into an effective new strategy. The following real example shows how one very large enterprise integrated the kinds of formal analyses just described with careful consensus-building processes to formulate its new strategy.

● In the late 1970s a major nation's largest bank named as its new president and CEO a man with a long and successful career, primarily in domestic operating positions. The bank's chairman had been a familiar figure on the international stage and was due to retire in three to five years. The new CEO, with the help of a few trusted colleagues, his chief planner, and a consultant, first tried to answer the question, "If I look ahead seven to eight years to my retirement as CEO, what would I like to leave behind as the hallmarks of my leadership? What accomplishments would define my era as having been successful?" He distilled these to the following: (1) to be the country's number one bank in profitability and size without sacrificing the quality of its assets or liabilities, (2) to be recognized as a major international bank, (3) to substantially improve the image, public perception, and employee identity of the bank, (4) to maintain progressive policies which prevent unionization, (5) to be viewed as a skillful, professional, well-controlled bank with strong planned management continuity, (6) to be clearly identified as the country's most professional corporate finance bank, with a strong base in the country but with foreign and domestic operations growing in balance, (7) to have women in top management and achieve full utilization of the bank's female resources, and

(8) to have a tighter, smaller headquarters with a more rationalized, decentralized corporate structure.

The CEO brought back to the corporate offices the head of his overseas divisions to be COO and a member of the small line Executive Committee which ran the company's affairs. The CEO discussed his personal views concerning the bank's future with this group and individually with several of his group vice presidents. Then to arrive at a cohesive set of corporate goals, the Executive Committee investigated the bank's existing strengths and weaknesses (again with consultants' assistance) and extrapolated its existing growth trends seven to eight years into the future. The results of this exercise quickly highlighted that the bank's foreseeable growth would require: (1) that the whole bank's structure be reoriented to make it a much stronger force in international banking, (2) that the bank must decentralize operations much more than it ever had, (3) that the bank find or develop at least 100 new top-level specialists and general managers within a few years, (4) that it reorganize around a "four-bank" principle (i.e., an international, a commercial, an investment, and a retail bank) with entirely new links forged between these units, (5) that these links and much of its new international thrust should probably be built on the bank's expertise in certain industries which were the primary bases of its parent country's international trade, and (6) that the bank's profitability must be improved across the board, but especially in its diverse retail banking units.

To develop more detailed data for specific actions and to develop consensus further around needed moves, the CEO commissioned two consulting studies: one on the future of the bank's home country and the other on changing trade patterns and relationships worldwide. As these studies became available, the CEO allowed an ever wider circle of top executives to critique the studies' findings and share in their insights. Finally, the CEO and Executive Committee were willing to draw up and agree to a statement of some ten broad goals (quite parallel to the CEO's original goals but enriched in flavor and detail). By then some steps were already under way to implement specific goals, such as the four-bank concept. But the CEO wanted further participation of his line officers in the formulation of the goals and the strategic thrusts they represented across the whole bank. By now 1½ years had gone by, but there was widespread consensus of the top management group on major goals and directions.

The CEO then organized an international conference of some 40 top officers of the bank and had a background document prepared for this meeting, containing: (1) the broad goals agreed on, (2) the ten major thrusts the Executive Committee thought were necessary to meet these goals, (3) the key elements needed to back up each thrust (1-1½ pages per thrust), and (4) a summary of the national and economic analyses the thrusts were based on. The 40 executives had two full days to critique, question, improve, and clarify the ideas in this document. Small work groups of line executives reported their findings and concerns directly to the Executive Committee. At the end of the meeting the Executive Committee tabled one of the major thrusts for further study, agreed to refined wording for some of the bank's broad goals, and modified details of the major thrusts in line with expressed concerns.

The CEO then announced that within three months each line officer would be expected to submit his own statement of how his unit would contribute to the major goals and thrusts agreed on. Once these unit goals were discussed and negotiated with the appropriate top executive group, the line officers would develop specific budgetary and nonbudgetary programs showing precisely how their unit would carry out each of the major thrusts in the strategy. The COO was asked to develop measures both for all key elements of each unit's fiscal performance and for performance against each agreed-upon strategic thrust within each unit. The total process from concept formulation to implementation of the control system would span some three to four years, with new goals and thrusts emerging as external events and opportunities developed.

Measure and reward thrusts

During the long evolution of such a process, it is difficult to maintain the organization's interest and continuity of thought on essential strategic issues. Concentrating on a few strategic thrusts helps. Even the most successful top manager can rarely push more than a few—typically a half dozen or less—basic changes without the organization's losing focus or building a huge back-pressure of resistance. Individual operating managers cannot maintain a sense of priorities among a cluster of potentially conflicting goals that are too diverse. And the problems of effectively and fairly measuring performance across various divisions skyrocket as the number of thrusts increases.

One of the binding principles in establishing critical thrusts for or across divisions is that they be important enough to measure progress and reward success against them in a highly visible way. Without such a capacity the strategy will soon be wrecked on the shoals of expediency. At a minimum the control system should ensure that (1) resource-commitment patterns support the intended thrusts, (2) action plans are aligned behind the thrusts, (3) performance against each is measured, and (4) successful achievement toward them gets rewarded. Measurements and adjusting actions are, of course, tactical operations. The strategist's concern is that proper systems are in place to align, evaluate, and reward performance toward the strategy at all levels. Unless such systems are carefully designed around major strategic thrusts, they will inevitably mutate behavior toward other—typically short-term and suboptimizing—actions.

Use of strategic criteria for focus and flexibility

Unfortunately, during the long processes of strategy creation and implementation, politics—and the compromises it entails—tends to soften or eliminate the distinctive profile that well-conceived strategies should have. Just as federal and state governments do, businesses and other organizations tend to allocate resources to help everyone a little bit and to cause no powerful individual great pain. During both formal planning and incremental processes, top managers need to discipline themselves to step back periodically and review the entity's emerging strategic posture. They should test it against the kind of criteria outlined in the early sections of this chapter. Focusing on even the few key criteria suggested can help enforce some of the central discipline that well-formed strategies should have, yet is so seldom present in formal business strategies. While, for reasons cited, one cannot expect written statements of all strategic goals, policies, and sequences, planners and executives should at least intellectually evaluate their emerging strategies against appropriate criteria. This is just one of many areas where the professional planner can intervene helpfully to improve both formal and incremental strategic processes.

INTERVENING IN INCREMENTAL STRATEGIC PROCESSES

Professional planners can help make their formal plans more useful through the formal methodologies and conceptual approaches described previously. But much more important are the ways they can contribute to and intervene in the incremental process steps outlined in Chapters 2-4. The most successful professional planners I have known essentially delegate running the annual planning process to someone else. Instead they concentrate on a series of almost ad hoc interventions designed to: (1) sense developing strategic needs, (2) teach top managers about the future, (3) build awareness about new options, (4) broaden support and comfort levels for action, (5) crystallize and communicate partial consensus as it emerges, (6) stimulate a few key executives' personal commitment toward new options, and (7) build communication channels and resource buffers that make the organization more open and flexible toward change. Because these interventions take on so many different forms, I will only suggest—not catalog—how some planners who have been most effective in stimulating strategic change approached these processes.

Sensing strategic needs

Virtually all such planners had developed extensive internal and external information networks and a purposely structured schedule of stimuli to make sure they kept in touch with events likely to affect their companies. They were often among the company's most prolific conference goers and executive course attendees. Rather than build their own permanent staffs, they preferred to bring in a stream of outside experts on subjects of interest and to have special studies done by knowledgeable consultants or staff people elsewhere in the company. They said this helped avoid personal biases and built credibility for new ideas presented. Many had individual experts or teams come in and lead small seminars on provocative topics well beyond the ordinary time horizons of their companies.

• Said the chief planner of a large chemical company, "For the price of one professional and his secretary, I can design for myself and a few key executives a biweekly series of seminars led by the very best people in the world. There's just no comparison between the potential impact of the two investments. And keeping my staff to minimum levels avoids political exposure."

By its very nature, real need sensing cannot depend solely on formal analytical structures. Instead, successful planners must place themselves at the center of the richest possible flows of information about the company and its future and imaginatively try to distill key concepts from this flow. As noted, much of this process is highly unstructured and intuitive.

Teaching managers about the future

This was among the three main tasks of the most successful planners. For good reasons, most line managers are preoccupied with urgent current problems. Successful planners learned when each key executive was most relaxed and likely to be open to more philosophical conversations or practical speculations about the future. After-hours talks, cocktails, lunch, golf links, carpools, and business trips all provided occasions for informally leading executives into the future.

• Said the vice president of planning of an electronics company: "When a provocative idea leads an executive to the inevitable 'I'd like to know more about that,' I try to put together some short publications, a study, or a seminar tailored to that executive's specific needs. I talk to him or her not just about potential future events, but how longer term forecasts are made, how accurate they are, and who the best individual sources may be. I may bring the executive into contact with some of these experts or arrange visits to advanced laboratories at universities and suppliers' or customers' factories. There the executive can see and feel the initial reality of new concepts."

The teaching process tended to be highly personalized, occasionally interspersed with more formal programs and environmental forecasting sessions for larger groups. Planners knew they were making progress when their executive "students" began to ask new and more penetrating questions during planning and budget review sessions.

Building awareness about new options

If initial creation of awareness could be stimulated by such planned "whispering in the ears of the gods," the next step was to intensify or amplify the reality of new options. This usually required some wider, more participatory actions.

- For example, when he thought his company's strategic viewpoints had become too myopic, one company's planning director, with the consent of the CEO, formed a strategic options group of highly regarded younger executives from all major divisions. This group was to propose a series of strategic questions it thought the company should consider and some new options the executive committee might want staffs to work through in more detail. The CEO said, "This got our next generation of executives looking at some important issues, taught them a good deal about the total company's viewpoint, gave us some fresh thoughts, and made sure we didn't overlook anything important. Some of the issues raised became subjects for specific inquiries by the executive committee."

On other occasions planners might get individual executives to sponsor internal ad hoc studies; they might arrange a conference on a specific issue; or they might have a prestigious external group make a presentation posing a selected opportunity or threat so unambiguously that management requested further inquiries and began to take a more personal interest. The seeds were sown outside the formal planning process, but the planner tried to ensure that later planning reviews inquired about the issues raised and executive questioners followed up on them in formal control processes.

Broadening support and comfort levels for action

As a new issue picked up momentum, successful planners often actively sought out the main sources of support and opposition to it. Frequently opponents were simply uninterested, ill-informed, or too busy to give new ideas serious consideration. In such cases, planners could begin a series of secondary education projects.

- Quoting an effective chief planner of a large consumer products company: "I may first have to build up a more adequate data base on the subject. Then I may arrange for some articulate proponents or neutral parties to prepare background papers on the topic with no recommended actions presented. As these endeavors accumulate weight and/or support, I may set up an informational meeting or two to inquire where we should go from here and what the prime concerns of opponents are. My office can often coordinate the accumulation of necessary data for the next stage of discussions. Finally, if necessary, I can arrange for a line executive to establish a carefully selected committee to look into the issue and come forward with recommendations. Or, if I can get a particular manager to sponsor the idea, it can be put forward as a trial balloon in his next formal plan."

All these are legitimate interventions to help a new option over the hurdles of ignorance and suspicion it always encounters. As an idea gains momentum, planners can further stimulate its acceptance by having their staffs prepare special studies on it and by including inquiries about it in the instructions issued for drawing up long-range plans.

Crystallizing consensus or commitment

An important role of effective planners and the planning process is to help crystallize or affirm consensus and commitment as they occur. As noted, formal plans typically corroborated broad goals where consensus existed or benefits might result from their formal expression. Such plans also confirmed more specific goals negotiated between subordinates and higher executives during planning exchanges. But crystallization occurred in other ways too. Typically it was the chief planner who first drafted the broad goal statements used to guide subordinates' plans. It was the planner who first summarized understandings reached in more formal goal-setting meetings like General Mills' "goodness to greatness" conference. It was the planners who helped subordinate groups draft their own goal statements or interpret the meaning of general enterprise goals from above. And it was the planners who first questioned the adequacy of divisions' submitted goals and supporting plans during planning cycles. Although line executives, of course, carried out the final negotiations and reached agreements with lower levels on goals, the planners' influence—inside and outside the formal planning process—could be very great in crystallizing consensus. The most effective planners were deeply aware of the practical politics that goal setting involved. And they adroitly balanced the caveats concerning generality versus specificity, and written versus unwritten goals noted in Chapter 3.

Successful planners operated in less formal ways too.

● Said the vice president of strategic planning of a large information products company: "I move when I know a top executive is about to make a speech or internal presentation where a reference about the future would be useful. I brief him or his speechwriters on potentially exciting developments or ideas I think may be ready for public exposure. Sometimes this is just a device to increase the executive's awareness of needs the company must respond to. Once an executive has spoken publicly about an issue, he is much more likely to feel he understands it and is committed to doing something about it. If I can get him to implicitly endorse a goal or a specific option in public, he will feel even more committed."

This is a realm where planners or other staff people must tread with care, but it was a common technique for sinking the hook of commitment. Planners also used the device of including statements of consensus in the "assumptions" instructions for annual plans sent to divisional planning groups or operating executives. Or they could escalate line executives' commitment to various problems by having the CEO include pertinent "questions to be answered" in these same instructions. All these measures tended to move issues proactively from awareness to commitment levels.

Planning communications and resources for flexibility

A high-yield, though often overlooked, service of the planning function was to stimulate actions that would ensure that the enterprise had the planned capability to respond flexibly to changes in the environment. When observed, this involved two central dimensions: (1) developing an open and opportunistically tuned communication system and (2) building sufficient resource buffers or slacks to respond flexibly to new stimuli without upsetting basic strategic balances. One of the important functions of a well-designed planning system is to encourage more open, data-rich communications about overall directions, opportunities, and threats. One company developed this concept quite fully in what it called its "opportunity planning" system.

- Planning sessions were not held just annually, but whenever either a division or a corporate officer identified a major opportunity which needed strategic investigation. At these sessions the emphasis was not placed on detailed numbers, but on the concept, its opportunity potential, and its strategic fit with the division's or company's other activities. Opportunity planning was a line activity with just the president, group vice president, division head, and perhaps one or two line functional managers present. The president took the attitude that resources were unlimited—

the company could always obtain capital for sufficiently good ideas. Using staff information and all the other external data sources about potential ventures available to an active president, he pressed his line managers to "shoot high enough." An opportunity missed was just as damaging to the line manager as an operating loss would be, and line managers were rewarded when their opportunities paid off. Only after an opportunity was thoroughly investigated and approved on a conceptual level—using a few broad numbers—was it thoroughly analyzed in financial terms and put through a separate, more detailed process for actual approval. The company backed this opportunity planning system with a very informal, open, electronic communication system which emphasized personal and verbal interactions, rather than formal memoranda.

Planning groups could also be instrumental in getting these executive groups to build the resource flexibilities needed to move opportunistically. Such flexibility required not idle resources but a consciously designed capability to expand or shift resources. For example, a company could build flexible capital access even though it might use its full capability only in spurts. By designing the organization with quality replacements at many levels, a company could—as IBM or Polaroid so often have done—assemble task forces or teams on short notice to carry out major ventures. And purposely developed organization policies could encourage and reward those involved in such shifts. The planning function could sensitize top management to the need for such planned flexibilities, estimate the nature of the opportunities and threats they should be designed for, and generate scenarios showing potential costs and benefits. The process of flexibility creation called for many of the same skills and approaches suggested for other forms of incremental consensus building.

Thus, effective professional planners worked both within the planning process and outside it to influence and support the incremental activities that typically led to strategy formation. When they integrated the two activities, the inputs of formal planning enriched and brought cohesion to the strategy. In fact the formal analytical skills of planners could be vital inputs to strategy formulation at many different points in the logical incremental process. When planners operated solely or even dominantly within the formal planning process, however, they missed some of the most important contributions they could make to strategy formulation. Consequently, as noted, most successful planners learned to delegate the mechanics of the annual planning process to juniors and actively participated at the heart of strategic processes. They joined in the management of logical incrementalism.

SUMMARY AND CONCLUSION

Most sophisticated observers agree on the value of incrementalism in strategic decision making. This book has tried to explain the reasons why incrementalism is logical—indeed essential—in such complex decisions. It has sought to present top managers' own rationales for acting as they do, and it has attempted to constructively relate their pragmatic practices to existing theory in order to obtain a synthesis that is more useful for both the theoretician and the practitioner. Knowledgeable top executives consciously design logical incrementalism into their decision processes. They also wisely use more formal management practices to ensure the continuity, balance, and cohesion of actions taken in this incremental mode. While such formal tools are important in the strategy formulation process, they are not the essence of its management. The kinds of approaches described in the first four chapters are.

An integrative paradigm

To be most effective, formal strategic analyses should be integrally related to many different phases of this logically incremental process of strategy formation. Where they are used, their prescriptions should reflect certain basic principles and balances best defined in the classic literature about military-diplomatic strategies. These strongly suggest that effective strategies concentrate resources and management attention on a few critical thrusts, which cohesively integrate the entity's major goals, policies, and action sequences into a uniquely strong and flexible posture that specifically considers a number of definitive evaluation criteria. Once arrived at, the requisites of this posture should override all other suboptimizing decision rules—like the short-term profit thrusts of individual divisions or the present value and rate of return criteria that subvert so many industrial strategies.

These major integrating strategic thrusts should consciously reflect the multiplicity of important goals any healthy enterprise has and align its resources across all units to achieve the full range of intended goals in a balanced and focused way. Properly developed formal strategic analyses, reflecting the criteria described in this chapter, can provide a powerful methodology for analyzing, conceptualizing, affirming, or calibrating either subsystem or overall strategies. And they can be designed to support important elements in the incremental and power-behavioral processes of developing strategies.

Subsystems of strategy

Typically, however, the actual processes of generating major enterprise strategies tend to occur outside its usual formal planning process. Strategies tend to form within several more or less discrete subsystems, each involving different sets of people, sequences of action, and pacing parameters. The somewhat random and independent timing of critical decisions within each subsystem—as well as the virtual impossibility of dealing simultaneously with all the different intellectual and behavioral dimensions of a complex enterprise's overall strategy—dictates that most macro-strategies evolve incrementally as a series of partial, tentative, somewhat fragmented decisions and personal commitments rather than as fully integrated conceptual totalities. Yet this incremental process of overall strategy formulation—practiced by most successful enterprises—is neither haphazard nor true "muddling," as that term is ordinarily used.

Instead executives can, and do, proactively manage the development of strategies in a logical incremental fashion. In the absence of overwhelming crises they consciously: (1) establish systematic means to help them sense new strategic needs well in advance, (2) build awareness and legitimize viewpoints about perceived new options, (3) broaden support and build psychological comfort levels for action, (4) start and stimulate ad hoc programs to generate partial solutions, (5) avoid early identification with specific solutions to maintain flexibility, organizational decentralization, and personal motivation of lower echelons, (6) manage political coalitions to develop and crystallize consensus as it emerges, (7) get individuals to identify personally with intended strategies, and (8) actively shape accepted proposals toward patterns which support goals that may be only broadly conceived at first but evolve interactively along with action alternatives toward more precise ultimate commitments. Many of the guiding strategists' methodologies are not of the usual textbook variety. They are astute combinations of formal analytical, behavioral, and political processes adapted to the realities of large organizations and the particular situation.

A continuous, evolving political consensus

Although crises can collapse time frames or cause abrupt shifts in direction, most strategic decisions in large enterprises emerge as continuous, evolving political consensus-building processes with no precise beginning or end. Managing the generation and evolution of this consensus is one of the true arts of management, calling for the best practices of both behavioral and decision scientists. This work has attempted to report how executives in major companies actually practice this art and why they seem to act as they do. It has also suggested how specific portions of the research literature apply to this process. And it has tried to show how both viewpoints can be synthesized around a logical incremental paradigm, supported by properly integrated formal strategic analyses. Along the way it has tried to provide some detailed insights and examples, which it hopes the reader has found new, provocative, and enlightening. Much of its data base is available in published form. I believe these publications thoroughly justify the limited conclusions set forth here. When the full data base is finally released, I—and I hope others—will continue the search for further useful insights.

But one must regard all analytical methodologies or structures—including logical incrementalism—as mere intellectual frameworks and be very cautious about their overuse in detail. One should remember Von Clausewitz's wise counsel about the inadequacy of prescriptive systems when faced with the infinite resources of the mind and spirit. "All theory can do is give . . . points of reference and standards of evaluation in specific areas of action, with the ultimate purpose not of telling [one] how to act, but of developing his judgment." Such has been the purpose of each chapter of this book. I have not sought a new panacea to replace faded predecessors. Instead I have sought to understand better how large organizations really do derive their strategies, to blend insights from this endeavor with those of existing theories, and perhaps to offer some new references and standards of action more useful to strategy makers and students of strategy.

NOTES

1. Sun Tzu, *The Art of War,* translated by S. B. Griffith (New York: Oxford University Press, 1963), original 500 B.C.

2. N. Machiavelli, *The Prince, and the Discourses* (New York: Modern Library, 1950).

3. Napoleon, I., "Maximes de Guerre," in T. R. Phillips, ed., *Roots of Strategy* (Harrisburg, Pa.: The Military Service Publishing Company, 1940).

4. C. Von Clausewitz, *On War,* translated by M. Howard and P. Paret (Princeton, N.J.: Princeton University Press, 1976).

5. F. Foch, *Principles of War,* translated by J. DeMorinni (New York: AMS Press, Inc., 1970), original (London: Chapman & Hall, Ltd., 1918).

6. V. I. Lenin, *Collected Works of V. I. Lenin,* edited and annotated (New York: International Publishers, 1927), especially vol. 21, "Toward the Seizure of Power."

7. B. H. L. Hart, *Strategy* (New York: Frederick A. Praeger, Publishers, 1954).

8. B. L. Montgomery, *The Memoirs of Field-Marshal The Viscount Montgomery of Alamein* (Cleveland: World Publishing Co., 1958).

9. Mao Tse-Tung, *Selected Military Writings, 1928-1949* (San Francisco: China Books, 1967).

10. V. J. Varner and J. I. Alger, eds., *History of the Military Art: Notes for the Course* (West Point, N.Y.: U.S. Military Academy, Department of History, 1978); and P. Green, *Alexander the Great* (New York: Praeger Publishers, 1970).

11. As described in Von Clausewitz, *On War,* p. 8.

12. In Phillips, ed., *Roots of Strategy.*

13. D. F. Von Bülow, *The Spirit of the Modern System of War*, translated by C. M. de Martemont (London: C. Mercier and Co., 1806).

14. A. H. Jomini, *Art of War*, translated by G. H. Mendell and W. P. Craighill (Westport, Conn.: Greenwood Press, 1971) original (Philadelphia: J. B. Lippincott & Co., 1862).

15. Von Clausewitz, *On War*.

16. Napoleon, "Maximes de Guerre."

17. The battle of Arnheim [see C. Ryan, *A Bridge Too Far* (London: Coronet Books, 1974)] suggests the disasters of inflexibility.

18. As described in B. W. Tuchman, *The Guns of August* (New York: The Macmillan Company, 1962), from the original G. Von Schlieffen, *Gesammelte Shriften* (Berlin: E. S. Mittler, 1913).

19. Foch, *Principles of War*.

20. As described in Tuchman, *Guns of August*.

21. Ibid. Also see M. H. Halperin, *Limited War in the Nuclear Age* (New York: John Wiley & Sons, 1963), and R. E. Osgood, *Limited War; The Challenge to American Strategy* (Chicago: University of Chicago Press, 1957) for the recognition of policy limits to the use of power in war.

22. Hart, *Strategy*.

23. M. Matloff and E. M. Snell, *Strategic Planning for Coalition Warfare (1941-42)* (Washington, D.C.: Office of the Chief of Military History, Department of the Army, 1953).

24. W. Stevenson, *A Man Called Intrepid: The Secret War* (New York: Harcourt Brace Jovanovich, 1976).

25. F. C. Pogue, *George C. Marshall: Ordeal and Hope, 1939-1942* (New York: Viking Press, 1966), pp. 303-20.

26. D. C. James, *The Years of MacArthur, 1941-1945* (Boston: Houghton Mifflin Company, 1970).

27. H. Essame, *Patton: A Study in Command* (New York: Charles Scribner's Sons, 1974); and L. Farago, *Patton: Ordeal and Triumph* (New York: I. Obolensky, 1964).

28. D. Irving, *The Trail of the Fox* (New York: E. P. Dutton, 1977); and D. Young, *Rommel: The Desert Fox* (New York: Harper & Row, 1974).

29. R. N. Anthony, *Planning and Control Systems: A Framework for Analysis* (Boston: Division of Research, Graduate School of Business Administration, Harvard University, 1965), is one of the first books to rigorously define goals into the business strategic structure.

30. D. Braybrooke and C. E. Lindblom, *A Strategy of Decision: Policy Evaluation as a Social Process* (New York: Free Press, 1963).

31. T. H. White, in *In Search of History: A Personal Adventure* (New York: Warner Books, 1978), calls this "the law of unforeseen consequences." Also see J. W. Forrester, "Counterintuitive Behavior of Social Systems," *Technology Review* (January 1971), pp. 52-68, and C. E. Lindblom, "The Science of 'Muddling Through,'" *Public Administration Review* (Spring 1959), pp. 79-88.

32. R. F. Vancil and P. Lorange, "Strategic Planning in Diversified Companies," *Harvard Business Review* (January-February 1975), pp. 81-90; and R. F. Vancil, "Strategy Formulation in Complex Organizations," *Sloan Management Review* (Winter 1976), pp. 1-18.

33. S. Tilles, "How to Evaluate Corporate Strategy," *Harvard Business Review* (July-August 1963), pp. 111-21; Boston Consulting Group, *Perspectives on Corporate Strategy* (Boston: BCG, 1968); and C. R. Christenson, K. R. Andrews, and J. L. Bower, *Business Policy: Text and Cases,* 3d ed. (Homewood, Ill.: Richard D. Irwin, 1973), pp. 114-17.

34. Von Clausewitz, *On War,* p. 15.

35. P. Lorange, in "Divisional Planning: Setting Effective Direction," *Sloan Management Review* (Fall 1975), pp. 77-91, suggests planning *across* functions or divisions and budgeting within divisions to avoid this. Control systems (and budgets) must reflect the plan to make this work, which means that the strategy must purposely override internal allocation procedures and controls.

36. D. S. Sherwin, in "Management *of* Objectives," *Harvard Business Review* (May-June 1976), pp. 149-60, suggests why this happens in functional organizations.

37. J. Jewkes, D. Sawers, and R. Stillerman, *The Sources of Invention* (New York: St. Martin's Press, 1958); Battelle Memorial Laboratories, "Science, Technology and Innovation," Report to National Science Foundation, 1973; and Arthur D. Little, Inc., *Barriers to Innovation in Industry,* prepared for the National Science Foundation, Washington, D.C., 1973.

38. J. B. Quinn, *Pilkington Brothers, Ltd.,* copyrighted case, The Amos Tuck School of Business Administration, Dartmouth College, Hanover, N.H., 1978.

39. The tendency of these measures to drive out other considerations is noted in K. J. Cohen and R. M. Cyert, "Strategy: Formulation, Implementation, and Monitoring," *The Journal of Business* (July 1973), pp. 349-67.

40. Tuchman, *Guns of August.*

41. Braybrooke and Lindblom, *Strategy of Decision.*

42. E. E. Carter, in "The Behavioral Theory of the Firm and Top-Level Corporate Decisions," *Administrative Science Quarterly* (December 1971), pp. 413-28, suggests that uncertainty in the environment influences the actual number of goals. Others like S. Kakar, in "Rationality and Irrationality in Business Leadership," *Journal of Business Policy* (Winter 1971/72), pp. 39-44, suggest that *homo maximus* is a mythical beast, and that other human instincts must come into all goal choices.

43. H. I. Ansoff, "The Concept of Strategic Management," *Journal of Business Policy* (Summer 1972), pp. 2-7.

44. Several writers, notably J. T. Cannon, in *Business Strategy and Policy* (New York: Harcourt, Brace & World, 1968), and P. F. Drucker, in *The Practice of Management* (New York: Harper & Row, 1954), have correctly noted that profits are *a measure* rather than *the goal* of business success.

45. J. G. March and H. A. Simon, *Organizations* (New York: John Wiley & Sons, 1958), chap. 7.

46. R. E. Miles and C. C. Snow, *Organizational Strategy, Structure, and Process* (New York: McGraw-Hill Book Co., 1978).

47. B. M. Bass and L. D. Eldridge, in "Accelerated Managers' Objectives in Twelve Countries," *Industrial Relations* (May 1973), pp. 158-71, conclude that even high-level business performers are driven by multiple goals. The exception to this tends to be the broad goal of "survival" as broadly defined in E. Rhenman, *Organization Theory for Long-Range Planning* (New York: John Wiley & Sons, 1973), p. 51.

48. J. G. March, "Business Decision Making," in H. J. Leavitt and L. R. Pondy, eds., *Readings in Managerial Psychology* (Chicago: University of Chicago Press, 1964).

49. W. D. Guth, "Toward a Social System Theory of Corporate Strategy," *The Journal of Business* (July 1976), pp. 374-88.

50. C. I. Barnard, in *The Functions of the Executive* (Cambridge, Mass.: Harvard University Press, 1938), saw organizations as incentive distribution devices where people contribute toward a mixture of their own goals in return for relative rewards.

51. J. M. Pfiffner, in "Administrative Rationality," *Public Administration Review* (Summer 1960), pp. 125-32, develops in some detail how these nonfinancial factors cause deviations from a maximizing model.

52. Miles and Snow, *Organizational Strategy;* and Cohen and Cyert, "Strategy Formulation, Implementation, and Monitoring."

53. R. M. Cyert and J. G. March, in *A Behavioral Theory of the Firm* (Englewood Cliffs, N.J.: Prentice-Hall, Inc., 1963), refer to these as side payments. E. E. Carter, in "Behavioral Theory of the Firm and Top Level Corporate Decisions," also reflects this proposition.

54. Pfiffner, "Administrative Rationality."

55. H. A. Simon, *Models of Man* (New York: John Wiley & Sons, 1957); G. A. Steiner, "The Changing Role of Tomorrow's Corporate Planner," International Conference on Corporate Planning, Montreal, 1972, and in Chapters 6-7 of *Top Management Planning* (New York: Macmillan & Company, 1969); and R. A. Gordon, *Business Leadership in the Large Corporation* (Washington, D.C.: The Brookings Institution, 1945).

56. E. H. Bowman, in "Epistemology, Corporate Strategy, and Academe," *Sloan Management Review* (Winter 1974), pp. 35-50, points out some of the traps the one goal thesis presents unless modified by utility theory.

57. H. A. Simon, in "On the Concept of Organizational Goals," *Administrative Science Quarterly* (June 1964), pp. 1-22, suggests how to handle this mathematically for a simple choice problem. For major organizations, such optimizations through mathematics are doubtful.

58. R. E. Neustadt, *Presidential Power: The Politics of Leadership* (New York: John Wiley & Sons, 1960).

59. This effect was classically described by D. Halberstam in *The Best and the Brightest* (New York: Random House, 1972) concerning the military's tendency to move into policy vacuums in Vietnam in order to optimize its own goals.

60. E. P. Learned, et al., *Business Policy: Text and Cases* (Homewood, Ill.: Richard D. Irwin, 1969). This is the original of C. R. Christensen, et al., *Business Policy: Text and Cases,* 4th ed. (Homewood, Ill.: Richard D. Irwin, 1978).

61. R. L. Katz, in *Cases and Concepts in Corporate Strategy* (Englewood Cliffs, N.J.: Prentice-Hall, Inc., 1970), develops these points well in his discussions of strategy formulation and structure.

62. Drucker, *Practice of Management,* chap. 7.

63. R. M. Cyert, H. A. Simon, and D. B. Trow, in "Observation of a Business Decision," *The Journal of Business* (October 1956), pp. 237-48, discuss these as "unprogrammable decisions." H. Mintzberg, D. Raisinghani, and A. Théorêt, in "The Structure of Unstructured Decision Processes," *Administrative Science Quarterly* (June 1976), pp. 246-75, provide a framework for considering some of the main components of these decisions.

64. A clear example is set forth in W. D. Guth and R. Tagiuri, "Personal Values

and Corporate Strategy," *Harvard Business Review* (September-October 1965), pp. 123-32.

65. General Electric Co. uses a stoplight grid to calibrate such intuition while Exxon works with a series of "envelopes of scenarios" to help calibrate judgment. See "Corporate Planning: Piercing Future Fog in the Executive Suite," *Business Week* (April 28, 1975), pp. 46-54.

66. See J. B. Quinn, *General Motors Corporation: The Downsizing Decision*, copyrighted case, The Amos Tuck School of Business Administration, Dartmouth College, Hanover, N.H., 1978.

67. B. D. Henderson, *Henderson on Corporate Strategy* (Cambridge, Mass.: Abt Books, 1979).

68. D. J. Smalter and R. L. Ruggles, Jr., in "Six Business Lessons from the Pentagon," *Harvard Business Review* (March-April 1966), pp. 64-75, develop this form of missions planning in detail.

69. Otherwise, as happens in many companies, strong divisions get their way without regard to the welfare of the whole. See J. Pfeffer, G. R. Salancik, and H. Leblebici, "The Effect of Uncertainty on the Use of Social Influence in Organizational Decision Making," *Administrative Science Quarterly* (June 1976), pp. 227-45.

70. For one example of setting goals in this fashion, see Sherwin, "Management of Objectives."

71. C. J. Hitch, *Decision-Making for Defense* (Berkeley: University of California Press, 1965), is the classic statement of this kind of analysis, which became the basis for systems planning and PPBM methodologies.

72. M. Jelinek, *Institutionalizing Innovation: A Study of Organizational Learning Systems* (New York: Praeger Publishers, 1979); and *Texas Instruments Inc.* case, © President and Fellows of Harvard College, 1977.

73. Lorange, in "Divisional Planning," suggests a structure for accomplishing this in part.

74. M. E. Salveson, in "The Management of Strategy," *Long Range Planning* (February 1974), pp. 19-26, describes some of this complexity. Later, other matrices representing coordinated functional and geographical thrusts had to be laid across even the SBU structure.

Bibliography

Ackoff, R. L. *A Concept of Corporate Planning.* New York: Wiley-Interscience, 1970.

————. "Management Misinformation Systems." *Management Science,* December 1967, pp. B147-56.

Aguilar, F. J. *Scanning the Business Environment.* New York: Macmillan, 1967.

Alexander, T. "The Wild Birds Find a Corporate Roost." *Fortune,* August 1964, pp. 130-34+.

Allison, G. T. *Essence of Decision: Explaining the Cuban Missile Crisis.* Boston: Little, Brown & Co., 1971.

Anderson, C. R., and F. T. Paine. "PIMS, A Reexamination," *Academy of Management Review,* July 1978.

Ansoff, H. I. "The Concept of Strategic Management." *Journal of Business Policy,* Summer 1972, pp. 2-7.

————. *Corporate Strategy: An Analytic Approach to Business Policy for Growth and Expansion.* New York: McGraw-Hill Book Co., 1965.

————. "Managerial Problem-Solving." *Journal of Business Policy,* Autumn 1971, pp. 3-20.

Anthony, R. N. *Planning and Control Systems: A Framework for Analysis.* Boston: Division of Research, Graduate School of Business Administration, Harvard University, 1965.

Argyris, C. "Double Loop Learning in Organizations." *Harvard Business Review,* September-October 1977, pp. 115-25.

————. "Interpersonal Barriers to Decision Making." *Harvard Business Review,* March-April 1966, pp. 84-97.

————. *Organization and Innovation.* Homewood, Ill: Richard D. Irwin, 1965.

————. "Personality and Organization Theory Revisited." *Administrative Science Quarterly,* June 1973, pp. 141-63.

Barnard, C. I. *The Functions of the Executive.* Cambridge, Mass.: Harvard University Press, 1938.

Bass, B. M., and L. D. Eldridge. "Accelerated Managers' Objectives in Twelve Countries." *Industrial Relations,* May 1973, pp. 158-71.

Battelle Memorial Laboratories. "Science, Technology and Innovation." Report to National Science Foundation, 1973.

Bauer, R. A., and K. J. Gergen, eds., *The Study of Policy Formation.* New York: Free Press, 1968.

Baumol, W. J. *Business Behavior, Value and Growth.* New York: Macmillan, 1959.

Bengston, P., and T. Hunt. *Packer Dynasty.* Garden City, N.Y.: Doubleday & Company, Inc., 1969.

Bennis, W. G. *Changing Organizations: Essays on the Development and Evolution of Human Organization.* New York: McGraw-Hill Book Co., 1966.

Blankenship, V., and R. E. Miles. "Organizational Structure and Managerial Decision Behavior." *Administrative Science Quarterly,* June 1968, pp. 106-20.

Boston Consulting Group. *Perspectives on Corporate Strategy.* Boston, 1968.

————. *Perspectives on Experience.* Boston, 1972.

Bower, J. L. *Managing the Resource Allocation Process: A Study of Corporate Planning and Investment.* Boston: Division of Research, Graduate School of Business Administration, Harvard University, 1970.

————. "Planning within the Firm." *The American Economic Review,* May 1970, pp. 186-94.

Bowman, E. H. "Epistemology, Corporate Strategy, and Academe." *Sloan Management Review,* Winter 1974, pp. 35-50.

Braybrooke, D., and C. E. Lindblom. *A Strategy of Decision: Policy Evaluation as a Social Process.* New York: Free Press, 1963.

Brim, O. G., et al. *Personality and Decision Processes; Studies in the Social Psychology of Thinking.* Stanford, Calif.: Stanford University Press, 1962.

Brown, S. H. "How One Man Can Move a Corporate Mountain." *Fortune,* July 1, 1966, pp. 81-83+.

Cannon, J. T. *Business Strategy and Policy.* New York: Harcourt, Brace & World, 1968.

Carter, E. E. "A Behavioral Theory Approach to Firm Investment and Acquisition Decisions." Unpublished doctoral dissertation, Graduate School of Industrial Administration, Carnegie-Mellon University, Pittsburgh, 1970.

————. "The Behavioral Theory of the Firm and Top-Level Corporate Decisions." *Administrative Science Quarterly,* December 1971, pp. 413-28.

Chandler, A. D. *Strategy and Structure: Chapters in the History of the Industrial Enterprise.* Cambridge, Mass.: M.I.T. Press, 1962.

Chevalier, M. "The Strategy Spectre Behind Your Market Share." *European Business,* Summer 1972, pp. 63-72.

Christenson, C. R., K. R. Andrews, and J. L. Bower. *Business Policy: Text and Cases,* 4th ed. Homewood, Ill.: Richard D. Irwin, 1978.

Cleland, D. I., and W. R. King. "Developing a Planning Culture for More Effective Strategic Planning." *Long Range Planning,* June 1974, pp. 70-74.

Cohen, K. J., and R. M. Cyert. "Strategy: Formulation, Implementation, and Monitoring." *The Journal of Business,* July 1973, pp. 349-67.

Collins, L., and D. Lapierre. *Freedom at Midnight.* New York: Simon & Schuster, 1975.

Collins, O. F., and D. G. Moore. *The Organization Makers: A Behavioral Study of Independent Entrepreneurs.* New York: Appleton-Century-Crofts, 1970.

Conot, R. E. *A Streak of Luck.* New York: Seaview Books, 1979.

"Corporate Planning: Piercing Future Fog in the Executive Suite." *Business Week,* April 28, 1975, pp. 46-54.

Cummin, P. C. "TAT Correlates of Executive Performance." *Journal of Applied Psychology,* February 1967, pp. 78-81.

Cyert, R. M., and J. G. March. *A Behavioral Theory of the Firm.* Englewood Cliffs, N.J.: Prentice-Hall, Inc., 1963.

⸺, W. R. Dill, and J. G. March. "The Role of Expectations in Business Decision Making." *Administrative Science Quarterly,* December 1958, pp. 307-40.

⸺, H. A. Simon, and D. B. Trow. "Observation of a Business Decision." *The Journal of Business,* October 1956, pp. 237-48.

Daniel, D. R. "Reorganizing for Results." *Harvard Business Review,* November-December 1966, pp. 96-104.

deCarbonnel, F. E., and R. G. Dorrance. "Information Sources for Planning Decisions." *California Management Review,* Summer 1973, pp. 42-53.

Demaree, A. T. "RCA after the Bath." *Fortune,* September 1972, pp. 123-28+.

Dessauer, J. H. *My Years with Xerox: The Billions Nobody Wanted.* Garden City, N.Y.: Doubleday, 1971.

Diesing, P. "Noneconomic Decision Making," in M. Alexis and C. A. Wilson, eds., *Organizational Decision Making.* Englewood Cliffs, N.J.: Prentice-Hall, Inc., 1967.

"Don't Jump Too Quickly into Goal-Setting." *Industry Week,* February 11, 1974, pp. 48-50.

Drucker, P. F. "Entrepreneurship in Business Enterprise." *Journal of Business Policy,* Autumn 1970, pp. 3-12.

⸺. *The Practice of Management.* New York: Harper & Row, 1954.

⸺. "What We Can Learn from Japanese Management." *Harvard Business Review,* March-April 1971, pp. 110-22.

Dubin, R., J. E. Champoux, and L. W. Porter. "Central Life Interests and Organizational Commitment of Blue-Collar and Clerical Workers." *Administrative Science Quarterly,* September 1975, pp. 411-21.

Dufty, N. F., and P. M. Taylor. "The Implementation of a Decision." *Administrative Science Quarterly,* June 1962, pp. 110-19.

Durant, W. *The Age of Napoleon.* New York: Simon & Schuster, 1975.

Essame, H. *Patton: A Study in Command.* New York: Charles Scribner's Sons, 1974.

Etzioni, A. *Modern Organizations.* Englewood Cliffs, N.J.: Prentice-Hall, Inc., 1964.

Farago, L. *Patton: Ordeal and Triumph.* New York: I. Obolensky, 1964.

Fayol, H. *General and Industrial Management,* translated by C. Storrs. London: Pitman, 1949. First published in 1916.

Feldman, J., and H. E. Kanter. "Organizational Decision Making," in J. G. March, ed., *Handbook of Organizations.* Chicago: Rand McNally, 1965.

Felton, S. "Case of the Board and the Strategic Process." *Harvard Business Review,* July 1979.

Foch, F. *Principles of War,* translated by J. DeMorinni. New York: AMS Press, Inc., 1970. First published London: Chapman & Hall, Ltd., 1918.

Forrester, J. W. "Counterintuitive Behavior of Social Systems." *Technology Review,* January 1971, pp. 52-68.

Frank, A. G. "Goal Ambiguity and Conflicting Standards: An Approach to the Study of Organizations." *Human Organization,* Winter 1958-59, pp. 8-13.

French, J. R., and B. Raven. "Bases of Social Power," in D. Cartwright, ed., *Studies in Social Power.* Ann Arbor: University of Michigan Press, 1959, pp. 150-67.

Friedman, M. *Capitalism and Freedom.* Chicago: University of Chicago Press, 1962.

Georgiou, P. "The Goal Paradigm and Notes Towards a Counter Paradigm." *Administrative Science Quarterly,* September 1973, pp. 291-310.

Gilmore, F. F. "Overcoming the Perils of Advocacy in Corporate Planning." *California Management Review,* Spring 1973, pp. 127-37.

Glueck, W. F., and R. Willis, "Documentary Sources and Strategic Management Research." *Academy of Management Review,* January 1979.

Gordon, R. A. *Business Leadership in the Large Corporation.* Washington, D.C.: The Brookings Institution, 1945.

Gore, W. J. *Administrative Decision-Making: A Heuristic Model.* New York: John Wiley & Sons, 1964.

_____. "Administrative Decision-Making in Federal Field Offices." *Public Administration Review,* 1956, pp. 281-91.

Goronzy, F., and E. Gray. "Factors in Corporate Growth." *Management International Review,* vol. 14, no. 4-5, 1974, pp. 75-90.

Green, P. *Alexander the Great.* New York: Praeger Publishers, 1970.

Grinyer, P. H., and D. Norburn. "Planning for Existing Markets: Perceptions of Executives and Financial Performance." *Journal of the Royal Statistical Society,* Series H, 1975, pp. 70-97.

Guth, W. D. "Formulating Organizational Objectives and Strategy: A Systematic Approach." *Journal of Business Policy,* Autumn 1971, pp. 24-31.

_____. "Toward a Social System Theory of Corporate Strategy." *The Journal of Business,* July 1976, pp. 374-88.

_____, and R. Tagiuri. "Personal Values and Corporate Strategy." *Harvard Business Review,* September-October 1965, pp. 123-32.

Guzzardi, W., Jr. "I.T. T. Gets the Message." *Fortune,* February 1961, pp. 112-18.

Halberstam, D. *The Best and the Brightest.* New York: Random House, 1972.

Hall, W. K. "Strategic Planning Models: Are Top Managers Really Finding Them Useful?" *Journal of Business Policy,* Winter 1972/73, pp. 33-42.

Halperin, M. H. *Limited War in the Nuclear Age.* New York: John Wiley & Sons, 1963.

Hamilton, T. S. "Management by Agreement." Hartford, Conn.: Hartford Hospital, 1968.

Hardwick, C. T., and B. F. Landuyt. "Timing and Surprise," in *Administrative Strategy and Decision Making,* 2d ed. Cincinnati: South Western Publishing Co., 1966.

Hart, B. H. L. *Strategy.* New York: Frederick A. Praeger, Publishers, 1954.

Head Ski Company, Inc. Case © President and Fellows of Harvard College, Cambridge, Mass., 1967.

Heany, D. F. "Is TIMS Talking to Itself?" *Management Science,* August 1966, pp. B146-55.

Henderson, B. D. *Henderson on Corporate Strategy.* Cambridge, Mass.: Abt Books, 1979.

_____. "The Non Logical Strategy." Boston: The Boston Consulting Group, 1973.

Hitch, C. J. *Decision-Making for Defense.* Berkeley: University of California Press, 1965.

_____, and R. N. McKean. *The Economics of Defense in the Nuclear Age.* Cambridge, Mass.: Harvard University Press, 1960.

Holloway, C., and G. T. Jones. "Planning at Gulf–A Case Study." *Long Range Planning,* April 1975, pp. 27-39.

Hunger, J. D., and L. W. Stern. "An Assessment of the Functionality of the Superordinate Goal in Reducing Conflict." *Academy of Management Journal,* December 1976, pp. 591-605.

Irving, D. *The Trail of the Fox.* New York: E. P. Dutton, 1977.

Irwin, P. H. "Towards Better Strategic Management." *Long Range Planning,* December 1974, pp. 64-67.

Ivancevich, J. M. "Changes in Performance in a Management by Objectives Program." *Administrative Science Quarterly,* December 1974, pp. 563-74.

James, D. C. *The Years of MacArthur, 1941-1945.* Boston: Houghton Mifflin Company, 1970.

James, R. M. "Corporate Strategy and Change–The Management of People." Monograph, University of Chicago, 1978.

Jelinek, M. *Institutionalizing Innovation: A Study of Organizational Learning Systems.* New York: Praeger Publishers, 1979.

_____. *Texas Instruments Inc.* Case © President and Fellows of Harvard College, Cambridge, Mass., 1977.

Jewkes, J., D. Sawers, and R. Stillerman. *The Sources of Invention.* New York: St. Martin's Press, 1958.

Jomini, A. H. *Art of War,* translated by G. H. Mendell and W. P. Craighill. Westport, Conn.: Greenwood Press, 1971. Original Philadelphia: J. B. Lippincott & Co., 1862.

Kahn, H., and A. J. Wiener. *The Year 2000: A Framework for Speculation on the Next Thirty-Three Years.* New York: Macmillan, 1967.

Kakar, S. "Rationality and Irrationality in Business Leadership." *Journal of Business Policy,* Winter 1971/72, pp. 39-44.

Katz, R. L. *Cases and Concepts in Corporate Strategy.* Englewood Cliffs, N.J.: Prentice-Hall, Inc., 1970.

_____. *Management of the Total Enterprise.* Englewood Cliffs, N.J.: Prentice-Hall, Inc., 1970.

Kelso, L. O., and M. J. Adler. *The Capitalist Manifesto.* New York: Random House, 1958.

Kessel, E. *Moltke.* Stuttgart: K. F. Koehler, 1957.

Kramer, J. *Instant Replay.* New York: The New American Library, Inc., 1968.

Lasagna, J. B. "Make Your MBO Pragmatic." *Harvard Business Review,* November-December 1971, pp. 64-69.

Latham, G. P., and J. J. Baldes. "The 'Practical Significance' of Locke's Theory of Goal Setting." *Journal of Applied Psychology,* February 1975, pp. 122-24.

_____, and G. A. Yukl. "A Review of Research on the Application of Goal Setting in Organizations." *Academy of Management Journal,* December 1975, pp. 824-45.

Lawrence, L. C., and P. C. Smith. "Group Decision and Employee Participation." *Journal of Applied Psychology,* vol. 39, 1955, pp. 334-37.

Lenin, V. I. *Collected Works of V. I. Lenin,* edited and annotated. New York: International Publishers, 1927, especially vol. 21, "Toward the Seizure of Power."

Levinson, H. "Management by Whose Objectives?" *Harvard Business Review,* July-August 1970, pp. 125-34.

Lindblom, C. E. *The Policy-Making Process.* Englewood Cliffs, N.J.: Prentice-Hall, Inc., 1968.

_____. "The Science of 'Muddling Through.'" *Public Administration Review,* Spring 1959, pp. 79-88.

Litschert, R. J., and T. W. Bonham. "Conceptual Models of Strategy Formulation." *Academy of Management Review,* April 1978.

Little, Arthur D., Inc. *Barriers to Innovation in Industry.* Prepared for the National Science Foundation, Washington, D.C., 1973.

Livingston, J. S. "Myth of the Well-Educated Manager." *Harvard Business Review,* January-February 1971, pp. 79-89.

Locke, E. A. "Toward a Theory of Task Motivation and Incentives." *Organizational Behavior and Human Performance,* vol. 3, 1968, pp. 157-89.

Lorange, P. "Divisional Planning: Setting Effective Direction." *Sloan Management Review,* Fall 1975, pp. 77-91.

Mace, M. L. "The President and Corporate Planning." *Harvard Business Review,* January-February 1965, pp. 49-62.

_____, and G. G. Montgomery, Jr. *Management Problems of Corporate Acquisitions.* Boston: Division of Research, Graduate School of Business Administration, Harvard University, 1962.

MacGinnitie, W. J. "How to Design a Strategic Planning System." *Best's Review,* Property/Liability Insurance Edition, May 1973, pp. 108-12.

Machiavelli, N. *The Prince, and the Discourses.* New York: Modern Library, 1950.

Mao Tse-Tung. *On Protracted War,* 3d ed. San Francisco: China Books, 1967.

_____. *Selected Military Writings, 1928-1949.* San Francisco: China Books, 1967.

March, J. G. "Business Decision Making," in H. J. Leavitt and L. R. Pondy, eds.,

Readings in Managerial Psychology. Chicago: University of Chicago Press, 1964.

_____, and H. A. Simon. *Organizations.* New York: John Wiley & Sons, 1958.

_____, J. P. Olsen, S. Christensen, et al. *Ambiguity and Choice in Organizations.* Bergen, Norway: Universitetsforlaget, 1976.

Marshak, J. "Toward an Economic Theory of Organization and Information," in R. M. Thrall, C. H. Coombs, and R. L. Davis, eds., *Decision Processes.* New York: John Wiley & Sons, 1954.

Matloff, M., and E. M. Snell. *Strategic Planning for Coalition Warfare (1941-42).* Washington, D.C.: Office of the Chief of Military History, Department of the Army, 1953.

Maurer, J. K. "Work as a 'Central Life Interest' of Industrial Supervisors." *Academy of Management Journal,* September 1968, pp. 329-39.

McDonald, J. *Strategy in Poker, Business and War.* New York: W. W. Norton & Company, Inc., 1950.

McGregor, D. *The Human Side of Enterprise.* New York: McGraw-Hill Book Co., 1960.

McKenney, J. L., and P. G. W. Keen. "How Managers' Minds Work." *Harvard Business Review,* May-June 1974, pp. 79-90.

Metcalf, H. C., and L. Urwick, eds. *Dynamic Administration: The Collected Papers of Mary Parker Follett.* New York: Harper & Brothers, Publishers, 1941.

Meyerson, M., and E. C. Banfield. *Politics, Planning, and the Public Interest: The Case of Public Housing in Chicago.* Glencoe, Ill.: Free Press, 1955.

Miles, R. E., and C. C. Snow. *Organizational Strategy, Structure, and Process.* New York: McGraw-Hill Book Co., 1978.

Miller, D., and P. H. Friesen. "Archetypes of Strategy Formulation." *Management Science,* May 1978.

Miller, E. C. *Advanced Techniques for Strategic Planning.* New York: American Management Association, 1971.

Mintzberg, H. "Book Review of Herbert A. Simon, *The New Science of Management Decision.*" *Administrative Science Quarterly,* June 1977, pp. 342-51.

_____. "Emerging Strategy of Direct Research." *Administrative Science Quarterly,* December 1979.

_____. *"The Nature of Managerial Work.* New York: Harper & Row, 1973.

_____. "Patterns in Strategy Formulation." *Management Science,* May 1978.

_____. "Research on Strategy-Making." *Academy of Management Proceedings, Thirty-second Annual Meeting,* August 13-16, 1972, pp. 90-94.

_____. "Strategy-Making in Three Modes." *California Management Review,* Winter 1973, pp. 44-53.

_____, D. Raisinghani, and A. Théorêt. "The Structure of 'Unstructured' Decision Processes." *Administrative Science Quarterly,* June 1976, pp. 246-75.

Mitroff, I. I., and J. R. Emshoff. "On Strategic Assumption Making." *Academy of Management Review,* January 1979.

_____, et al. "Assumption Analysis: A Methodology for Strategic Problem Solving." *Management Science,* January 1979.

Montgomery, B. L. *The Memoirs of Field-Marshal The Viscount Montgomery of Alamein.* Cleveland: World Publishing Co., 1958.

Murray, E. A. "Strategy Formulation as a Negotiated Outcome." *Management Science,* May 1978.

Napoleon, I. "Maximes de Guerre," in T. R. Phillips, ed., *Roots of Strategy.* Harrisburg, Pa.: The Military Service Publishing Company, 1940.

Neustadt, R. E. *Presidential Power: The Politics of Leadership.* New York: John Wiley & Sons, 1960.

Newell, A., and H. A. Simon. *Human Problem Solving.* Englewood Cliffs, N.J.: Prentice-Hall, Inc., 1972.

Newman, W. H. *Administrative Action: The Techniques of Organization and Management,* 2d ed. Englewood Cliffs, N.J.: Prentice-Hall, Inc., 1963.

Nicolaidis, N. G. "Policy-Decision and Organization Theory." D.P.A. dissertation, University of Southern California, Los Angeles, 1960.

Nord, W. R. "Developments in the Study of Power," in W. R. Nord, ed., *Concepts and Controversy in Organizational Behavior.* Pacific Palisades, Calif.: Goodyear Publishing Co., 1976.

Normann, R. *Management for Growth,* translated by N. Adler. New York: John Wiley & Sons, 1977.

_____. "Organizational Innovativeness: Product Variation and Reorientation." *Administrative Science Quarterly,* June 1971, pp. 203-15.

Nyström, H. "Uncertainty, Information and Organizational Decision Making: A Cognitive Approach." *Swedish Journal of Economics,* vol. 76, 1974, pp. 131-39.

Osgood, R. E. *Limited War; The Challenge to American Strategy.* Chicago: University of Chicago Press, 1957.

Perrow, C. "The Analysis of Goals in Complex Organizations." *American Sociological Review,* February 1961, pp. 854-66.

"Personal Management Styles." *Business Week,* May 4, 1974, pp. 43-51.

Pettigrew, A. M. "Information Control as a Power Resource." *Sociology,* May 1972, pp. 187-204.

Pfeffer, J., G. R. Salancik, and H. Leblebici. "The Effect of Uncertainty on the Use of Social Influence in Organizational Decision Making." *Administrative Science Quarterly,* June 1976, pp. 227-45.

Pfiffner, J. M. "Administrative Rationality." *Public Administration Review,* Summer 1960, pp. 125-32.

Phillips, T. R., ed. *Roots of Strategy.* Harrisburg, Pa.: The Military Service Publishing Company, 1940.

Pogue, F. C. *George C. Marshall: Ordeal and Hope, 1939-1942.* New York: Viking Press, 1966.

Porter, M. E. "How Competitive Forces Shape Strategy." *Harvard Business Review,* March 1979.

Pounds, W. F. "The Process of Problem Finding." *Industrial Management Review,* Fall 1969, pp. 1-19.

Quinn, J. B. *Bell Laboratories.* Copyrighted case, The Amos Tuck School of Business Administration, Dartmouth College, Hanover, N.H., 1965.

_____. *Chrysler Corporation.* Copyrighted case, The Amos Tuck School of Business Administration, Dartmouth College, Hanover, N.H., 1977.

_____. *Exxon Corporation.* Case manuscript, The Amos Tuck School of Business Administration, Dartmouth College, Hanover, N.H., 1974.

_____. *General Motors Corporation: The Downsizing Decision.* Copyrighted case, The Amos Tuck School of Business Administration, Dartmouth College, Hanover, N.H., 1978.

_____. *Germanium Power Devices Corporation.* Copyrighted case, The Amos Tuck School of Business Administration, Dartmouth College, Hanover, N.H. 1979.

_____. *KMS Industries.* Copyrighted case, The Amos Tuck School of Business Administration, Dartmouth College, Hanover, N.H., 1976.

_____. "Norway: Small Country Plans Civil Science and Technology." *Science,* January 18, 1974, pp. 172-79.

_____. *Pilkington Brothers, Ltd.* Copyrighted case, The Amos Tuck School of Business Administration, Dartmouth College, Hanover, N.H., 1977.

_____. "Strategic Goals: Process and Politics." *Sloan Management Review,* Fall 1977, pp. 21-37.

_____. "Technological Innovation, Entrepreneurship, and Strategy." *Sloan Management Review,* Spring 1979, pp. 19-30.

_____. *Xerox Corporation (A).* Copyrighted case, The Amos Tuck School of Business Administration, Dartmouth College, Hanover, N.H., 1977.

_____. *Xerox Corporation (B).* Copyrighted case, The Amos Tuck School of Business Administration, Dartmouth College, Hanover, N.H., 1977.

_____, and M. Jelinek. *General Mills, Inc.* Copyrighted case, The Amos Tuck School of Business Administration, Dartmouth College, Hanover, N.H., 1978.

_____, and M. Jelinek. *Pillsbury Company.* Manuscript in preparation.

_____, and J. A. Mueller. "Transferring Research Results to Operations." *Harvard Business Review,* January-February 1963, pp. 49-66.

Raia, A. P. "Goal Setting and Self-Control: An Empirical Study." *The Journal of Management Studies,* February 1965, pp. 34-53.

Reitman, W. R. "Heuristic Decision Procedures, Open Constraints, and the Structure of Ill-Defined Problems," in M. W. Shelly, II, and G. L. Bryan, eds., *Human Judgments and Optimality.* New York: John Wiley & Sons, 1964.

Rhenman, E. *Organization Theory for Long-Range Planning.* New York: John Wiley & Sons, 1973.

Riker, W. H. *The Theory of Political Coalition.* New Haven, Conn.: Yale University Press, 1962.

Ronan, W. W., G. P. Latham, and S. B. Kinne III. "Effects of Goal Setting and Supervision on Worker Behavior in an Industrial Situation." *Journal of Applied Psychology,* December 1973, pp. 302-307.

Rothschild, W. E. *Putting It All Together: A Guide to Strategic Thinking.* New York: AMACOM (a division of American Management Association), 1976.

Ryan, C. *A Bridge Too Far.* London: Coronet Books, 1974.

Salveson, M. E. "The Management of Strategy." *Long Range Planning,* February 1974, pp. 19-26.

Sawyer, G. "Use of Strategic Models in Setting Goals." *MSU Business Topics,* Summer 1979.

Sayles, L. R. *Managerial Behavior: Administration in Complex Organizations.* New York: McGraw-Hill Book Co., 1964.

Schaffir, W. B. "What Have We Learned about Corporate Planning?" *Management Review,* August 1973, pp. 19-26.

Schoeffler, S., R. D. Buzzell, and D. F. Heany. "Impact of Strategic Planning on Profit Performance." *Harvard Business Review,* March-April 1974, pp. 137-45.

Shank, J. K., E. G. Niblock, and W. T. Sandalls, Jr. "Balance 'Creativity' and 'Practicality' in Formal Planning." *Harvard Business Review,* January-February 1973, pp. 87-95.

Sherwin, D. S. "Management *of* Objectives." *Harvard Business Review,* May-June 1976, pp. 149-60.

Shubik, M. *Games for Society, Business, and War: Towards a Theory of Gaming.* New York: Elsevier, 1975.

Simon, H. A. *Administrative Behavior.* New York: Macmillan, 1947.

_____. *Models of Man.* New York: John Wiley & Sons, 1957.

_____. *The New Science of Management Decision.* New York: Harper & Row, 1960.

_____. *The New Science of Management Decision,* rev. ed. Englewood Cliffs, N.J.: Prentice-Hall, Inc., 1977.

_____. "On the Concept of Organizational Goals." *Administrative Science Quarterly,* June 1964, pp. 1-22.

Skibbins, G. J. "Top Management Goal Appraisal." *International Management,* July 1974, pp. 41-42.

Smalter, D. J., and R. L. Ruggles, Jr. "Six Business Lessons from the Pentagon." *Harvard Business Review,* March-April 1966, pp. 64-75.

Snyder, R. C., and G. D. Paige. "The United States Decision to Resist Aggression in Korea: The Application of an Analytical Scheme." *Administrative Science Quarterly,* December 1958-59, pp. 340-78.

Soelberg, P. O. "Unprogrammed Decision Making." *Industrial Management Review,* Spring 1967, pp. 19-29.

Springer, C. H. "Strategic Management in General Electric." *Operations Research,* November-December 1973, pp. 1177-82.

Steiner, G. A. "The Changing Role of Tomorrow's Corporate Planner." International Conference on Corporate Planning, Montreal, 1972.

_____. *Top Management Planning.* New York: Macmillan & Company, 1969.

Stevenson, W. *A Man Called Intrepid: The Secret War.* New York: Harcourt Brace Jovanovich, 1976.

Stonich, P. L. "Formal Planning Pitfalls and How to Avoid Them." *Management Review,* June 1975, pp. 4-11.

Sun Tzu. *The Art of War,* translated by S. B. Griffith. New York: Oxford University Press, 1963, Original 500 B.C.

Taylor, B. "Strategic Planning for Resources." *Long Range Planning,* August 1974, pp. 12-26.

"Texas Instruments Shows U.S. Business How to Survive in the 1980s." *Business Week*, September 18, 1978.

Thompson, J. D. "The Control of Complex Organizations," *Organizations in Action*. New York: McGraw-Hill Book Co., 1967.

————, and A. Truden. "Strategies, Structures, and Processes of Organizational Decision," in J. D. Thompson, et al., eds., *Comparative Studies in Administration*. Pittsburgh, Pa.: University of Pittsburgh Press, 1959.

Tilles, S. "How to Evaluate Corporate Strategy." *Harvard Business Review*, July-August 1963, pp. 111-21.

Tosi, H. L., and S. J. Carroll. "Managerial Reaction to Management by Objectives." *Academy of Management Journal*, December 1968, pp. 415-26.

————, J. R. Rizzo, and S. J. Carroll. "Setting Goals in Management by Objectives." *California Management Review*, Summer 1970, pp. 70-78.

Tuchman, B. W. *The Guns of August*. New York: Macmillan Company, 1962.

Vancil, R. F. "Strategy Formulation in Complex Organizations." *Sloan Management Review*, Winter 1976, pp. 1-18.

————. "What Kind of Management Control Do You Need?" *Harvard Business Review*, March-April 1973, pp. 75-86.

————, and P. Lorange. "Strategic Planning in Diversified Companies." *Harvard Business Review*, January-February 1975, pp. 81-90.

Varner, V. J., and J. I. Alger, eds. *History of the Military Art: Notes for the Course*. West Point, N.Y.: U.S. Military Academy, Department of History, 1978.

Von Bülow, D. F. *The Spirit of the Modern System of War*, translated by C. M. deMartemont. London: C. Mercier and Co., 1806.

Von Clausewitz, C. *On War*, translated by M. Howard and P. Paret. Princeton, N.J.: Princeton University Press, 1976.

Von Neumann, J., and O. Morgenstern. *Theory of Games and Economic Behavior*. Princeton, N.J.: Princeton University Press, 1944.

Warren, E. K. *Long-Range Planning, The Executive Viewpoint*. Englewood Cliffs, N.J.: Prentice-Hall, Inc., 1966.

Weir, G. A. "Developing Strategies: A Practical Approach." *Long Range Planning*, October 1974, pp. 7-12.

White, G. R., and B. R. Graham. "How to Spot a Technological Winner." *Harvard Business Review*, March 1978.

White, T. H. *In Search of History: A Personal Adventure*. New York: Warner Books, 1978.

Whitehead, C. T. "Uses and Limitations of Systems Analysis." Ph.D. dissertation, Sloan School of Management, Massachusetts Institute of Technology, Cambridge, 1968.

Wise, T. A. "I.B.M.'s $5,000,000,000 Gamble." *Fortune*, September 1966, pp. 118-23+.

————. "The Rocky Road to the Marketplace." *Fortune*, October 1966, pp. 138-43+.

Witte, E. "Field Research on Complex Decision-Making Processes—The Phase Theorem." *International Studies of Management and Organization*, Summer 1972, pp. 156-82.

Womack, W. W. "The Board's Most Important Function." *Harvard Business Review,* September 1979.

Wrapp, H. E. "Good Managers Don't Make Policy Decisions." *Harvard Business Review,* September-October 1967, pp. 91-99.

_____. "A Plague of Professional Managers." *New York Times,* April 8, 1979.

Young, D. *Rommel: The Desert Fox.* New York: Harper & Row, 1974.

Zaleznik, A. "Management of Disappointment." *Harvard Business Review,* November-December 1967, pp. 59-70.

_____. "Power and Politics in Organizational Life." *Harvard Business Review,* May-June 1970, pp. 47-60.